BLOSSOMING HOPE

The Black Christian Woman's Guide to Mental Health and Wellness

Tonya D. Armstrong, Ph.D., M.T.S.

Overflowing Hope Media
Durham, North Carolina

Blossoming Hope: The Black Christian Woman's Guide to Mental Health and Wellness

First Printing, 2018
Copyright © 2018 by Tonya D. Armstrong, Ph.D., M.T.S.

ISBN: 978-0-9993894-1-6

Published by Overflowing Hope Media. P.O. Box 13068, Durham, NC 27709

Library of Congress: 2017915641

Book interior by CSinclaire Write-Design
Cover design and imagery by Obelia Exum

For my parents,
Leo and Jeanette Farmer and Calbert and Willa Carlton,
whose love for music, learning, and service
to humankind have inspired me;
my husband, Corwin Armstrong,
whose compassion, generosity, and humor sustain me;
and my children, Gabrielle and Dexter Armstrong,
whose talents, curiosity, and promise
propel me forward.

Acknowledgements

Truly, this book has been a "village" experience. Many thanks to my beta-readers who assisted me with earlier drafts of this manuscript: Renee Clark-Bush, Israel Durham, Adrienne Hart, Dr. Raquel Lettsome, Dr. Amelia Roberts-Lewis, and Dr. Bernadette Watts. I am indebted to a number of consultants who helped me learn the lay of the land of publishing and marketing: Joy Cook, Dr. Sackeena Gordon-Jones, Diana Graham, Dr. Dan Grandstaff, Lee Heinrich, Dr. Nicole Swiner, and Dr. Daphne Wiggins. I express gratitude for the clients and families of The Armstrong Center for Hope (ACFH) for their support in inspiring me with their profoundly touching stories and their courageous actions toward blossoming. Furthermore, I appreciate the staff of the ACFH for their competence which is only made sharper by their commitment to excellence and fun-loving natures: Dr. Kristen Bell Hughes, Raven Brooks, Esther Cooper, Dr. Sherry Eaton, Clifton Garner, Natalie Gidney-Cole, Dr. Lorraine Graves, Sharyn Holland, HarDarshan Khalsa, Jesús Sánchez Ohep, and Dr. Milicia Tedder. Additionally, I would like to thank my editor, Anita Bunkley; book cover designer, Obelia Exum; text designer, Charlotte Sinclaire; and indexer, Nanette Norris. I also give a hearty thanksgiving for Mingie Song, my personal assistant who provided technical and research support for this project.

I am grateful for the inspiration offered by the Black Women in Business, founded by Ingrid Jones, for the many sisters who have shared their writings, business strategies, and other creative musings. Also, I am delighted to be a member of the Nonfiction Authors Association, Durham/Chapel Hill Chapter, headed by Diana Needham, for teaching me about many of the concrete skills needed to bring this project to pass. My therapist-friends in the accountability group Uzima (Anita Daniels, Ava Hinton, and Dr. Paula Newman) and my Girls Night Out friends from childhood (Lynecia Cooper and Kimberly Stevens) help immensely in my quest for self- and communitarian care. Moreover, I thank God for *my* mental health professionals who have supported me over the years since graduate school and have allowed my passion for this work to expand.

Many thanks are owed to Pastor Emeritus Kenneth Ray Hammond, who instituted the Ministry of Congregational Care and Counseling (MC3) at Union Baptist Church in 2000, and Pastor Prince Raney Rivers, who continues to provide support for this ministry. I cherish my MC3 co-laborers (Charlene Barbour, Kiki Barnes, Anita Daniels, Ava Hinton, Landa Giles, Brenda Hall, Ida Ham, Harriet Holloway, Nellie Jones, Dr. Micheline Malson, Sonya Mathias, Kim Nichols, Angela Pittman, and Angela Teal), who have taught me much about receiving and sharing compassionate care at the ministry, church, and community levels. Providing leadership and teaching at Apex School of Theology has been a joyous experience, thanks to President Joseph E. Perkins, his doting wife, Dr. Carrie Perkins, and the faculty, staff, administrators, and students. I am especially thankful for lessons learned from the faculty of the Counseling Studies Department, with whom I closely work: Jennifer Dashiell-Shoffner and Drs. Cornelius Battle, Carol Bunch, Sharon Lee, and Mary Morgan.

I am very thankful for the producing, singing, and songwriting of my recording partners, Ray Watkins and Joe Jones. Thanks to Willa Carlton, Gabby Armstrong, and Anita Daniels for their participation in the recording of "Sisters." Finally, thanks to my family for supporting me steadfastly along this journey: Corwin, Gabby, and Dexter Armstrong; Michael L. Farmer; Connie Otutu; Willa and Calbert Carlton; Leo and Jeanette Farmer; Barbara J. Farmer; Daryl and Marcie Carlton; Rick and Jocelyn Carlton; Gary Carlton; Vincent and Sheba Brown; Sterling and LaShonda Jordan; Nickolas and Shannon Jordan; and numerous aunts, aunts, uncles, cousins, and godfamily and fictive family members.

Table of Contents

x

BLOSSOMING HOPE

The Black Christian Woman's Guide
to Mental Health and Wellness

Introduction

"Hope is a song in a weary throat."
*Rev. Dr. Pauli Murray, attorney, author, and first
Black woman ordained as an Episcopal priest*

Perhaps Dr. Maya Angelou said it best: We are phenomenal women! Despite our shared history of oppression due to gender and race, God has indeed created us to be phenomenal women. We display our gifts, abilities, and creativity through our multiple roles, including those of wife, mother, daughter, sister, friend, homemaker, employee, entrepreneur, church worker, and community organizer. In spite of our inherent beauty and strength, we often sell ourselves short. Many times, we don't believe that we are making a significant difference in our world, and more importantly, in the lives of those around us. We don't perceive that we are already thoroughly equipped for every good work for which we were created (2 Timothy 3:17). Well before we were in our mothers' wombs, God designed us with ultimate purpose, a unique *raison d'être*, or reason for existence, that the world is waiting for. Yet, the trials and distractions of life often leave us wandering in the proverbial wilderness, not only moving away from our God-ordained calling, but also sometimes questioning whether we ever were called or whether we can ever be redeemed and resume our purpose.

My Professional Journey

The path to writing this book has been an extensive one. I completed my undergraduate training at Yale University in 1992, where I double-majored in psychology and music. I then trained in clinical psychology at the University of North Carolina at Chapel Hill, receiving my Ph.D. in 1998, and completed a post-doctoral fellowship funded by the National Institute on Drug Abuse with the Center for Developmental Epidemiology at Duke University Medical Center. After completing my clinical hours at the Northside Child and Family Counseling Center in Chapel Hill, I earned my license in 2001 and began practicing part-time at the Alase Center for Enrichment in Durham while I pursued a Master of Theological Studies degree at Duke University Divinity School in 2003. Shortly after completing my degree, I joined the faculty there, teaching and conducting research with the Pastoral Care Department, the Institute for Care at the End of Life, and the Duke/UNC Master of Divinity/Master of Social Work dual-degree program. These rich training experiences prepared me to impart my clinical training and theological insights on a broader scale.

Around the same time that I was honing my professional identity as a clinical psychologist, I was also called into the ministry. I accepted the call, and after a series of conversations with then-Pastor Kenneth R. Hammond, I was appointed Minister of Congregational Care and Counseling at Union Baptist Church in Durham, N.C., in 2000. With a dedicated team of God-sent co-laborers, we provide mental health and wellness services through licensed mental health professionals, trained laypersons called Stephen Ministers, and grief support group facilitators. This ministry provides confidential, competent, and compassionate care at no cost to the members (or "disciples") of our congregation, and where feasible, to members of the broader community. Providing and supervising these services has given me great insight into the needs, struggles, and strengths of Black Christians, particularly women.

In 2010, I prepared my business plan, received a business loan from the Small Business Administration (SBA), and took the leap of faith in launching a group practice called The Armstrong Center for Hope, where we specialize in psychological and spiritual wellness for all ages. Our staff is comprised of women and men diverse in age, ethnicity, mental health discipline, and faith tradition. Our clients are similarly diverse. Training faculty and students to develop excellence in counseling has been an exciting role at Apex School of Theology in Durham, which provides another angle for multiplying the impact of sound psychological principles across our communities.

As a practicing clinical psychologist in both the private practice and church community roles, I am privileged to witness and support daily individuals of all ages who are struggling with myriad issues and situations, particularly Black Christian women. Women, often well put together on the outside, nevertheless feel that they are crumbling on the inside due to pressures at work, challenges in their romantic and platonic relationships, and seemingly impossible obstacles on their path to fulfilling their vision. These problems are exacerbated by difficulties with sleep, appetite, mood, past traumas, fears and worries, and negative habits that seem to take them even further away from their dreams. Counseling and psychotherapy provide greater understanding of how these patterns operate in our lives, and equip us with the skills and strategies to become liberated from the burdens that encumber us. Faith and spirituality help us to understand who we are, whose we are in the context of a tremendous legacy of race, gender, class, and faith, and to endow us with the practices of prayer, meditation, study, and other disciplines that strengthen us to blossom. In over twenty years of caring for clients and their families, I have witnessed the strength of the human spirit in prevailing over stigma to overcome all kinds of pain, suffering, and trauma. Even more importantly, I have watched the power of the Holy Spirit in creating lasting change in the lives of those persons who engage in the work of psychotherapy and blossom into the persons they were created to be. Each story is different, yet there are many common threads that unite us.

This book is written to help us more fully appreciate who we are as individuals and as a collective, to more fully perceive the extent of God's purpose operating in our lives, and to clarify the concrete skills for unleashing that purpose, one day at a time. Although we come from different walks of life (e.g., geographic location, class, family configuration, experiences across faith and denominational traditions), we are united in our painful past and in our desire to rise above oppression and marginalization to carry on to completion the good work that God has begun in us (Philippians 1:6). One of the features throughout this book is the inclusion of quotes from Black women across time, space, and vocation. I have used these quotes to highlight the wisdom of each sister, and also to demonstrate the breadth and depth of our achievements as Black women. May you be inspired to blossom in spite of the barriers that stand before you.

You will note that I have intentionally used the term "Black" to recognize the breadth of our locations and experiences across the African Diaspora. Whether we live in the U.S., South America, the Caribbean, other countries, or on the great continent of Africa, Black woman share many commonalities and mutual empathy. Additionally, I have referred to God throughout this book by using gender-neutral language. The Word of God declares that God is Spirit (John 4:24), which transcends a male or female identity; however, there is often significant cultural pressure to refer to God as male. Succumbing to this pressure can have negative effects on our ability to fully identify and connect with our Creator, particularly as women longing to see aspects of ourselves in God's image.

Finally, this book seeks to give broad coverage of a number of factors that affect our wellness, including fitness, nutrition, and finance. Although I am not an expert in these fields, I have observed time and time again how these areas are affected for better or for worse by our psychological health. I encourage you to consult experts in these areas as you become more intentional about blossoming in these particular ways.

Our Queendom

In order for us to more fully understand our capacity for wellness, it is important for us to have a broad historical foundation. While our history is often narrated by others from the time frame of our enslavement in the Americas, it is crucial that we remember the strong tradition of queendom in our past (Films Media Group, 2006; Van Sertima, 1984)! Centuries before our people were sold into slavery, black women demonstrated strong leadership, not only as the wives of great rulers, but also in their own right. Hatshepsut, a female pharaoh who lived circa 15 BC, is known as one of the most successful and prolific rulers in Egypt's history. She was responsible for hundreds of construction projects in upper and lower Egypt, including the acclaimed Djeser-Djeseru, a breath-taking monument built in her honor. Queen Nefertiti, circa 1330 BC, is one of the most commonly recognized icons of ancient Egypt. She and her husband, King Akhenaten, were credited with founding monotheistic religion in Egypt against the prevailing polytheistic practices of the day. Amina was a fierce warrior and leader of 16th century Zazzua, known today as Zaria, a province of Nigeria. She was best known for her accomplishments in the military, for steadily expanding the borders of Zazzua during more than thirty years of her reign. In modern-day Angola, Mbande Nzinga reigned over the Ndongo and Matamba kingdoms during the 17th century. Celebrated for her brilliant political and military strategies, Queen Nzinga negotiated a peace treaty with Portugal and exerted control over slave trade routes.

Perhaps best known to Christians was the Queen of Sheba, also known as Makeda (Van Sertima, 1984) who is mentioned multiple times in Scripture (e.g., I Kings 10:1-13; Matthew 12:42; Luke 11:31). Understood to be the queen of Egypt, Ethiopia, and Arabia, Queen Sheba famously visited King Solomon to ask him hard questions. Scripture records that she was overwhelmed, both by the king's wisdom and his wealth. The fact that she brought gifts of gold, precious stones, and unprecedented amounts of spices tells us something about the magnitude of her reign and accomplishments. The stories of these ancient queens have stood the test of time, but know that queens are still being made. Your story may not be well known now, but God is in the process of developing a legacy in you that can inspire countless generations to come.

This book also seeks to provide healthy alternatives to the written and lived phenomenon of countless Black women who have lost themselves in the service of others. In the late 1970's, Michele Wallace (1978) introduced the myth of the Superwoman as a way of examining the challenges imposed upon Black women. Authors Charisse Jones and Kumea Shorter-Gooden (2003) described the Sisterella Complex, a syndrome in which the Black woman honors others rather than herself, a behavioral pattern which contributes to a plethora of challenges including depression, emotional overeating, somatization (i.e., expression of psychological concerns into physical symptoms), obsession with one's appearance, and overachieving workaholism. Psychologist and pastoral theologian Chanequa Walker-Barnes characterizes the "Strongblackwoman" as a woman whose caregiving, independence, and emotional strength are demonstrated at all costs, even to the detriment of her own health. "Imprisoned within the unholy trinity of self-denial, suffering, and silence, the Christian Strongblackwoman serves as the modern sacrificial lamb, with the church functioning as both the officiating priest and the altar of ungodly fire" (Walker-Barnes, 2014, p. 6). Acknowledging the reality that many have experienced Black culture and even Christianity as systems that exploit Black women, this book provides practical guidance for how Black Christian women can transcend these unhealthy identities. More specifically, the Black Christian woman's ownership of Christian beliefs, principles, and practices can strengthen the Black woman, even to the point of allowing vulnerability. Ironically, this vulnerability provides the strength needed for Black Christian women to work individually and collectively to overcome systemic oppression.

What is Wellness?

As a student of the discipline of psychology in the early 1990s, I learned early on about psychopathology, or the scientific study of mental and behavioral disorders. In my "Abnormal Psychology" class, we learned about the syndromes and disorders of mental illness that constituted the Diagnostic and Statistical Manual of Mental Disorders (American Psychiatric Association, 2013), or the DSM, in its third revision at that time. Under the DSM classification system, mental illnesses are grouped around a common theme, such as mood, anxiety, or psychosis. Persons who meet the required number of symptoms, as measured by frequency, intensity, and duration, and demonstrate sufficient impairment in daily functioning, are diagnosed with one or more disorders. While the medical model has its shortcomings, I believe that mental illnesses are valid phenomena, and I've witnessed first-hand the devastating effects of untreated or undertreated mental illness, including severely limited quality of life, broken relationships, and shortened life spans. Even if we never receive a formal clinical diagnosis, sometimes we may suffer from debilitating symptoms for years.

At the same time, it seems most useful to conceptualize the health and wellness of ourselves, fully mind, spirit, body, and soul, on a continuum. Rather than dividing ourselves into categories of having or not having a mental illness, I believe it's more important to reflect authentically on the degree to which we may have symptoms of an illness or suffer from dysfunction. Additionally, it is crucial to consider to what extent we possess the thoughts, feelings, and behaviors that support the flourishing of our wellness. The model on the following page, developed by John Travis (Travis & Ryan, 2004), demonstrates how mental health is more than the absence of mental illness; instead, it represents our movement toward a high level of wellness through awareness, education, and growth. It is my hope that the pages of this book will inspire you to strive toward wellness, a state in which God's fullest purpose for your life is realized.

As we prepare to elevate to the next level of wellness, it's important to

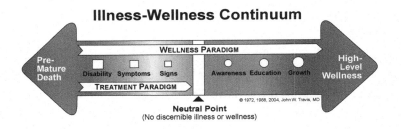

recognize common impediments to wellness. The distractions of life are everywhere. There is always more housework to be done, another family member or friend wanting to "shoot the breeze," more bills to be paid, more projects at various stages of incompletion, more TV shows or movies waiting to be watched, and so on. Then there are the barriers of limited resources. Not enough money to make ends meet, let alone cover the expense of a new venture. Not enough time to finish what we've started, not enough support or encouragement to inspire us to achieve our best, not enough energy to accomplish the things that we need to do, let alone want to do. When we confront these barriers, which have a way of presenting themselves in great numbers and sheer intensity, the attitude we can quickly develop is that mediocrity is sufficient. We can unknowingly be lulled into a false sense of complacency about the issues of life, leaving the most important things off the radar while we pursue the things that seem most urgent. Before we know it, we've fallen into a pattern of pro- crastination where it becomes the norm to delay the fulfillment of our priorities until the last minute, where they are much more likely to get "the short end of the stick." In the worst cases, our priorities are completely disregarded and ultimately die.

The Blossoming Hope Wellness Model

In a culture where Black Christian women are rumored to be "coming up on the rough side of the mountain" and barely "keeping our heads above water," it is vital that we remember that our Cre- ator has endowed us with the ability to prosper in every life sphere. Rather than merely surviving, we are intended to thrive and flourish. One particularly beautiful and organic way that we can depict this slowly unfolding process of flourishing in our lives is to compare it to a blossoming flower. The Blossoming Hope Wellness Model is depicted below through the images of a dogwood tree and its flowers. The dogwood image was chosen for several reasons. First, the dogwood is the state flower of North Carolina, my beloved home state. Second, variations of the flower come in pinks and purples, colors that reflect our range of hues and our propensity for the color purple! Third, the tree has been known for its medicinal properties. The tree blossoms every spring around Easter, and there is even a legend that suggests that dogwood was used in the crucifixion of Jesus.

The dogwood flower in Figure 1 is not only appealing in its beauty and aroma, but also successful in drawing others to the glory of our Maker. With appropriate sunlight, soil, and water, what begins as an humble bud will develop into an amazing reflection of God's glory. Similarly, when we have the appropriate nourishment of mind, spirit, soul, and body, we blossom fully.

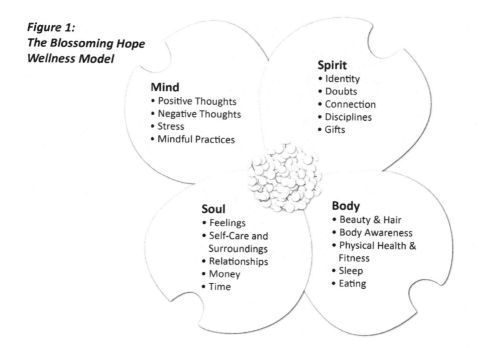

Figure 1:
The Blossoming Hope
Wellness Model

Spirit
- Identity
- Doubts
- Connection
- Disciplines
- Gifts

Mind
- Positive Thoughts
- Negative Thoughts
- Stress
- Mindful Practices

Soul
- Feelings
- Self-Care and Surroundings
- Relationships
- Money
- Time

Body
- Beauty & Hair
- Body Awareness
- Physical Health & Fitness
- Sleep
- Eating

In this model, our essence is visually presented through four main components: mind, spirit, body, and soul. As you can see from the model, these components are very closely related, and in fact, often overlap. They all stem, literally, from the branches that are ultimately rooted in the Triune God. The multiple facets of our functioning, including physical, emotional, spiritual, sexual, mental, financial, occupational, and environmental facets are all subsumed in this four-part model. The subsequent chapters provide significant detail about each of these components.

The tree (Figure 2, below), with its proliferation of limbs, branches, and flowers, represents our connection to our families and communities, all rooted in the life of the Triune God, that is God the Father/Mother, God the Son, and God the Holy Spirit.

The Body of Christ

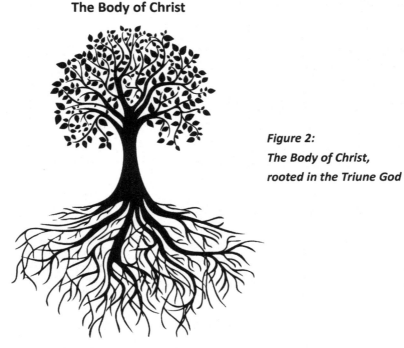

Figure 2:
The Body of Christ,
rooted in the Triune God

The Triune God

The dogwood tree provides a visual representation of how the Church and the community draw life and hope from God. Although intangible, hope is an essential component of wellness. Hope, or an expectation of good to come, is what allows us to get up morning after morning and continue to put one foot in front of the other, even when we don't feel like it or when circumstances seem bleak. Hope is the opposite of hopelessness, which is the despair that is one of the hallmark symptoms of depression. Hopelessness is what makes us want to give in, throw in the towel, and go home. Under a hopeless outlook, life is too hard, has dealt us too many blows, and is only getting worse, not better. Psychological research has repeatedly demonstrated through clinical and community studies that hope, a concept that has most robustly emerged out of the positive psychology movement, is associated with positive outcomes such as life satisfaction, optimism, gratitude, and lowered levels of psychological distress (e.g., Weis & Speridakos, 2011).

However, well before the field of psychology was born in a laboratory in Leipzig, Germany in 1879, there was ancient wisdom regarding the importance of hope, and perhaps more importantly, the originator of hope: The Psalmist David declared "Yes, my soul, find rest in God; my hope comes from him" (Psalm 62:5). God promises back to the faithful, "For I know the plans I have for you," declares the Lord, "plans to prosper you and not to harm you, plans to give you hope and a future" (Jeremiah 29:11). And even when our hope waxes thin, we must remember:

> But those who wait for the Lord [who expect, look for, and hope in Him] will gain new strength *and* renew their power; They will lift up their wings [and rise up close to God] like eagles [rising toward the sun]; They will run and not become weary, They will walk and not grow tired.
> (Isaiah 40:31, Amplified Version)

Thus, multiple sources of wisdom agree to the significance of hope for fulfilling the purposes of our lives. As Christians, we know that our God is the source of our hope: "May the God of hope fill you with all joy and peace as you trust in him, so that you may overflow with hope by the power of the Holy Spirit" (Romans 15:13).

Thus, our hope is rooted in God, and is blossoming as we pursue wellness in mind, spirit, body, and soul. One of the major emphases of this book is the importance of taking inventory of the various components of our wellness, and making the minor to major adjustments needed to establish and maintain balance in these areas.

The Blossoming Hope Wellness Inventory

Now that I have presented the Blossoming Hope Wellness Model, you may take the following inventory to better assess your own level of wellness:

The Blossoming Hope Wellness Inventory

Rate the quality of your wellness in each of the areas below. Circle the most accurate response using the following scale:

1 = Never a part of my regular routine
2 = Rarely a part of my regular routine
3 = Occasionally a part of my regular routine
4 = Usually a part of my regular routine
5 = Almost always a part of my regular routine

• Mind •

1) *Promotion of positive thoughts*
    1   2   3   4   5

2) *Elimination of negative thoughts*
    1   2   3   4   5

3) *Effective management of stress*
    1   2   3   4   5

4) *Mindfulness practices*
1   2   3   4   5

5) *Clarity of life purpose*
1   2   3   4   5

6) *Consistent pursuit of life purpose*
1   2   3   4   5

7) *Use of preparation strategies*
1   2   3   4   5

Reflections on Blossoming in Mind: _____

_____

_____

_____

• Spirit •

8) *Increasing clarity about spiritual identity*
1   2   3   4   5

9) *Use of a safe space/person for sharing your doubts*
1   2   3   4   5

10) *Dedicated space and time for spiritual devotion/renewal*
1   2   3   4   5

11) *Use of one or more spiritual disciplines (e.g., prayer,
journaling, study of holy writings, fasting, silence)*
1   2   3   4   5

12) *Use of one or more spiritual gifts*
1   2   3   4   5

13) *Daily use of spiritual disciplines(s)*

1   2   3   4   5

14) *Daily use of spiritual gift(s)*

1   2   3   4   5

Reflections on Blossoming in Spirit: _____

_____

_____

_____

• Body •

15) *Appreciation for your beauty*

1   2   3   4   5

16) *Maintenance of your hair*

1   2   3   4   5

17) *Awareness of your bodily sensations*

1   2   3   4   5

18) *Exercise (150 minutes per week)*

1   2   3   4   5

19) *Adequate sleep*

1   2   3   4   5

20) *Adequate hydration with water*

1   2   3   4   5

21) *Nutritious meals and snacks*

1   2   3   4   5

Reflections on Blossoming in Body: _____

_____

_____

_____

• Soul •

22) *Emotional regulation*

   1   2   3   4   5

23) *Self/communitarian care*

   1   2   3   4   5

24) *Managing your physical surroundings—beauty and organization at home, work, school, in car*

   1   2   3   4   5

25) *Positive family relationships*

   1   2   3   4   5

26) *Life-giving friendships*

   1   2   3   4   5

27) *Healthy intimate relationships*

   1   2   3   4   5

28) *Social activism*

   1   2   3   4   5

29) *Sound money management skills*

   1   2   3   4   5

30) *Effective use of your time*

   1   2   3   4   5

Reflections on Blossoming in Soul: _____

_____

_____

_____

Add up your total points. How did you do? If you scored 121-150 points, you have likely mastered several areas of wellness and can serve as a guide to others in their quest toward wellness. If you scored 91-120 points, you are strong in at least one to two areas and are building great progress toward blossoming. A score of 61-90 points suggests that you are making moderate progress—be encouraged! If you scored 31-60 points, you probably have several areas where you can implement wellness practices. Also, pay attention to your reflections in each area, for they may potentially contain important information about your barriers and how to get beyond those barriers.

These numbers and comments are not magical, but they do provide a reasonable barometer for your blossoming baseline. Keep your original score in mind as you read the book and pick up more strategies along the way for specific ways to blossom in each area. **For a free bonus, visit** *drtonyaarmstrong.com/blossominghope* **for "111 Blossoming Tools," a list of activities that can contribute to your life enrichment.** Enjoy the journey!

Organization of This Book

While not exhaustive, this book attempts to address many of the common issues with which we struggle by offering practical suggestions for overcoming stress and psychological distress. Part One of this book, "Understanding Mental Illness," uses vignettes informed not only by my own life experiences, but also by the experiences of hundreds of women I have supported in therapy. This particular point of departure helps us to become familiar with the end of the health and wellness spectrum where sisters are suffering most acutely in the form of active mental illness. At any given time, most of us do not meet the full criteria for any mental illness; however, across the life span many more of us will experience clinical or sub-clinical symptoms of at least one disorder. Certainly, someone we love will receive a clinical diagnosis of mental illness. The stories shared herein represent a compilation of the different challenges encountered by these clients, and the specific details related to any one client have been changed to protect the identity of each client.

In Part Two, I present the many aspects of Blossoming in Mind, covering our thoughts about stress, self-worth, and our perception of our capacity to move forward with our vision. Part Three explores Blossoming in Spirit, with its components of our spiritual identity, our doubts, approaches to nurturing our spiritual life, and concrete discussions of spiritual disciplines and spiritual gifts. In Part Four, we examine the internal and external components of Blossoming in Body, including ways we've historically related to body awareness, and contemporary practices of sleep, fitness, nutrition, and beauty. Part Five addresses the important facets of Blossoming in Soul, e.g., the seat of our emotions, our relationships, our environment, our money, and our time. Scattered throughout the book are "Take a Moment" icons (🕰️) that signal a recording available for your listening pleasure. Whether song or spoken word exercise, listening to the recording can help deepen your experience of the wellness principle being shared.

You may find it helpful to read the book from cover to cover. Alternatively, you may choose to focus on the sections that are most relevant for you at this time. There are several instances throughout the book in which I use internal dialogue to demonstrate what we are often thinking but may never say out loud. Remember, don't believe everything you think! Instead, take every thought captive and make it obedient to Christ (2 Corinthians 10:5). You may also find that working with a coach, spiritual director, pastoral counselor, or therapist can maximize your progress toward mental health and wellness.

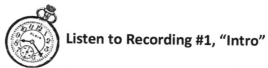 **Listen to Recording #1, "Intro"**

Part One

Understanding Mental Illness

"… I began to discover that telling the truth [about my depression]
is addictive—time I did it, and survived, I wanted to do it again.
The more I took off my mask, the more I shared my story,
the more folks shared back with me."
Terrie M. Williams, entrepreneur, psychotherapist, and author of
Black Pain: It Just Looks Like We're Not Hurting

At some point in our lives, or in the lives of our loved ones, the odds are that someone will be diagnosed with mental illness. In 2014, about 16 percent of African Americans had a diagnosable mental disorder (Center for Behavioral Health Statistics and Quality, 2015). Sadly, the percentage of African Americans who were actually diagnosed and received treatment was much lower. Part of the challenge of getting the help we need at these crisis moments is the stigma that is associated with undergoing evaluation by a mental health professional (Armstrong, 2016; Corrigan, 2004). We feel that discussing mental challenges is taboo, or we fear that others will think we are crazy. We resist the label of a psychiatric diagnosis, choosing instead to continue our suffering, and that of our family and community members. Even if we receive a diagnosis, we are less likely to pursue treatment, for several reasons. Often, even under the Affordable Care Act (still in effect as of this writing), millions of African Americans have been uninsured or underinsured. Persons with Medicaid, public insurance for low-income individuals, occasionally have difficulty identifying therapists who accept their insurance. If affordability is not an issue, therapist suitability often is. While much healing can occur with anyone skilled in the art and science of psychotherapy, we usually find it easier to connect with another sister. Ignorance about mental disorders and how they are classified is another barrier, one that is addressed here.

The Diagnostic and Statistical Manual of Mental Disorders-Fifth Edition (DSM-5; American Psychiatric Association, 2013) is the globally-recognized classification system for mental disorders. It is used by mental health professionals and health insurers as a common language for discourse about various mental, behavioral, and emotional challenges of human beings. It is divided into several sections, including the following:

- Neurodevelopmental disorders
- Schizophrenia spectrum and other psychotic disorders
- Bipolar and related disorders
- Depressive disorders
- Anxiety disorders
- Obsessive-compulsive and related disorders
- Trauma- and stressor-related disorders
- Dissociative disorders
- Somatic symptom and related disorders
- Feeding and eating disorders
- Elimination disorders
- Sleep-wake disorders
- Sexual dysfunctions
- Gender dysphoria
- Disruptive, impulse-control, and conduct disorders
- Substance-related and addictive disorders

- Neurocognitive disorders
- Personality disorders
- Medication-induced movement disorders and other adverse effects of medication

As you can see, this represents a fairly comprehensive list of mental and emotional challenges. Clinical disorders are diagnosed based on the frequency, intensity, and duration of the clinical signs (i.e., objective indicators of disease) and symptoms (i.e., subjective indicators of disease) that comprise the disorder. Another important factor in diagnosis is significant evidence that the individual demonstrates considerable functional impairment, meaning that the individual is not able to function in a number of life spheres, such as work, family, and/or community roles. Because we clinicians generally seek to avoid over-diagnosis, we also take precautions to consider other explanatory factors that may better account for someone's symptoms. For example, if a woman takes a new pain medication following surgery and begins to hallucinate, we recognize that she is suffering from medically-induced psychosis rather than schizophrenia. We also take into account cultural variables that may better explain a person's symptoms in the context of her culture.

In order for you to better understand the lived symptoms of these disorders, I have presented vignettes representing some of the most common disorders and life challenges. Each of these cases is a compilation of the histories of various Black Christiain women I have treated over the last twenty years. Identifying information has been omitted to protect the privacy of each client. These narratives reflect their struggles, their faith, and their hope in God to support them through their challenges. In each case, I describe the sister's story within her cultural context. Next, I present a broad summary of criteria for her clinical diagnosis based on the guidelines of the DSM-5 (American Psychiatric Association, 2013). Finally, I briefly discuss how each woman benefitted from her experience in therapy. You are encouraged to use the Reflection Questions in Appendix A to record your thoughts and feelings regarding each story.

Chapter One

Vignettes of Black Christian Women with Mental Illness

Bipolar I Disorder

"I feel as if I am out of control!" This plea for help came from Darlene, a 53-year-old Caribbean-born woman who had been struggling for years to achieve her goal to start her own baking company. Control was an important concept to her. A Christian since her teens, she knew that self-control was one of the fruits of the Spirit, and she felt deeply convicted that she should have developed this fruit by now. As a transplant from the Islands, she was well accustomed to a round-the-clock work ethic. Nevertheless, this entrepreneurial goal had been elusive. Despite her obvious talents in the kitchen and growing admiration of her baked goods from family and friends, Darlene stated that she had been unable to "keep herself together" long enough to get her business off the ground.

During her early adolescence, she recalled the vague feeling that she was different from others, but by the time she got to college, she knew that there was something wrong. Darlene would alternate between bouts of depression where she could not get to class for days or weeks at a time, and time periods where she felt on top of the world and was driven by an intense energy. During those periods, Darlene would stay up late and wake up early, surviving for days at a time on just two hours of sleep per night. By the first semester of her sophomore year, right around midterm examinations, Darlene was convinced that she could turn her off-campus apartment cupcake business into an overnight franchise. She spent all of her savings, and maxed out her credit cards to obtain professional-grade baking equipment, the finest ingredients, and flashy marketing materials.

From all indications, Darlene did have superb instincts and she made great progress on her business goals. Nonetheless, the weight of her academic demands combined with her business aspirations and a flourishing mania was too much to handle, and Darlene ended up being involuntarily committed at the local inpatient psychiatric facility.

At age nineteen, she was diagnosed with Bipolar I Disorder, meaning that she'd exhibited sufficient symptoms for both depression and mania. (The medical team had also learned that her paternal aunt had been previously diagnosed with Bipolar II Disorder, as that aunt had only experienced hypomanic episodes that did not meet criteria for full mania.) While Darlene did not have full agreement or support from her family who lived 150 miles away, she began medication to treat her condition, and was able to return to school the following semester. After a few months, Darlene felt stable and experienced almost no side effects. However, she felt so revitalized that by the time she performed well on her spring semester finals, Darlene felt that God had answered her prayers and delivered her from her bipolar condition. Thus, she discontinued the medication.

By the beginning of her junior year, Darlene was in the throes of another manic episode, which ultimately compromised her academic scholarship. Without financial support and not fully knowing her rights and possible accommodations as a disabled student, Darlene dropped out of college and returned to her hometown to work in a franchise bakery.

Over the years, she attempted medication a few more times. However, she often felt guilty about taking the medication when she knew God to be *Jehovah Rophe*, the LORD who heals, and knew that her local pastor had been staunchly against psychiatric medication. (Everybody in the small church knew that Pastor Boyd had always taken his diabetes medication religiously, but, well, that was apparently a different story.)

Darlene showed up for therapy with me for several reasons: Pastor Boyd, her pastor from childhood, had recently passed away and a more progressive pastor had succeeded him. This pastor spoke of God's healing in both supernatural and natural terms, recognizing health care providers as often representing the hands and feet of Jesus. Additionally, Darlene's only son, Zahn, had graduated from high school and was on his way to an out-of-state college in a few months. She thanked God for such a loyal and compliant son, yet still had her concerns about his vacillating moods. She wanted Zahn to get professional help before college turned out to be an unsuccessful experience for him, and she also wanted to influence him by modeling help-seeking behavior herself. Finally, while God had been gracious enough to allow her to climb the ladder at the bakery, Darlene had gone as far as her education would take her. Her business ideas were so much more imaginative than what her cookie-cutter company would allow, and she still harbored the dream to have a business she could grow as her own. All shame and ambivalence aside, Darlene was sick and tired of being sick and tired, and was ready to rise to the fullness of God's purpose for her life, her son, and her business.

Major Symptoms of Bipolar I Disorder

- Experiencing a depressive episode:
  - Feeling depressed most days of the week

- – Losing interest or pleasure in activities previously enjoyed
- – Significant increase or decrease in sleep and/or appetite
- – Feelings of fatigue or low energy
- – Feeling worthless
- – Having thoughts of death or self-harm

- Experiencing at least one manic episode:
  - – Irritable mood most days of the week
  - – Needs less sleep than usual
  - – Talking more than usual
  - – Feeling that thoughts are racing
  - – Engaging in highly risky activities that may have negative consequences
  - – At least one depressive episode

How Psychotherapy Helped Darlene

By Darlene entering psychotherapy for the first time during her mid-life period, she had witnessed firsthand how neither her human effort nor an overspiritualized view of healing had yielded the quality of life she desired. Thus, she was eager to work toward positive transformation. Darlene used therapy as a place to explore the lingering sense of inadequacy she had felt since her youth and to appropriate her Christian beliefs to better see herself as made in God's image and empowered to do God's work through her baking business. Having suffered through broken relationships, Darlene was able to better understand her relationship with Zahn's father, and she developed better communication skills with Zahn. Also during psychotherapy, Darlene was able to acknowledge that her best functioning had occurred during times when she was on medication. While this recognition might have seemed like admitting defeat in an earlier life stage, Darlene was now prepared to accept this reality as God's grace and underwent concurrent treatment for psychiatric evaluation and medication management.

Cannabis Use Disorder

Felicia arrived on her college campus full of expectation and standing on the shoulders of her ancestors. Her family made sure she knew that she was the first in the family to go to college, and she was excited about the opportunity to represent them well. Felicia's mother, Harriet, was her cheerleader. Harriet had dropped out of school at sixteen after she gave birth to Felicia. Her father Charley had managed to graduate from high school, yet found that his wages as a brick mason didn't always cover the needs of the family. Felicia was the oldest of five children, and she felt responsible for setting a good example for her siblings. Her church, a small storefront she'd been raised in since infancy, didn't have a lot of external resources, but it raised $1,000 through a fish fry to send her off to school with a scholarship. Although this scholarship only helped to cover the cost of her books for her freshman year, her church's gesture meant a lot to Felicia. Not only did the body of believers rally around her to offer support, but their efforts reminded her that God was on her side as she advanced her education.

Felicia had chosen her school based on its fit with her career interest, which was to become a neurosurgeon. Felicia studied hard from the first week of class, but was not prepared for the onslaught of assignments and academic pressures she felt in her pursuit to excel. In hindsight, she wasn't so sure that her small-town high school had prepared her adequately to be a "pre-med" student at the state university. Also, she noticed it was a bit difficult to make friends, since she was the only woman from her high school to be accepted there. She couldn't dress as stylishly as the other Black women on campus, and was not in a network with the more popular students. Felicia was only 40 miles away from home, but had a hard time getting home, since her family members were either working two jobs each, or didn't have adequate transportation to pick her up. She missed her grandmother's good cooking, her father's corny jokes, and Mother Brown's weekly words of encouragement.

Although she'd never even attended a party until attending college,

Felicia found that she liked the tremendous sense of relief she felt on the dance floor after a long week of studying. She would take a drink every now and then at the parties, but wasn't really looking for a high. She just wanted to relax and step away from her troubles for a while. At one particularly festive party after midterms, however, Felicia realized too late that she was partying with a group of suitemates who were smoking weed, and she experienced a contact high. She could not deny that she enjoyed the feeling, but she swore to herself that she could not compromise her academic future by experimenting with weed. However, after an especially harrowing biology final, Felicia's friend offered her a blunt, and she tried it. Felicia liked it, and smoked it, reasoning to herself that she would be away from the temptation when she returned home in a few weeks.

Unfortunately, Felicia had not quite estimated just how slippery her slope had become. By the end of the next semester, Felicia was smoking weed regularly and had regular rendezvous with her weed man. She knew that her family would be disappointed in her because they needed their first college graduate, not another family member with substance abuse issues. There was already Grandpa, who'd drunk himself out of several jobs well before retirement age. Then there was Aunt Sally, who was a paraplegic after driving while intoxicated and causing an accident with two fatalities. And don't forget about Cousin Shaun, who was in the slammer for decades based on mandatory sentencing for dealing crack cocaine.

Felicia knew she could not be competitive in her classes with her growing substance abuse problems. Still, she craved the experience of escape that she felt when she smoked. Truthfully, the feeling was not the same as when she began. She found herself having to smoke more often, to find more exotic blends, and to be more and more creative about how to accommodate her growing habit along with her student lifestyle. Felicia would sometimes miss class in order to meet her weed man, and grew less and less concerned about class attendance, her assignments, and ultimately, her grade point average (GPA). When her weed man suggested that she try some heroin to intensify her high, she froze in her tracks. Felicia had flashbacks of Cousin Dana who, although just a few years older than she, had overdosed on heroin at age seventeen. Felicia was at a crossroads and needed to make a decision not just to maintain her family's and church's pride, but also to sustain her own long-term interests.

Major Symptoms of Cannabis Use Disorder

- Craving cannabis
- Using more cannabis for longer periods of time
- Spending more time pursuing, using, or recovering from cannabis
- Difficulty controlling cannabis use
- Problems fulfilling work, family, or social roles
- Symptoms of tolerance (i.e., needing more cannabis to achieve the same effect)
- Symptoms of withdrawal

How Psychotherapy Helped Felicia

Given Felicia's symptoms of substance abuse and her student status, she sought out a mental health professional who also had specialty credentials in treating addictions through Student Health Services. After undergoing withdrawal from cannabis and achieving stabilization, Felicia's therapist helped to connect her to community resources, including a Marijuana Anonymous group and a Celebrate Recovery ministry at a local church. Because of Felicia's academic challenges, her therapist referred her for psychological testing, which revealed a learning disorder in written language. Further, the therapist was able to help advocate for Felicia to maintain her hard-earned scholarship with accommodations for her learning disorder that were authorized by her university's Disability Services Department. As Felicia's crises stabilized, she was able to immerse in deeper work around the spoken and unspoken pressures placed on her by her family and community. After a few sessions involving Felicia and her parents, Felicia lovingly renegotiated her relationships with them as an adult child. She was also supported by her therapist in developing healthy social supports in her home away from home.

Major Neuro-Cognitive Disorder Due to Alzheimer's Disease

No one had to say it. Just as sure as the sun rises every morning, everyone in the family just knew that Willie Mae was their loyal and reliable matriarch. A strong, statuesque woman, she had learned early on to lean on the Lord after her husband left her (and six hungry children) for another woman. Willie Mae was proud to say that she'd brought up all of her children to fear the Lord, and put every one of them in college, vocational school, or the military. Willie Mae was also there for her family down through the generations. She watched grandchildren, and then great-grandchildren, raising those little ones to respect God, family, and themselves. She "loaned" money when it was needed, although she rarely was re-paid for those loans. She provided counsel to her children, putting some marriages together and stopping some train wrecks on their tracks. Long after retirement age, Willie Mae was still working long hours as a home health care nurse to put food on her table, which was really a very long table to make room for all of her extended family members. At Sunday dinners after church (which she prepared each week by herself), her family used to joke, "A mighty fortress is our Mama Mae!"

Willie Mae got her ways honestly. She came from a long line of strong women who worked as far back as slavery, serving others in their homes while maintaining their own homes. Her father, raised in an orphanage, died from polio, and she never knew her mother's father. Sisters had to do for themselves! When she was growing up, there was no such thing as a Black woman becoming anything other than a washerwoman. As her children grew older, she began hearing of Black women who were becoming secretaries, or even teachers. However, with her seventh-grade education and the role of sole breadwinner, Willie Mae felt resigned to domestic work.

However, after her children finished high school, she did pass the GED exam, picked up some classes at the local community college, and became a certified nursing assistant. Helping people was in her blood.

Therefore, no one was prepared for the subtle, and increasingly, not-so-subtle cognitive changes that Willie Mae began to exhibit. Initially, she would forget what she was doing in the middle of a task, or would forget her loved ones' names. This was easy enough to cover up because Willie Mae had always been an affectionate woman, so she just increased her use of terms of endearment for everyone, like "darling" and "sweetie pie." She certainly didn't forget how to share her charming smile. Next, she began to repeat the same stories over and over again, which caught the attention of her family members and friends. She was embarrassed when they would beat her to the end of the story with the punchline, but she didn't know what to do.

After a while, her personality began to change. While Willie Mae had always been clear and direct, she had never communicated harshly to anyone. Now, depending on the day, Willie Mae might yell at others when something wasn't completed to her liking, or call people names. Not surprising to anyone, Willie Mae became even meaner once she lost her driving privileges. Her frustrations over not being able to come and go as she pleased, and having a growing awareness of her memory challenges, were taken out on the two children who lived close by, especially the daughter who lived with her. Not able to get to church regularly, she felt ashamed about her cognitive and spiritual declines, and was increasingly isolated from the strongest sources of support at her church. Willie Mae's health was fairly stable, so her challenges with memory and learning could not be attributed to a stroke or any other medical condition.

Willie Mae, so fiercely independent since age twelve, was finally diagnosed with Alzheimer's Disease, a form of dementia. Her family members were devastated. They had depended on her for so long and for so many things that they had taken for granted that they didn't know what to do. They knew she needed medical intervention, and had even heard that there might be medication that could help slow the progression of her memory issues. The family was less sure about the need for any psychological interventions. What good would it do to put Mama Mae in therapy when she couldn't even remember what parts of her history she had already talked about, nor could she remember new material from week to week? Some agreed that in theory, at least, therapy might help them deal with Mama Mae's changes and to learn strategies to keep the family functioning as effectively as possible given these changes. However, finding the time to take care of themselves seemed like a luxury few could afford as they spent their time "stressing out" over their new roles and responsibilities.

Major Symptoms of Major or Mild Neurocognitive Disorder Due to Alzheimer's Disease

- Greater impairment in one or more cognitive domains
- Family history or evidence through genetic testing of Alzheimer's Disease
- Decline in memory and learning
- Decline in thinking

How Psychotherapy Helped Willie Mae and her Family

Alzheimer's Disease and other types of dementia are progressive cognitive disorders. Because of the course of decline, traditional cognitive-based interventions are less effective forms of psychotherapy. If we emphasize the tremendous need for support for both Willie Mae and her family members, however, we can value psychotherapy for helping the family unit to cope with what is. To the extent that Willie Mae was still verbal and interactive, psychotherapy created a space for venting her frustrations through telling her story, no matter how many times she might have told the same story before. She still received the same nonjudgmental listening and validation, week after week. During family therapy sessions, the family members as a whole discussed their concerns, and one daughter safely voiced her anger at God for letting this happen to their mother. Their therapist affirmed the difficulties of their roles, instructed them in empathic communication with Willie Mae and each other, and engaged them in practical problem-solving strategies, where possible. The therapist was also able to connect the family with culturally relevant resources within their local health system.

Depression

Cassie was a bright young woman full of promise. Despite her intellectual gifts, her winning smile, and her passion for the arts, Cassie had long since convinced herself that the world was against her. When she began spiraling down, usually in the late fall of the year, she would find herself becoming easily annoyed with the co-workers, family members, and even her friends. As a result, she would withdraw from as much social contact as possible. On days when she was feeling better and did want some company, she often found that her loved ones seemed distant and rejecting, confirming her earlier thoughts that they did not want to be around her.

Cassie could go for days without getting out of bed. She used to be "forced" to get out of bed when her dog Pacho was alive, but ever since Pacho died from cancer eight months prior, Cassie told herself during her slumps that she had no reason to get moving if she didn't feel like it. She counted herself blessed to have a job that allowed telecommuting, but even her accommodating boss had been pressing her about missed deadlines lately. Cassie knew that she couldn't afford to lose her job because most of her relationships were strained and she couldn't imagine having to move back in with "The Critic," the nickname she used for her mother behind her back. Her debts were mounting, not only from student loans she'd accrued many years earlier, but also from daily fast-food deliveries, which had become more and more frequent over the last few months. Cassie knew that her lack of exercise and her unhealthy diet were both contributing to her weight gain, but she felt out of control to stop her downward spiral.

Cassie felt like the harder she tried to improve her life conditions, the deeper her despair grew. She had become so lonely that she often questioned whether anyone would miss her when she was gone. As a Christian, Cassie told herself that she would never kill herself, because she knew she would be violating one of the Ten Commandments and bring shame on her family. After all, everybody in her town always said that people who committed suicide go straight to hell, she reminded herself. That commitment to preserving her life, however, did not stop Cassie from praying each night that she simply would not wake up the next morning.

Major Symptoms of Major Depressive Episode

- Feeling depressed most days of the week
- Losing interest or pleasure in activities previously enjoyed
- Significant increase or decrease in sleep and/or appetite
- Feelings of fatigue or low energy
- Feeling worthless
- Having thoughts of death or self-harm

How Psychotherapy Helped Cassie

Because Cassie reached out for help, her therapist was able to quickly diagnose her depression. Her recovery resulted from a combination of interventions: neurochemical stabilization through her psychiatrist prescribing an antidepressant, and Cassie's eventual transparency about her despair, especially as it differed so greatly from the messages of hope she'd always heard at church. Once Cassie understood that she was larger than her depression, she was able to get her vocational plans back on track. Cassie was also able to learn skills for thinking more positively about herself, others, and her future. Even more importantly, Cassie gained courage and developed skills for reconnecting genuinely to others through old and new social relationships.

Chapter Two

Lessons Learned from the Vignettes

As diverse as these women's stories are, notice that each woman demonstrated increases in the frequency, duration, and/or intensity of her symptoms as her story unfolded. For example, Cassie found that her symptoms of sadness and hopelessness intensified each fall. In looking back over her life, Darlene discovered that she had experienced occasional manic episodes since her adolescence. Much like with physical illnesses, without intervention symptoms are likely to worsen over time. These women also displayed functional impairment in that their daily routines at work, school, and/or home were disrupted by the symptoms of their illnesses. Felicia questioned whether she could remain a student as her cannabis addiction progressed and interfered with her life. Willie Mae was not able to care for her own needs, let alone the needs of her extended family, as her symptoms of Alzheimer's Disease worsened.

Because of these challenges, as well as longer-term life experiences, many of these women felt a sense of shame, which sometimes prevented them from seeking help sooner than they did. This shame was sometimes heightened by their faith commitments, whether a religious institution or family member spoke against the pursuit of counseling or therapy, or whether the woman herself interpreted God's Word as condemning any interventions other than spiritual ones. Darlene had been told by her previous pastor, Rev. Boyd, that medication for her bipolar disorder was not a Christian choice. Felicia's church family was visibly quite supportive of her matriculation, but she feared they might also judge her setbacks harshly, let alone her pursuit of therapy and support groups.

What these women shared in common was the great benefit of the nonjudgmental listening each received from her therapist. In some cases, a sister was able to release a long-term secret that had crippled her progress for years. In other cases, receiving support and coping skills for the day-to-day challenges of her symptoms was the most substantial factor in her healing. Willie Mae experienced a supportive environment for venting her frustrations, which she found was lacking amongst her family members. Cassie was able to be transparent about her thoughts of harming herself and gained access to effective techniques for viewing herself and the world in a better light.

Goals of therapy will vary greatly based on the mental disorder diagnosed, the pattern of symptoms, and the theoretical orientation of the therapist. Still, there are some recurring themes that a woman can expect to encounter in treatment, particularly when her treatment is informed by a Christian perspective. These themes include compassionate listening; the remittance of acute symptoms; the recognition of faith as a resource rather than a hindrance to be condemned; empowerment of the self by the Holy Spirit; new ways of looking at one's situation; engagement of distinctively Christian spiritual coping tools; enhancement of communication skills; transparent conversation about relationship issues such as forgiveness and restitution, and reflection on a need or desire for family healing.

If you'd like to read more about other forms of mental illness and life challenges, additional vignettes may be found in Appendix B. In the meantime, let's examine how a sister might begin the journey toward psychotherapeutic healing.

Chapter Three

Choosing Positive Change
Through Psychotherapy

"The stigma of mental illness runs rampant in our community.
People really need to try really hard to get over that
because it is pressing."
Jenifer Lewis, actor starring in Black-ish and
living with bipolar disorder

Have you ever felt like you woke up in a bad mood? Or like everything that can go wrong *is* going wrong? Everybody has this feeling every now and then, a feeling that the day starts out bad and gets worse from there. Throbbing headache. Child confessing in the carline that homework is undone. Doubly congested traffic. One fire after another at work. Phone calls about extended family issues. And that's all before lunch! But sometimes, these challenges can last for more than a day, or even a week. If you find that your mood is low, or that your blues have been lasting for longer than two weeks, you might be dealing with a depressive disorder. (As you've seen from the previous section, major depression is just one of many diagnoses that can benefit from psychotherapy, but is elaborated here due to its high prevalence among Black women.) Major depression can occur in a single episode, or in recurring episodes. Symptoms include depressed mood, feelings of worthlessness, changes in your sleeping and eating patterns, low energy, a loss of pleasure or interest in things or activities previously enjoyable, low motivation, social isolation, and sometimes suicidal ideation. Your experience of these symptoms may be mild, moderate, or severe. You may find it increasingly difficult to function in even your primary roles as a wife, mother, or employee.

 Listen to Recording #2, "Chest of Cares"

While most women with depression find that their symptoms respond fairly well to psychotherapy and/or antidepressant medication, many Black women in my clinical experience take years before they seek professional treatment. For one thing, many in our community do not believe that depression is a true phenomenon. Persons who exhibit these symptoms are often described as lazy, avoidant, attention-seeking, or just needing to "get herself together." We attribute the weight gain or loss that can occur with depression as just an inevitable change in life. At other times, some women feel great shame in seeking help. Perhaps we've been told that building more faith or a stronger prayer life can bring about healing. We may be warned by family members not to "air dirty laundry" or share family business with strangers. Many of us don't understand the degree to which depression can be in our family history, and thus we are exposed to greater risk, through no fault of our own. It is quite common for us to seek help from our pastor or another member of the clergy, which can be an important first step (Chalfant, Heller, Roberts, Briones, Aguirre-Hochbaum, & Farr, 1990; Chatters, Mattis, Woodward, Taylor, Neighbors, & Grayman, 2011; Wang, Bergland, & Kessler, 2003). However, if this person is not adequately trained in mental health issues, a referral to a mental health professional is usually warranted. (Positively, more and more churches are developing church-based mental health programs for their congregants [e.g., Armstrong, 2016; Hankerson & Weissman, 2012].)

The good news, though, is when we do finally decide that life can be better, and make up our minds that it's time to get help, treatment can make a significant difference in our quality of life. Depending on how intense our mood challenges are, we may benefit from following a prescribed regimen of antidepressant medication. Many options are available on the market, and although many primary care providers (PCPs) can provide a prescription, it is often helpful to see a psychiatrist who has expertise in antidepressants and other types of psychotropic medications and can facilitate your transition to the most effective option for you while minimizing side effects.

Your first visit will probably include a psychiatric evaluation, where the psychiatrist will ask about your symptoms, your personal and family medical history, and your preferences. Your subsequent visits will probably be shorter medication management visits, where your psychiatrist will evaluate the effectiveness of your medication and make any needed changes to your dosage, or perhaps change you to a different medication altogether if needed. Some medications require long-term maintenance to properly manage your symptoms, while other medications may be taken on a shorter-term basis. Be sure to speak openly with your psychiatrist at the initial evaluation if you have concerns about the longevity of your pharmacological treatment.

Whether you require medication to support mood stability, psychotherapy is a crucial tool for creating and sustaining positive life changes. Everybody has a story to tell, but few people have shared their story with an impartial, confidential, and nonjudgmental listening ear that can also impart skills for creating positive change or for effective coping in situations that cannot be changed. There's an old hymn that says, "I feel better, so much better, since I laid my burdens down." How true! Jesus invites us: "Come to me, all you who are weary and burdened, and I will give you rest. Take my yoke upon you and learn from me, for I am gentle and humble in heart, and you will find rest for your souls" (Matthew 11:28-29). Your therapist or counselor can assist you in manifesting this "burden transfer" in your life!

So, what can you expect when you seek psychotherapy or counseling? In order to ensure the best fit with a mental health professional, do your homework:

1. Ask your girlfriends or colleagues if they can make any personal recommendations, as word of mouth goes a long way in inspiring confidence to take this big step. (You might be surprised by the number of people who actually have already pursued therapy! As Bill Withers famously sang, "We all need somebody to lean on.")

2. Conduct an Internet search. There are many, many referral directories online (see Appendix C for some suggestions). Many of them are searchable by type of therapist (e.g., counselor, clinical social worker, psychologist, clinical addiction specialist, marriage and family therapist, psychiatric nurse, psychiatrist), areas of expertise, faith commitment (if any), geographical location, schedule availability, forms of payment/insurance accepted, theoretical orientation, and cultural fit; such as race, ethnicity, gender, sexual identity, and disability;

3. Ensure that each person you are considering is licensed and/or certified in their area(s) of expertise. This information will often be reflected in the referral directory or on the individual's website, but you can also confirm that this information is up-to-date by going to the website of their respective professional board for license verification.

4. Once you have a reasonable list of potential therapists, call their respective offices. Although many therapists are in session with other clients during most of their business hours, they may have a receptionist or answering service who handles their calls, or they may have an outgoing greeting on their voicemail that

encourages you to leave a confidential message. Other therapists may have a website presence or a directory listing that allows you to submit a confidential email. Some therapists may even offer a free consultation in case you would like to speak to or meet her/ him before committing to the process of therapy.

5. Inquire about payment arrangements. Many therapists will accept at least a few forms of health insurance for a presenting problem that demonstrates "medical necessity" (i.e., your symptoms meet criteria for a mental disorder in the DSM-5 [American Psychiatric Association, 2013]). Health insurance plans are required to cover mental health and substance abuse conditions, but pay attention to your responsibility for copays, coinsurance, and/or a deductible that must be met before your insurance will cover your visits. Alternatively, you may wish to pay out-of-pocket rates for your sessions. Some women opt to do this if it is affordable, or if they desire to not have information about their mental health history and treatment included in their medical record. For women who do not have insurance coverage and may not qualify for public insurance (i.e., Medicaid), many therapists have sliding scale fees available that may correspond to your income level. Finally, some cities and towns have a network of therapists who agree to provide some *pro bono* counseling sessions. While the number of these sessions is often limited, a *pro bono* counselor can greatly assist in stabilizing a client during or after a crisis situation.

What might you expect during your first psychotherapy session? You will hopefully find a comfortable waiting area with soothing sights and sounds. A receptionist or other notification system will let your therapist know that you have arrived. If you have not already completed initial paperwork online or via email, arrive with enough time to finish prior to the starting time of your scheduled appointment. Your paperwork will likely include your consent to treatment, contact information, questions about your physical and psychosocial history, including any family history of mental challenges, and a mental

health screening tool. Once your appointment begins, your therapist will bring you to her office, review guidelines of the practice, offer you an opportunity to ask questions, and invite you to begin sharing your story. If you have previously received emotional and/or spiritual care from another caregiver, your therapist may request permission to speak with that caregiver to facilitate your treatment. Research demonstrates that such collaboration, especially between therapists and clergy, can be fruitful for long-term client outcomes (e.g., Ennis, Ennis, Durodoye, Ennis-Cole, & Bolden, 2004). Additionally, you and your therapist will probably collaborate on creating a treatment plan that will direct your clinical journey.

As you've seen in the vignettes, working with a licensed mental health professional offers several benefits, including the opportunity to share your story in a safe and confidential space. It offers you the powerful release of burdensome thoughts, feelings, and behaviors in a nonjudgmental atmosphere; the development of a positive and trusting relationship with your therapist, which can foster motivation and transformation; and the accumulation of practical strategies for thinking about and navigating your interactions with the world in a healthier manner. You can expect some difficult days on the therapeutic journey. You may leave some of your sessions feeling frustrated or even angry at your therapist because of the way s/he challenges old patterns that no longer work for you as s/he promotes your positive change. However, there should also be times when you laugh in therapy and rejoice in the transformation happening in your life.

Even when you haven't struggled or are no longer struggling with the symptoms of a defined disorder, you will continue to confront the phenomenon of stress on a daily basis. Because the mind is significantly involved in how daily stressors are perceived and responded to, let's now take a closer look at the components of the mind.

Part Two

Blossoming in Mind

In this section, we explore the mind, which is the seat of our thoughts, both positive and negative. Positive thoughts often facilitate our blossoming, so we'll want to promote those thoughts as much as possible. Negative thoughts, on the other hand, typically discourage us and distract us from the tasks or goals at hand, so we'll want to eliminate those thoughts as much as possible. Additionally, it is important to understand how stress works in our lives, and how we can plan for success even in the midst of stress. Finally, this section ends with a description of mindfulness and several suggested practices for stabilizing the mind.

Chapter Four

Promoting Positive Thoughts

Purpose and Destiny

"When they go low, we go high."
Michelle Obama, attorney and first Black First Lady of the United States

Once a woman knows her purpose, nothing can stop her from reaching her destiny! King David describes God's knowledge of us through creation:

> You have searched me, LORD,
>   and you know me.
> You know when I sit and when I rise;
>   you perceive my thoughts from afar.
> You discern my going out and my lying down;
>   you are familiar with all my ways.
> Before a word is on my tongue
>   you, LORD, know it completely.
> You hem me in behind and before,
>   and you lay your hand upon me.

(Psalm 139: 1-5)

Purpose is something that is God-given well before we are born. Psalm 139:16b declares that God ordained all of our days before one of them came to be. Thus, our life purpose is not so much something to be found as to be discovered. We discover purpose as we steadfastly pursue a thriving relationship with God, for God holds our purpose. God knows all about our wants and our needs, assets and our liabilities, our strengths and our weaknesses, our traumas and failures, our personalities, our family histories, our hopes and dreams. Purpose lines up with our natural talents, our spiritual gifts, our knowledge of the world, and our lived experiences. When you are living "on purpose," you find joy and passion in your everyday existence, even when bogged down in the mundane. You will confront obstacles along the way, but because you have tenaciously traversed your journey thus far, you remained undeterred. Everyone can always use a little extra encouragement and support, but even if these courtesies are absent, you have sufficient internal motivation and the Holy Spirit's encouragement to keep moving forward.

Psychological theory teaches us that children rarely enter the world with a proclivity to doing the things that are good for them, such as eating their vegetables, doing their homework, or practicing their musical instrument. However, with sufficient guidance, repetition, and oversight from loving adults, external motivation such as verbal praise, pats on the back, stickers, and other rewards will ultimately be transformed into internal motivation. Once your internal motivation begins to grow, as a child of God, you have the benefit of the communion of your spirit continually being fed by the Holy Spirit. The Spirit intercedes for you on your behalf, especially when you do not know what to pray about, or what to pray for. So as you grow closer to God, not only do you know more and more of your purpose, but you are given a daily boost of inspired power to accomplish it!

One word about detractors, better known as haters. Sometimes, the closer you get to your purpose, the more likely others, who are not focused on their purpose, are to question you. They might express doubts or disbelief about your destiny (e.g., "Now you know no Black woman has ever done that before!"), about the magnitude of your dream, about your strategies for reaching your destiny, or about the faith walk that enables your success. So, when they pass you the cup of "haterade," you just remember, in the words of our sister Kimberly "Sweet Brown" Wilkins, "Ain't nobody got time for that!" We must be careful in how we expend our energy toward negative, versus positive, endeavors. I often find great encouragement to remain focused in the Scripture recorded in Hebrews 12:1-2:

> Therefore, since we are surrounded by such a great cloud of witnesses, let us throw off everything that hinders and the sin that so easily entangles. And let us run with perseverance the race marked out for us, fixing our eyes on Jesus, the pioneer and perfecter of faith. For the joy set before him he endured the cross, scorning its shame, and sat down at the right hand of the throne of God.

Especially in times of challenge and strain, we focus our attention on Jesus, the One who attended to the joy that was ahead rather than the pain of the immediate moment. We also focus on Jesus because Jesus intercedes for us and reminds us that we are empowered to do even greater works than Jesus had been doing during His earthly ministry (John 14:12). The psychological theories of social modeling and the power of focus reinforce the idea that our altitude depends on where we place our attention and concentration.

Wholeness

> **"Greatness can be captured in one word: lifestyle.**
> **Life is God's gift to you, style is what you make of it."**
> *Mae Jemison, engineer, physician, and*
> *first Black woman to travel in space*

There are many examples in the gospels where Jesus tells someone he has healed that "your faith has made you whole." (Matt 9:22; Matt

14:36; Matt 15:28; Mark 5:34; Mark 6:56; Mark 10:52). In one particular Gospel account (John 5), however, Jesus asks "Will you be made whole?" or "Do you want to get well?" Knowing that our God is all powerful, this is not a moment of doubt for Jesus about whether he is able to heal the man. After all, Jesus Christ was clear in his identity as the Son of God and had already established an incredible track record of healings. Rather, Jesus is asking this man whether he has gotten comfortable, even complacent, with his 38 years of disability. Much like today, there was probably some benefit that the man derived from his disability. Perhaps it wasn't a check from the government, but he probably did receive special consideration, and perhaps donations from the community, particularly from those who pitied his plight. Furthermore, he had probably developed relationships with others who congregated at this pool called Bethesda. There, they could commiserate together about their woes and their limitations. Since habits are formed in as few as 21 days, 38 years had surely perfected his daily routines. Even in his status as an "invalid," this man had probably long adopted the broader society's view of him as invalid, or no good.

How similar to the predicament in which we find ourselves today! As distressing as our shortcomings and limitations may be, they can grow to be as comfortable as a well-worn shoe. We can begin to believe the reports of others over the report of the Lord. Even our family members and friends can have blind spots when it comes to what our true capabilities are. We might be accustomed to a lifestyle of repose and low functioning, because Uncle Sam requires anyone receiving disability payments *not* to demonstrate any significant productivity. So even today, Jesus' question is relevant to us: "Do [we] want to be well?"

If we are prepared to accept the risk that accompanies healing, that is, unfamiliar territory, financial instability, interdependence on others, and change or turbulence in our social relationships, then yes, Jesus is most ready to heal us! All of the years of our suffering can be ended with his touch, even at his word! Although such healing in our lives can generate the aforementioned changes, God is faithful as we adjust to our new identities. The good news, then, is that we can choose to participate in the healing that God offers us. The healing may be physical, psychological, spiritual, financial, or in some other area, and God may heal us differently than how we desire to be healed. Nevertheless, if you want to be well, God is waiting to show you the path. It may involve a few steps that you did not anticipate, such as washing seven times in the Jordan River (2 Kings 5:1-15), receiving your deliverance through unconventional means (John 9: 1-7), or accepting that God's grace is sufficient in spite of our thorns (2 Corinthians 12: 7-10). Indeed, God wants you to be well, and will facilitate your wellness. When the Lord answers our prayers, however, will we be ready to follow some strange instructions?

Stewardship

> His master replied, "Well done, good and faithful servant! You have been faithful with a few things; I will put you in charge of many things. Come and share your master's happiness!"
>
> (Matthew 25:21)

What does it mean to be a good steward of all that God has given us? Well, first it makes sense to define what a steward is, especially since that term is used less often in our common vernacular than it used to be. A steward is "A person who manages another's property or financial affairs; one who administers anything as the agent of another or others." When we consider that all that we have, including our bodies, minds, souls, spirits, relationships, and possessions, have been endowed by God, we realize that we don't actually own anything. Everything is on loan from God, and our role as servants of God is to manage God's gifts to us to the best of our abilities.

A good steward maintains her inheritances from God. The Merriam-Webster dictionary reveals that to maintain is "to keep in an existing state; to preserve from failure or decline." Not only maintenance, but also improvement is key to good stewardship. Imagine that

God gave you a car, still sparkling from the manufacturer, that was the top of the line and brimming with all of your desired features. Maintaining that car would include regular exterior and interior washing and detailing, regular check-ups on all of the systems of the car, and even the addition of enhancements such as a vanity plate, your favorite bumper stickers, and a fragrance system to keep your car smelling fresh. Many of us might invest significant time and money into the maintenance of a car, yet might neglect the maintenance of ourselves, our relationships, and our purpose. In order to properly maintain our heavenly gifts, our time, attention, and intention are required. Stewardship of our bodies includes a consistent fitness routine, nutritious eating, and quality sleep hygiene. Our minds and souls benefit from healthy emotional expressiveness, positive coping skills, reflection, fulfilling relationships, and self-awareness. Being a good steward in our relationships requires love, sacrifice, and courage. Relationships also require honesty, and even conflict at times, in order to grow stronger. Sometimes stewardship requires that an issue be lovingly confronted so that the relationship does not weaken due to growing distrust that has not been expressed. Maintaining our spiritual selves includes regular study of and meditation on God's Word, a lifestyle of prayer, gathering with other believers, and reflection on God's promises to you as well as God's mission for your life. All of these ways of blossoming are further elaborated throughout this book.

Locus of Control and Motivation

> **"I have learned over the years that when one's mind is made up, this diminishes fear; knowing what must be done does away with fear."**
> Rosa Parks, mother of the modern-day Civil Rights Movement

Agency. Power. Self-efficacy. All of these words have to do with what we believe we are able to accomplish. As a child, I inherited a dresser from my parents' bedroom suite that had the following message applied in sticker-like fashion to the upper-right corner of its mirror: "Whatever the mind believes, it can achieve." From an early age, this truth was imprinted on my mind. Even as a largely sheltered, occasionally overprotected child, I had my share of bumps and bruises as my "accidents of birth" (e.g., my gender, race, skin color) collided with the stereotypes and assumptions of my world in the South. I'd always heard warnings of having to work "twice as hard to achieve half as much." I observed from the people in power at my school, at my church, and in my community that racism and sexism were real. I knew from my classroom experiences and the evening news that discrimination was real; I knew from my interactions with other blacks, young and old, that colorism was real.

As an example of colorism, we as a community could be quick to describe, or even insult, another Black person based on the nuanced gradients of skin color, facial features, and of course, hair texture. (It seemed as though we never paused to think about what message we were sending to those not born with so-called "good hair.") Society has continued to correlate negative outcomes with things that are black or dark (e.g., black ice, black humor), and if we're not careful, we too can buy into making negative associations with all things black, including ourselves. We can take on the "victim" role and explain away our lack of accomplishments on "the system," "the Man," our absent father, our last boyfriend, or any convenient scapegoat. Psychologists describe this dynamic, one in which we utilize external factors to explain outcomes, as an external locus of control. From this viewpoint, things are as they are in our lives because the power to change important factors is outside our control. We failed in school because teachers didn't like us. We haven't been promoted on our jobs because the supervisors have their "picks." We can't eat with more healthy habits because fast food restaurants have taken over our neighborhood and the quality grocery stores have closed down, leaving only food deserts behind. Under this scheme, we are stuck in a web of diminishing opportunity and increasing negativity. Life's glass is half empty.

On the other hand, an internal locus of control represents our view that each individual, not external others, has the power to determine her destiny. Internal factors such as faith, hard work, perseverance, and commitment are the ultimate determinants of the future from this perspective. To be sure, women who embrace an external locus of control express positive character traits, and women who endorse an internal locus of control have their share of external barriers (e.g., racism, sexism, classism, and other -isms of the world) that serve as significant impediments to their success. On the balance, however, women who possess an internal locus of control are much more likely to achieve their goals. For these women, life's glass is half full.

If we take seriously God's promises to us as God's daughters (e.g., "You, dear children, are from God and have overcome them, because the one who is in you is greater than the one who is in the world" (I John 4:4), then we have to recognize the inevitability of our success, and to fully cooperate with it rather than resist it. In almost any human contest, there are obstacles that are encountered that must be overcome in order to win the prize. For some of us, we may have the obstacle of physical, mental, and/or emotional disability. For others, we start off in a seemingly compromised position because we were born into poverty or lack of resources. For still others, our family histories are full of dysfunction that both genetically and socially have placed us in a vulnerable position. Those challenges may slow us temporarily, but they can't stop us! God gives each of us the wherewithal to overcome our challenges and setbacks, and to "press toward the mark for the prize of the high calling of God in Christ Jesus" (Philippians 3:13). Continually, we need grace, mercy, encouragement, or strength. These contributions are important because they strengthen the mind and spirit to blossom. And we know that once the mind is made up and the spirit has been renewed, nothing can stop us! At other times, however, we need more practical helps, like financial assistance, or specific direction on our path, or a connection into networks that can equip us with tangible and intangible resources. God equips us with the natural and supernatural resources we need to fulfill God's purpose.

Self-Worth

**"A racist system inevitably destroys and damages human beings;
it brutalizes and dehumanizes them, black and white alike."**
*Drs. Kenneth and Mamie Clark, husband and wife team
and psychologists whose "Doll Test" studies were vital to the success
of the 1954* Brown v. Board of Education *case*

Much has been written about low self-esteem in Black women. But whereas self-esteem is about how we feel about what we have or have not accomplished, self-worth is much deeper: Self-worth is the value that we place upon ourselves. It's how we decide, even at a subconscious level, what we do and do not deserve. Amazingly, there is a deep connection between what we decide we deserve and how others arrive at the same conclusion, for better or for worse. After all, we have to train others in how to treat us. Those who are good students get to stay in our lives, and those who can't or won't comply with our lessons must fall by the wayside. Our worth is determined not by our pedigree, but by God, our Creator, who on the sixth day of creation, saw that what God made was "very good." Even after the fall of Creation, God sent God's only begotten Son to die for each and every one of us, covering ALL sins once and for all.

Despite the infinite value that God has placed on our lives, however, our worth has been and continues to be deeply questioned by society. It only makes sense, then, that out of a history of being marginalized, even explicitly oppressed as women and as blacks, we have more than our fair share of humiliation, mistreatment, and abuse. During centuries of chattel slavery in America, our bodies were not our own. Instead, we were subjected to long hours of labor under harsh, violent conditions and sexual assault at the hands of often vicious slaveholders. Our families were not our own. Our men were often intentionally separated from us, usually sent to another plantation for the purposes of avaricious breeding practices. Our children, too, were regularly sent away as generation after generation became depleted of their youthful vigor and hope. Even after slavery, we were relegated to second-class citizenship through Jim Crow and through work that was often limited to domestic roles in White homes. Despite our foundational roles in the Black Church and the Civil Rights Movement, our contributions have been minimized or ignored. These painful experiences, at the hands of Whites, men, and even ourselves, have often left us with a very dim, even destructive view of ourselves.

Fortunately, our Creator places infinite value on each and every one of us. God not only tells us, "I have loved you with an everlasting love (Jeremiah 31:3)," but also demonstrates love for us by taking on our brokenness, dying for us, and coming back to life with all power to share with us! God continues to encourage us with the message that "you are the apple of my eye" (Deuteronomy 32:10), meaning that when others are implicitly neglectful or even explicitly aggressive toward us or our culture, God still keeps focus on us and continues to develop the gifts and abilities with which we've been endowed. God gives and expands the value and range of our physical appearance, full figures, kinky hair, large nostrils, bodacious lips, and all! God orchestrates our psychological make-up, with all of the mother wit, emotional insight, nurturing presence, intellectual acumen, and intuitive wisdom that we bring to the table. God "stirs up" the deep reservoirs of our faith through our unique experiences and our abilities to pass along those lessons, especially to other Black women. Once we are secure in our own value, knowing that we possess **infinite worth**, we can be about the business of giving God glory on the world's stage through our blossoming lives and talents.

Perspective

"I freed a thousand slaves. I could have freed a thousand more if only they knew they were slaves."
Harriet Tubman, conductor extraordinaire of the Underground Railroad

Do you see your circumstances through a glass that is half full or half empty? Because of who we are in this world, we are often perceived as second, or third-class citizens, ones whose competence, beauty, and contributions lag far behind men and White women, according to mainstream culture. We experience oppression and discrimination from all sides, and this constant pressure takes its toll on us. "Death by a thousand nicks" is one way to describe the injury sustained by constant microaggressions that signal anything from benign neglect to outright rejection from those who presume superiority. No wonder the concept of the "Angry Black Woman" has taken hold! Through sheer conditioning, it seems reasonable that we could wake up every morning "on the wrong side of the bed" with our fists balled up, ready for the first confrontation to attack us. We could expect that any deck would be stacked against us and assume that the world is against us. We could interpret every slight as intentionally rude and every failure for another to be kind to us as a sign of disrespect or even malice.

Yet we must ask, are these the lenses that our Creator has given us for the day? Are we not blessed beyond measure not only by our material goods, but also by the progress of our circumstances? Would not our foremothers, on whose shoulders we now stand, be amazed at the advances of Black women in America, by our achievements in educational attainment, career opportunities, residential communities, and family leisure? Granted, we are each at different places in our individual journeys, but the blessings are no less real as we examine our own stories.

It would help greatly if we could start by counting what we often consider the "little things:" food and water, shelter, transportation, clothing, and safety. Those items may not be exactly as we like them; we may desire a late-model Jaguar but be currently driving a "hooptie," yet we can still get from Point A to Point B. We may wish to be dining in the region's finest steakhouse but currently are resigned to our homemade beans and rice. Nevertheless, we need only to consider those who do not possess these basic necessities to know that we are blessed in our current circumstances, even as God prepares us for greater blessings. The Apostle Paul poignantly stated, "I know what it is to be in need, and I know what it is to have plenty. I have learned the secret of being content in any and every situation, whether well fed or hungry, whether living in plenty or in want. I can do all this through him who gives me strength" (Philippians 4:12-13). Even though we often cite verse 13 as encouragement when we are seeking to undertake significant external feats, such as working toward a significant achievement on our jobs or facing a major foe, we can see here that real strength is needed to accomplish a great **internal** feat, that is, to reach contentment. Contentment, you see, is a state of mind. It reflects our ability to overcome the thoughts and feelings about our perceived shortcomings, and about what other people think about our shortcomings. Contentment is the strength to resist the urge of upward comparison, when we judge ourselves and our worth based on what it seems that others possess and achieve, especially through the lens of social media. Contentment reveals a trust in the God who has the power to bless us with immeasurable riches, and the desire to do so in due time as we allow and collaborate with that power to work within us (Ephesians 3:20). Contentment is not being resigned to the limitations of our current circumstances; rather, contentment is embodying gratitude even as we are blossoming toward where God is taking us next!

 **Listen to Recording #3, "Yes, I Can!"**

Habits

"Never be afraid to sit awhile and think."
Lorraine Hansberry, playwright of A Raisin in the Sun,
the first play written by a Black woman to be performed on Broadway

When you think about your habits, what comes to mind? Brushing your teeth morning and night? Using your turn signals when changing lanes? Late-night munching? From the ordinary to the extraordinary, habits can be positive or negative, taking us closer to or further away from our destiny. Conventional wisdom says that it takes 21 days to form a habit, so we need consistency and patience when we are attempting to develop new habits, such as a fitness routine or an alternative way of engaging social media. So yes, it is true that we have the capacity to form new habits all the time. If the truth be known, however, we are deeply formed by habits that we've demonstrated over years and years, habits so deeply entrenched that they've virtually become invisible to us. Our lives are shaped by the interchange of the week and the weekend: pay periods that may come on a weekly, biweekly, or monthly basis; holidays and their related traditions that form us year after year. That rhythm can be comforting to us, but can also lull us into a sense of complacency. For example, we're sometimes in the habit of going to weekly worship, but may just be going through the motions if we're not fully present in the experience. Think about your daily routines: What do you do when you first wake up in the mornings? What do you drink? What do you eat for breakfast? For lunch? What happens when you get off work? How do you occupy yourself during the evenings? What time do you go to bed? If you were to log all of your activities, you might be surprised by the rhythms of your daily and weekly schedules (and non-schedules).

Some of our best and worst habits are patterns that were introduced to us long ago. Whether it's flossing nightly or hanging out every weekend with a crowd that really doesn't reflect our values, we do many things automatically, mechanically, without consideration of how our lives might be better if we more closely inspected our habits. Herein lies the power of tracking of our behaviors. Not only can you keep a log of your exercise, your food intake, and your sleep patterns for the week, but you can also track your level of productivity at a library versus a coffeehouse, or examine how your devotional life tracks to your well-being, or the level of your attention given to your loved ones with and without your favorite electronic device close by. The timeless wisdom of Mahatma Gandhi, Indian civil rights activist and leader of the Indian Independence Movement, reminds us:

> Your beliefs become your thoughts,
> Your thoughts become your words,
> Your words become your actions,
> Your actions become your habits,
> Your habits become your values,
> Your values become your destiny.

Think intentionally, then, about how you'd like your routines to look. Don't be distracted by the wealth of obstacles that come to mind; they may seem formidable but can be overcome one at a time when you are determined to reach your goals. The barriers to success seem to preoccupy us so much that we never get to the important task of brainstorming freely, without censoring ourselves. But if you can get your mind to imagine or visualize the possibilities, the mind, greatly aided by the Holy Spirit, has a way of transcending those barriers. (This is the concept behind the saying "Where there's a will, there's a way.")

Just ask yourself this question: "If I were to wake up tomorrow and a miracle had occurred, what would my perfect day look like?" Would you be displaying habits that make you a better employee, like getting to work earlier, or communicating more effectively with teammates or customers? Might you show patterns that make you a better student, like studying on a consistent basis, not just the night before a test or paper? Would you be contributing more to humankind, such as making more time for community service, or following up with friends or family who could use your support? Or perhaps you would be preserving some precious time for yourself and for your favorite activities (such as taking that much-needed nap)? While perfection won't be realized on this side of glory, there are witnesses around us who manage to establish habits that reflect integrity with their deepest values. And those values aren't always connected to "doing," (i.e., identifying more business leads, running more marathons, or volunteering for more agencies). Sometimes the highest form of success comes in simply "being," without requisite productivity having to be engaged or documented. Dream carefully about the habits you're envisioning; they will become your destiny.

Power

**"The most common way people give up their power
is by thinking they don't have any."**
*Alice Walker, founder of womanism
and author of* The Color Purple

What comes to your mind when you think of power? Monarchs and
world leaders bending the will of their subordinates to their every
whim? Our elected representatives going through the motions on
Capitol Hill? White men in crisply tailored suits cutting deals in a
boardroom? Well, it's easy to think of worldly power in these ways
because we see so many examples of its use, and frankly, its abuse, in
our daily current events. Merriam-Webster's dictionary defines power
as "possession of control, authority, or influence over others." Power
often resides in political office, wealthy families, in the pulpit, or in
the C-Suite with a corporation's top executives. But do we sometimes
negate our own power? Women, as a group, even in the 21st century,
are often viewed as second-class citizens. Men may not recognize or
may deny our capabilities, particularly if they perceive those capabilities as a threat. As Black women who may also have the experience
or history of poverty, we find ourselves in "triple jeopardy," where the
world assigns us low status because of our race, gender, and socioeconomic class. As the world measures power, we are often on the lowest
rungs of the ladder, or at least farther behind our counterparts with
similar training and experience. If we are hoping to catch up through
sheer effort and determination alone, we may find ourselves in a world
of hurt.

But God! "He came to that which was his own, but his own did
not receive him. Yet to all who did receive him, to those who
believed in his name, he gave the right to become children of God"
(John 1:11-12). That's right—God empowered us to become God's
very own daughters, chosen to show God's love and works in this
world. Reflect on the following Scriptures, which remind us of our
power through God:

"Greater is he that is in me than he that is in the world" (I John 4:4, KJV).

"God is able to do immeasurably more than we could ever ask or think according to God's power at work within us" (Ephesians 3:20).

"No, in all these things we are more than conquerors through him who loved us" (Romans 8:37).

"I can do all things through Christ who strengthens me" (Philippians 4:13).

What would happen if we made these Scriptures and other godly statements the affirmations that we repeated day after day, loud enough for ourselves and those around us to hear, believe, and act upon? We would unleash power that could change us and our circumstances! We would witness the impact of God's truths on our families, our homes, our churches, our communities, and our society! Make your favorite affirmations visually and auditorily accessible in your journal, around your office, prayer closet, and vehicle. Say them out loud several times daily, remembering that "The tongue has the power of life and death, and those who love it will eat its fruit" (Proverbs 18:21).

 Listen to Recording #4, "Affirmations for Sisters"

Creativity

> **"The only limit to success is your own imagination."**
> *Shonda Rhimes, first Black woman writer, director, and producer of a Top 10 network series, "Grey's Anatomy"*

The book of Genesis offers two accounts of the creation story. One account is contained primarily in the first chapter, and the other account, which begins in the second chapter, gives specific details about the creation of woman out of man. (Some have quipped that when God made Eve, God was really showing off!) Both accounts demonstrate God's amazing ability to create something out of nothing, something as majestic as the heavens, the seas, the vegetation of the earth, the animals, and humans. And when God finished, God marveled that creation was good.

Even after millennia of human neglect and abuse of creation, we creatures can still observe the wonders that exist in nature. God's creation is still amazing, including what God has bestowed to us as creatures. I am often left speechless by how much creative power flows through our veins! Think about the incredible masterpieces that emerge from the chair of your favorite stylist, or the exquisite visual and gustatory stimulation rendered by that community sister who has mastered making beautiful cakes and other desserts for every occasion. Did you ever wonder how Mama So-and-So can run her full-capacity child care business like a champ, while you and I might struggle with just our few children after a couple of hours? Or maybe you've witnessed the C-suite sister who runs her department, or the whole business, with grace and superb effectiveness. All of this creative inspiration comes from our Creator and is elevated to a fine art by the Holy Spirit. But before you chalk the talents up to an inaccessible entity (e.g., "I wish I could, but that's not my gift."), think deeply about the spiritual gifts, talents, and abilities that have already been given to you. (See also Chapter 12 on Spiritual Gifts.)

It may be that the major difference between the heart-warming creativity of your neighbor and your own self-assessed mediocrity is practice. In this society of instant gratification, we expect that things in life will come easily to us. Technology and resources are often readily available, but they don't negate the need for good old-fashioned commitment, perseverance, and skill building in our craft. After commitment comes the vision for an outcome and the burgeoning of our creativity toward our desired end. "Whatever the mind believes, you can achieve." If you have a vision for an outcome, don't be deterred by anxieties about how it will come to pass. The Creator not only gives inspiration, but also will guide you every step of the way. If you're someone who likes to have the whole journey laid out before you begin, you may be in for a rude awakening, because that is often not how God works. Think about Abram's challenge in Genesis 12:

The LORD had said to Abram,

> "Go from your country, your people and your
>   father's household to the land I will show you.
> I will make you into a great nation,
>   and I will bless you;
> I will make your name great,
>   and you will be a blessing.
> I will bless those who bless you,
>   and whoever curses you I will curse;
> and all peoples on earth
>   will be blessed through you."

So Abram went, as the LORD had told him; and Lot went with him. Abram was seventy-five years old when he set out from Harran. He took his wife Sarai, his nephew Lot, all the possessions they had accumulated and the people they had acquired in Harran, and they set out for the land of Canaan, and they arrived there (verses 1-4).

As you can see from Abram's obedience to God's command at the ripe age of 75, as long as there is breath in your body, you are never too old to respond to God's command. Your obedience, and the resulting blessings, will powerfully affect your family, your employees, and your community. Abram was able to build on the resources that God had already bestowed upon him. God may not be calling you to uproot geographically; God may be calling you to uproot your old ways of thinking and to transition to a new mindset. New places are unfamiliar and sometimes intimidating. New ideas are foreign, yet can lead to the very blessings and refreshing for which we've been thirsting. With God on our side and God's creative power flowing through our veins, whom shall we fear (Psalm 27:1)? As a child of the Creator, be creative!

Chapter Five

Eliminating Negative Thoughts

Getting Unstuck

> "We have to talk about liberating minds
> as well as liberating society."
> *Angela Davis, political activist, and author of*
> The Prison-Industrial Complex

Have you ever found yourself fully aware of a million things you need to do—for work, for school, for your family, for your home, for your church, for yourself—but you're so overwhelmed that you don't know where to start? Your initial uneasiness and anxiety, your awareness that more and more time is passing without much (or any) productivity, and your panic about the imminent consequences of your tasks not getting done all culminate in debilitating paralysis. Some call this pattern "paralysis of analysis" because the more we think through the tasks, the more paralyzed we feel. This string of events is bad enough to experience once, but most of us have experienced this in a frustrating cycle. Sometimes we even create a catastrophe with our thoughts, which can leave us in a state of panic and catastrophizing. Such a scenario leaves us wondering, "How can I get unstuck?"

Listen to Recording #5, "Cutting the Catastrophizing"

In my experience, one of the factors that aggravates this cycle is not knowing exactly what we are trying to accomplish. When those million to-dos are swirling around in our heads, they take on a life of their own. So, one of the best ways to impose structure on this situation is to make a list. Write down all of the things that you need to do. Perhaps you use a calendar or planner, or maybe you prefer to record and store this data electronically. (Electronic storage carries the advantage of easy retrieval; however, some of us like the feeling of paper and pen, and all of us should be cautious about storing sensitive data in the Cloud, so proceed with caution.) No matter which way you go, you should write down every single task that has been, is now, or will be on your mind. This dumping of all contents of your to-do list will free your brain to use its resources on much more effective endeavors, including strategizing a plan.

I find it helpful to categorize my list by projects or segments of my life (e.g., home and family, work tasks, church responsibilities, me! See Appendix D for an example). It may work best for you to create this weekly list late Friday afternoon, while deliverables are still on your mind, or on Sunday evening, to mentally prepare for the work week. If you work a nontraditional schedule, adjust your preparation times accordingly. Even though the inevitably long list may initially intimidate you, it can also give you a sense of relief in that everything is written down, at least eliminating your worry that you are about to forget a major task! Also, putting down small items, such as returning phone calls, gives you a sense of victory and builds some helpful momentum.

Another strategy for getting unstuck is to envision or literally create a "reset button." While the sheer volume of what we may need to accomplish is significant enough, we make our tasks ten times more burdensome with the guilt and shame that we pile on ourselves:

"I should have done this a long time ago."

"I'm such a procrastinator!"

"Just like Aunt Vickie used to say, I'm just lazy."

We find it tremendously difficult to come out from hiding, so the inertia multiplies. But think about the power of a reset button on, say, a game you might play on your favorite device. No matter how complex the situation, no matter what mistakes you made in that game, the reset button sets all things right again. This reset button isn't just a figment of our imaginations, or an illusion we create to make ourselves feel better. This reset button is compliments of God! We serve a God not just of another chance, but a God of many, many chances:

> Who is a God like you,
>   who pardons sin and forgives the transgression
>   of the remnant of his inheritance?
> You do not stay angry forever
>   but delight to show mercy.
> You will again have compassion on us;
>   you will tread our sins underfoot
>   and hurl all our iniquities into the depths of the sea.
>   (Micah 7:18-19)

Thus, our guilt is thrown into the "sea of forgetfulness." Don't go out to sea and drag it back! Yes, I hear your protests:

"How can God forgive me when I keep repeating the same mistakes?"

"God does not give me license to continue to sin after bailing me out."

"I must not be really serious if I keep getting into the same problems over and over again."

When Peter queried Jesus about the limits of forgiveness in The Parable of the Unmerciful Servant (Matthew 18: 21-35), Jesus instructs Peter to forgive "not seven times, but seventy-seven times." While we do not like to be on the giving end of this much forgiveness, what a privilege to be on the receiving end of God's forgiveness! When we confess our sins, God *is* faithful and just to forgive our sins and cleanse us of all unrighteousness (I John 1:9). Yes, we sometimes take it upon ourselves to get sullied again, yet God's faithfulness remains. As we grow stronger in Christ, we are able to engage in the practice of *metanoia*, a Greek term that denotes agreeing with God's way and turning away from our transgressions. God increases our self-control, and also gives us grace to become less and less interested in situations that are not God-centered. Increasing your organizational skills and activating the forgiveness that God extends to all of us are two powerful ways to get unstuck and to start blossoming toward your goals.

Baby Steps

> **"As I look back on my life, I realize that every time I thought I was rejected from something good, I was actually being redirected to something better."**
> *Tamela Mann, award-winning gospel recording artist and actor*

Another important approach for managing stress is to realize and harness the power of "baby steps." As I mention baby steps to you, there's probably a part of you that cringes at the thought of not being able to beautifully execute a masterful feat in one fell swoop (which sounds eerily similar to "able to leap tall buildings in a single bound"). Well, fall back, Superwoman! As Strongblackwomen, envisioning achievement in this way not only creates ongoing physical challenges, leads to sleep deprivation, and contributes to the neglect of our homes and relationships, but it also produces a distorted view of who we are. Instead of operating in the Spirit and strength of God, we have re-written Scripture to say, "I can do all things through *myself* because I strengthen me." In reality, God tells us that God's grace is sufficient for us, for God's grace is made perfect in weakness, and when we are weak, then we are made strong (2 Cor 9:9-10).

Even though we are conscious of the notion that showing weakness is "not a good look," we also must acknowledge that the journey of a thousand miles begins with one step. No matter what the goal, it can successfully be broken down into smaller chunks. If you're having a difficult time identifying how to create manageable steps to solve a problem, enlist the help of a friend. Not only do you want to write down the larger issues, but you want to develop a timeline for the completion of each step. Since we are made in God's image, we are able to formulate our own plans. "Plans fail for lack of counsel, but with many advisers they succeed" (Proverbs 15:22). However, we must also keep in mind that although we have many plans in our hearts, the Lord's purpose will prevail (Proverbs 19:21). So, I heart-ily encourage you to prayerfully make your plans, but understand fully that those plans are subject to the LORD's revisions (which are always improvements as compared to our finite plans, in the final analysis)!

Once you establish your goal, break it into bite-sized pieces and have a plan for implementing each segment. Begin the work by using a healthy dose of self-control. Self-control, after all, is a fruit of the Spirit that God plants in us and allows to grow in us with loving care and maintenance. Self-control is exercising the power to do the things that we need to do, no matter how we feel. This is not easy, because we can always generate endless excuses for why we are not able to execute our goals at the appointed time:

"I don't feel well."

"I didn't get enough sleep last night."

"I've got a lot on my mind."

"So and so needs such and such..." and the list goes on. Even the

Word acknowledges that the spirit is willing but the flesh (human nature) is weak (Mark 14:38). Nevertheless, we do grow stronger in self-control as we remain connected to the Vine.

Another factor in successfully taking baby steps is through the creation of human connections that can gently hold you accountable in reaching your goals. You may find that it is helpful to have different accountability partners for different goals in areas that best fit those persons. For example, the person who holds me accountable for my financial goals is a friend who is an entrepreneur in the financial industry. The person who holds me accountable for my writing goals is a therapist who is a published author. While face-to-face accountability works best for me, it can also be achieved using other forms of technology, especially when it comes to long-distance confidantes. The key is making sure that your accountability system is consistent.

Nonjudgmental Love

"Everything I need is in the presence of God."
Tasha Cobbs Leonard, award-winning gospel recording artist

"Do not judge, or you too will be judged. For in the same way you judge others, you will be judged, and with the measure you use, it will be measured to you" (Matthew 7:1-2). Despite the fact that the Word of God commands us not to judge, we often find ourselves evaluating the "rightness" or "wrongness" of others:

"If I were her, I would let that man go!"

"How did she choose to wear *that* to church today?!"

"Why didn't he at least finish high school?"

These are some of the judgmental statements that we mutter under our breath, or even worse, that we say out loud, in the company of others who need more of our light and less of our darkness. It has become such an ingrained habit that we often judge automatically, without thinking about the repercussions of our thoughts and words. Sadly, many of our family and religious cultures support such judgmental practices. Gather most of our families together and you'll observe that we can quickly pile on judgment as a group, even feeding off of each other. And one of the most common criticisms of Christians, often appropriately earned, is that we are "too judgmental."

How have we fallen so far from grace, from the very commandment that instructs us not to judge? Well, part of the reality is that our human nature is given to tearing each other down rather than building each other up. It sometimes makes us feel better about ourselves when we can portray another in a less favorable light. Social psychologists use the theory of downward social comparison to explain how we often compare ourselves to others whom we believe are performing less well than we are to boost our self-esteem (Carmona et al., 2006). On the other hand, using upward social comparison to measure ourselves against those who we perceive are doing better than us has the effect of leaving us feeling worse about ourselves. So judging ourselves against "less successful" others seems to leave us with a psychological benefit.

That "benefit" is short-lived, however. Not only are we often incorrect in our perceptions of "right" and "wrong," but we typically can fall prey to the very weapon that we've used against others. Yes, we can become extremely judgmental of ourselves. I have observed countless clients talk themselves out of pursuing their dreams, or even reaching for a weekly goal, because they judged that there were "too _____" to get the job done. Often, this self-judgment is one that they've learned from early childhood or adolescence:

"You don't have the IQ to become a doctor."

"Your skin is too dark to become a model."

"You are too lazy to ever amount to anything!"

Or perhaps the messages were subtler: a disapproving look when you wore certain clothing, an abrupt change of subject when you raised issues important to you, or a lack of support or attendance at events that you were enthusiastic about. So, now as an adult, you have internalized the judgment and disdain to perfection, and it unleashes itself automatically in your mind.

One of the most important steps in releasing yourself from being judgmental is to first recognize how deeply entrenched it is in your life. How often do you catch yourself passing judgment on someone else? On yourself? Do your friends describe you as judgmental? Have your relationships suffered as a result of your sharing a critical viewpoint in a cold manner at a most inopportune time? Sadly, we are often standing in judgment about situations that we don't know the first thing about. We don't know the history, the lack of resources, negative messaging, or the other complex factors that contribute to another person's decision making. Even when it comes to judging ourselves, we often don't have full self-awareness of why we do the things we do, or don't do the things we don't do. Even the Apostle Paul struggled in this area, noting "I do not understand what I do. For what I want to do I do not do, but what I hate I do" (Romans 7: 15).

Once you recognize how pervasive the pattern is in your life, are you willing to turn the tide? You can become a less judgmental person by showing nonjudgmental love, that is, by taking on a more compassionate attitude toward others, *and toward yourself.* Being compassionate is not the same thing as ignoring or approving wrongdoing. Reflect on the story of the woman who was caught in adultery and brought before Jesus by the teachers and Pharisees (John 8:1-11). Her accusers demanded that she be stoned and were so bent on her condemnation that they even quoted the law of Moses to Jesus, as if he had forgotten the rules. (By the way, if you're noticing that the man caught in adultery with her did not appear in this passage, be aware that double standards have been with us for centuries!) Jesus initially ignored them, but as they pressed him for a response, he stated, "Let him who is without sin cast the first stone" (v. 7, King

James Version). Slowly but surely, her accusers departed. Jesus noted to the woman that no one had condemned her, and that he would not condemn her either, although as the Son of God without sin, he *could have* condemned her. So, did Jesus say, "Do you, Boo"? No! He told her to go and to leave her life of sin, giving a compassionate acknowledgement that she could do better, and empowering her to do so. Compassion empowers, while judgment destroys. We must remember that God is our ultimate Judge, and God will judge us in the end. Yet this is the same God who gives us countless chances to become more godly, the same God who is constantly looking beyond our faults to see and meet our needs.

Often, the best way to overcome thinking and saying judgmental statements is thinking and saying compassionate statements. Instead of thinking, "She knows better than to send those kids to school looking so unkempt," think, "I wonder what difficulty she is going through in her life right now. I will pray for the LORD to meet her needs." Or even more honestly, "I wonder what would happen in my relationship with my children if I didn't insist on them looking perfect all the time. I will pray for the LORD to help *me* with my perfectionism!" Confessing to God that you have judged when God told you not to judge, and committing to replace judgmental thinking with nonjudgmental love, especially toward yourself, will work amazing results in your life.

Chapter Six

Understanding Stress

"Although we cannot avoid stress, we do not have to be distressed.
We do not have to let stress conquer us. We can find
the strength and power we need for life's journey."
Rev. Dr. Suzan D. Johnson Cook, first female senior pastor of the
American Baptist Churches USA and first Black and first woman to
serve as U.S. Ambassador-at-Large for International Religious Freedom

E very day of our lives, we experience stress. The Merriam-Webster
Learner's Dictionary defines stress as "a state of mental tension
and worry caused by problems in your life, work, and so forth." Even
when we experience a positive outcome, such as being promoted at
work, we experience what pioneering stress researcher Hans Selye
referred to as "eustress," or good stress. Stress is disruptive to our
regular state of equilibrium. On our better days, stress is manageable—the dress we purchase doesn't come in our favorite color, or
our children are fussing with each other about whose turn it is to
ride shotgun. On more difficult days, however, we wonder whether
our resources—physical, psychological, financial, or otherwise—are

sufficient for coping with the demands that we face. We've heard the hymn, "There's A Bright Side Somewhere (Jenkins, 2001)," but we secretly wonder if this is true. For countless generations of Black women before us, stress was just a way of life, something to press through because their survival depended on it. The challenges of chattel slavery and its harsh realities—having little to no control over our bodies, our families, what work we would did, or the circumstances of our lives—were devastating to the psyche. Transitioning out of slavery into the reign of Jim Crow laws did not vastly improve our living conditions as we remained at the bottom of the social framework of society. With the victories of the Civil Rights Movement and the advancement of women's rights, we witnessed more glimmers of hope and some measurable progress in the quality of life of Black women, overall. Still, in contemporary society, we face the challenges of our intersectionality, that is, ways that our race, gender, class, and other unique factors converge to oppress us. On a daily basis, we may be confronted with microaggressions, which are statements, gestures, or events that demonstrate small, indirect, or nuanced forms of discrimination against members of a marginalized group (e.g., "You don't seem like a normal Black woman.")

Over the years, our ancestors have passed along our Christian faith, wisdom, encouragement, and practical strategies for how to survive under oppressive circumstances. In everything from raising children without paternal support to maintaining our coiffures with style and dignity, these maternal figures have helped us to "keep on keeping on." Some might suggest that Black women now have unprecedented opportunities to focus not merely on surviving, but blossoming!

Of course, blossoms don't occur in isolation. Our individual blossoms are inevitably connected to other blossoms, stemming from many branches on the Vine. God connects us to God as well as others, nurturing us from the deep roots that sustain us. We sisters are growing together!"

Listen to Recording #6 for "Sisters"

Striving to blossom, with all of its glorious potential, however, also has its challenges. Many of these challenges, such as pursuing advanced education, building a family of integrity, climbing the corporate ladder, establishing a non-profit organization, or starting your own business, can yield amazing outcomes, but also result in higher and higher levels of stress. Even more overwhelming can be the community and global stressors, such as gang violence, unfair educational practices in our children's schools, and the constant tele-vised or cyber-based, viral events connected to the criminal *injustice* system. Over time, stress is unpleasant or painful to experience, and it can also have a devastating impact on our life expectancy and other indicators of health and quality of life.

Approaches to stress management are often presented by focusing on one individual category of mind, spirit, body, or soul. The truth of the matter, however, is that many of the most effective strategies overlap with each other. That is, stress-relieving practices that are good for the spirit are also good for the body, and practices that are good for the body are also good for the mind. Take prayer, for example. As women of God, we understand intellectually and experientially that prayer is our deep-est form of communication with God, our connection to God's endless resources, and our reminder that we are creatures dependent on God's grace and mercy just to make it through. When prayer becomes our habit, it has a way of letting us know that since God is in control, we don't have to be, which is a tremendous stress reliever. As we experience God's work in our lives, God makes our yokes easier and our burdens lighter (Matthew 11:30). This spiritual relief, however, also shows up on the horizon of our mental and physical states. Although our circumstances may not have changed, with prayer we can experience less worry and fewer headaches, gastrointestinal (GI) problems, and muscle tightness. The next section offers several strategies that you can adopt into your regular routines to help relieve stress.

Planning for Success with Goal Setting

> **"You can pray until you faint, but unless you get up and try
> to do something, God is not going to put it in your lap."**
> *Fannie Lou Hamer, voting rights activist, philanthropist, and
> co-founder of the Mississippi Freedom Democratic Party and the
> National Women's Political Caucus*

Setting goals is a key component in successful outcomes. One of the most popular times to set goals is at the turn of the New Year when we are feeling most hopeful about the upcoming year. However, New Year's resolutions have begun to fade. Why is it that we as a society are reluctant to make and keep resolutions? In many cases, we've faced years of discouragement as we've witnessed the cycle of making, then breaking resolutions. We conclude that resolutions don't work, so we dismiss the entire practice. We know firsthand that resolutions can be difficult to sustain over time, and downright embarrassing if we have made public declarations that eventually call more attention to our failure. However, if we were to ask ourselves whether we plan to be better in the future than we have been in the past, many more of us would agree that improvement is a worthwhile goal.

So perhaps we might do better not to "throw out the baby with the bathwater," but to develop the best strategy for establishing and maintaining our resolutions, or our goals, more generally. First, we have to make sure that our goals are SMART—Specific, Measurable, Attainable, Realistic, and Time-bound. It is much more difficult to assess progress on a vague goal (e.g., "This year, I will lose weight") as compared to a SMART goal (e.g., "This year, I will lose 2 pounds per month."). We sometimes find more motivation in setting modest goals and surpassing them, rather than setting unrealistic goals and falling short.

In addition to our SMART goals, however, we also find success in introducing positive accountability into the equation. Research conducted by Richard Wiseman (2007) reported that men were 22 percent more likely to reach their goals when they engaged in the practice of goal setting. Further, Wiseman reported that women were 10 percent more likely to succeed in achieving their resolutions when they made their goals public and received support from their friends. While I have always exhibited a zest for accountability, I have learned from some of my clients that accountability can be perceived as a bad word. As I explored this dynamic further, I often found that clients had entrusted their precious goals to the hands of accountability partners who did not always have their best interests at heart. Perhaps they were ridiculed or subtly demeaned when they missed the mark. Or maybe they were neglected when partners did not check on their progress, or were ignored in the face of obvious progress. Maybe their partners were excessively harsh, or not skilled in providing useful support. So, it appears that good accountability partners possess the qualities of being trustworthy, supportive, prayerful, consistent, and "gently firm." You should sense in a good accountability partner, even one with whom you've become recently acquainted, that she expresses a genuine concern for you as a person, and understands the importance of protecting your privacy, at least to the extent that your goals are private. She is not only willing, but also action-oriented in checking on your progress. And in the case of mutual accountability, she is transparent about her own successes and failures along the journey to achieving a higher level of self-improvement.

One final word about goal setting: Rather than thinking about goals as either met or unmet, we can train our minds to think about goal achievement more like a marathon than than a sprint. If we find after two months that our goals have gone largely unachieved, we don't have to conclude that we have permanently failed our pursuits. Instead, we can re-evaluate what has and has not worked, and why. What barriers have presented themselves? What control do we have over those barriers? For those barriers outside of our control, what new adjustments must we make to stay on the path toward meeting our goals? Equipped with these reflections, we can make course corrections and continue blossoming!

Chapter Seven

Practicing Mindfulness

**"You have to dance unencumbered. There's no other
way to move. The idea of dance is freedom.
It is not exclusiveness, it's inclusiveness."**
*Judith Jamison, dancer, choreographer, and Artistic Director Emerita
of the Alvin Ailey American Dance Theater*

Mindfulness is the practice of nonjudgmental focus on the
present moment. Dr. Jeffrey Brantley, an expert in mindful-
ness-based stress reduction (MSBR), further notes, "Mindfulness
is practiced by paying attention on purpose, nonjudgmentally, and
with a welcoming and allowing attitude. It means turning toward
present-moment experience rather than away from it" (Brantley, 2007). Mindfulness is associated with lower levels of anxiety,
depression, anger, confusion, and chronic pain, and higher levels
of self-regulation, acceptance, empathy, and spirituality. Mindfulness meditation has been demonstrated to be effective with Black
women (e.g., Woods-Giscombé & Gaylord, 2014; Watson, Black, &
Hunter, 2016), particularly when cultural adaptations, such as focus
on Biblical texts and hymns, inclusion of other African Americans

in the practice, and the incorporation of writings and music from African Americans.

**Listen to Recording #7, "This Day,"
a mindful reflection on the present moment**

Centering Prayer is a form of meditative, silent prayer that leads us to experience closeness with God's presence, with the purpose of deepening our relationship with Jesus Christ (Keating, 2009). Centering Prayer is closely connected to a form of prayer known as contemplative prayer, which originated in the practices of the desert fathers and mothers during the early centuries of Christianity (Chryssavgis, 2008). To engage this practice, the individual is encouraged to sit comfortably in a quiet environment, and to focus on God's love and grace. Next, the individual focuses on a holy word that symbolizes the desire for closeness to God, such as "loving" or "faithful." As the individual focuses on this word, she also becomes aware of the thoughts, feelings, or images that surround her practice. She gently brings her attention back to the holy word, and experiences the presence and movement of God in that moment.

Deep breathing, also known as diaphragmatic or abdominal breathing, is an intentional discipline that undergirds many other relaxation practices. Qualitatively different from involuntary breathing, which occurs below our conscious awareness, deep breathing requires our awareness and attention to the breath, or our pattern of inhalation and exhalation. Engaging this practice effectively can reduce feelings of anxiety and panic and reduce arousal of the autonomic nervous system, which controls our fight-or-flight responses (Davis, Eshelman, & McKay, 2008). Deep breathing is one of the most practical and effective relaxation strategies we can use, for several reasons. First, it can be used virtually anywhere, whether in the classroom, in the boardroom, or in interstate traffic. Second, it is a private discipline. If you practice with gentle nose breathing, your deep breathing is nearly undetectable by others. Third, God's air is free, so there are no fees associated with this practice. Fourth, deep breathing can be highly effective. Practicing these steps for only three to five minutes per episode can yield demonstrable differences in your body's relaxation response. Deep breathing actually instructs the body to relax, a response that is incompatible with anxiety.

 Listen to Recording #8 for an example of deep breathing combined with the Jesus Prayer, described further in Chapter 11

Therapeutic massage and bodywork are modalities that bring a number of benefits to the body and mind, including stress reduction, improved circulation, stimulation of the lymphatic system (which helps rid the body of toxins), increased range of motion, enhanced joint flexibility, stretching and relaxation of tight or tired muscles, release of endorphins (i.e., the body's natural painkillers), and alleviation of pain. Therapeutic massage may be conducted on a table or in a specially designed chair, which makes it accessible in a variety of settings, including massage studios, day spas, and even many shopping areas. More specific forms of bodywork include deep tissue massage, Reiki, cupping, acupressure, acupuncture, and myofascial release. Oncology and prenatal massage options are also available.

Movement of the body is often a key component of stress relief and relaxation, since stress often resides in the body. Sedentary lifestyles are associated with greater incidence of cardiovascular disease, cancer, and type 2 diabetes, in addition to higher mortality rates across these diseases (Biswas et al., 2015). In addition to more traditional forms of exercise and dance, three popular forms of movement include yoga, Zumba, and tai chi.

In Sanskrit, **yoga** means "union with God." Yoga is an ancient practice of bringing into balance the breath, body poses, and meditation and to promote health and wellness. Originating in India over 5,000 years ago, yoga has been adapted across many cultures and faith traditions. Contrary to popular belief, yoga is not a religion and is not descended from Hinduism, as it existed long before Hinduism was established in India (American Yoga Association, 2006). Yoga is often practiced for 60-90 minutes per session, with one to three sessions per week for optimal wellness. Many people who practice yoga advise against eating two to three hours before the yoga session.

Zumba employs Latin and international music with a combination of low- and high-intensity movements to produce a dance fitness experience. Zumba classes emphasize cardio-vascular exercise, conditioning, balance, and flexibility. Class variations include aquatic exercise, chair dancing, a nutritional focus, and adaptations for children of all ages. Classes may be found at fitness centers, dance studios, skating rinks, schools, community centers, and churches.

Tai chi is an ancient Chinese practice that combines low-impact physical exercise, stretching, and mindfulness. It has been demonstrated to increase flexibility, balance, and sleep quality, and to reduce stress, anxiety, depression, as well as the number of falls among older persons (Nordqvist, 2016). The term "tai chi" derives from the term "t'ai chi ch'uan," which means "supreme ultimate fighting" (Palermo, 2015). Originally developed as a noncompetitive martial arts form, it is appropriate for people of all ages due to its gentle movements.

From my perspective, it is less important to choose the "right" stress-relieving technique, and more important to experiment with one or more of these approaches to find the ones that allow you to blossom. While they can greatly relieve the mind, they also can bring great benefits for body, soul, and spirit. We now turn our attention to the important components that promote blossoming in spirit.

Part Three

Blossoming In Spirit

We are spiritual creatures, yet we are not always familiar with the ways that we can expand our spiritual capacity. This section affirms our identity as daughters of God, an identity that forms the basis of our confidence for exploring the rich relationship that is available with our Creator. Through the real challenge of spiritual doubts, we emerge to explore the precious spiritual disciplines of Scripture reading, prayer, journaling, and other gems. As these regular practices shape us for service, we can discern which spiritual gifts have been endowed to us to translate our purpose into the world.

Chapter Eight

Uncovering Your Spiritual Identity

"Grace is not the absence of the struggle;
it is the presence of protection."
*Sarah Jakes Roberts, pastor, author, and business woman
with TDJ Enterprises*

How do we know who we are? As Black women of the 21st century, it can be difficult to answer this question. We are a people of the African Diaspora, meaning that we are spread far and wide from our motherland. Even with the current DNA testing that is available, we don't really know for sure the specifics of which village we are from, or which particular clan or tribe from which we are descended. For some of us, reconnecting to the African continent is an important aspect for our identity. For others of us, we simply desire to have more information about our family ties on this side of the Atlantic. That feat, too, can be difficult for several reasons, including the common lack of awareness of who our father or mother is. Sometimes the parent is absent due to decision, death, divorce, or other division between the parents. At other times, well-intentioned parents have been denied access to a child by the other parent or by their own extended family members. In these cases, it can be nearly impossible to learn about one side of our family, including information on traditions, major family events, medical history, and who is in the family. There can also be a lack of family history due to a premature death, records lost or destroyed, secrets, or a family cut-off where family members are no longer speaking to each other. Stories that we've heard about the identity of a parent sometimes conflict with other stories, even from members of the same family. Additionally, the shame experienced by the primary parent can prevent a disclosure of the other parent's identity, particularly where incest, teen pregnancy, adultery, or substance abuse has been involved. If we have a vague sense of who that parent is, we can mature to a point where we can do our own genealogical research. Some women are even fortunate enough to locate a "lost parent," to reconnect with them, and to forge a positive and growing relationship.

Thus, knowing your family history and your geographical location seem essential to knowing yourself. Think about the genealogies that are listed throughout the Bible, such as in the fourth chapter of Genesis, the third chapter of Numbers, the first chapter of Matthew, and the third chapter of Luke. We sometimes gloss over these long passages with the unfamiliar, difficult-to-pronounce names, yet God desires for us to know from whom we've come. Furthermore, the people of God experienced a deep connection to their land, which explains the traumatic nature of the fall of the holy city of Jerusalem and their subsequent exile. When taunted by their captors to joyfully sing a song of Zion, they communally and wistfully pondered, "How can we sing the LORD's song in a strange land?" (Psalm 137:4).

God wanted the Israelites, and by in-grafting, we Christians today, to know from where and from whom they came. Because one or both of these sources of knowing is obscured from most African American women, we often struggle to establish a firm identity. And sadly, when we don't know who we are, we are at great risk for attempting to assume the identity of someone else. Ask yourself: Am I trying to be like someone else? Do I imitate the hairstyles or fashion sense of my favorite celebrities to my own detriment? Do I wear the brands of the rich and famous, making the designers themselves even more rich and famous, while my own brand fades into obscurity?

If aspects of your cultural identity are hidden from you, don't despair. While knowing and being yourself is important in its own right, the richness of our faith lies in our eternal connection to the Triune God, the One who created, redeemed, and sustains us! We best know who we are when we know *whose* we are. The concept of the *Imago Dei*, the assurance that we are made in the image of God, means that we are capable of taking on the attributes of God, including the fruit of the Spirit: love, joy, peace, patience, kindness, goodness, faithfulness, gentleness, and self-control (Galatians 5:22-23). Our spirituality is a very important facet of our lives, with great implications for our connection to God *and* our connection to others (Armstrong, 1996). Embracing our spiritual identity means that we are more than conquerors, women with abundant life, sisters with a hopeful future, recipients of immeasurably more than we could ever ask or think according to God's power working in us! Hear God's word for us regarding our belonging:

> But now, this is what the LORD says—
>
> he who created you, Jacob,
>   he who formed you, Israel:
> "Do not fear, for I have redeemed you;
>   I have summoned you by name; you are mine.
> When you pass through the waters,
>   I will be with you;
> and when you pass through the rivers,
>   they will not sweep over you.
> When you walk through the fire,
>   you will not be burned;
>   the flames will not set you ablaze.
> For I am the LORD your God,
>   the Holy One of Israel, your Savior
>
> (Isaiah 43:1-3a)

Once again, the Word affirms that we belong to a caring and protective God. Whether we discover anything further about our human lineage, we are ultimately connected to the Root of Jesse, that is, Jesus Christ. As we acknowledge this connection, we are already on our way to deeper spiritual growth. However, just as we might hesitate before going deeper in human relationships, we might be cautious about launching out into the deep with God. We might think that we're not ready for such a commitment, or that we don't really have enough faith to present ourselves to the world as a believer. The next section of this chapter will help you move toward a closer relationship with God, even in the midst of your questions and misgivings.

Chapter Nine

"Help My Unbelief": Managing Your Doubts

"It is important for you not only to see who you can become
but to know that you are empowered to become what you see."
*Rev. Dr. Cynthia Hale, author and senior pastor of
the Ray of Hope Christian Church*

The ninth chapter of the Gospel of Mark reveals the story of a father who was desperate for the healing of his son, desperate enough to actually approach Jesus of Nazareth and to ask for healing. By the way, this was no run-of-the-mill illness that his son had, no blindness or leprosy or excessive bleeding. This child was viewed in his times as demon-possessed, or one with an impure or unclean spirit. His condition, known today as epilepsy, led the child to often fall into the fire, or commit some other types of what we would now term as self-injurious behaviors such as cutting or head-banging. Unlike many other miracles during which Jesus primarily healed the body and spirit, this boy's illness required a healing of the mind. Perhaps that is why when the father approached Jesus, he stated, "If you can do anything, take pity on us and help us." Jesus wondered aloud why the father said "if," and the father forthrightly acknowledged his ambivalence. "I do believe. Help me overcome my unbelief" (9:24). Notice that Jesus did not withhold a healing from this family due to the father's portion of unbelief. He did not rebuke the father for his less-than-stellar faith. Jesus did not shame him for not praying hard enough or not believing enough in his power. Instead, Jesus met him at his point of need, forgave his sins, and healed his son of epilepsy.

How is this relevant to us? Well, sometimes we condemn ourselves for not having enough faith to achieve our goals. We've prayed and we've prayed for God to do something for us or to give us something, and after a while, when we don't see "results," we begin to question ourselves. We wonder what's wrong with us that we haven't received an answer to prayer. We try even harder to live by God's law, to cross every "t" and dot every "i," as though God will then be obligated to move on our behalf. However, we've forgotten, or are learning for the first time, that God is sovereign and will not be domesticated. God is working behind the scenes on our behalf, and the results may not yet be visible, but that doesn't necessarily mean that God has said "no." God's seeming inaction or inattention often means that God has something better in store for us. So rather than attempting to earn quick answers to God's prayer by our own merit, we rest in God's wisdom and perfect timing. When we don't know what to pray, the Holy Spirit is interceding for us according to God's will (Romans, 8:26-27). Even with "faith the size of a mustard seed," God still accepts us and is working to help us blossom into someone who is stronger and better!

With the confidence that we don't have to possess perfect faith to be authentic Christians, let's examine how we become more deeply rooted to Jesus by nurturing our spiritual life through Scripture reading and prayer.

Chapter Ten

Nurturing Your Spiritual Connection Through Scripture Reading and Prayer

"LORD, deliver us from attending our daily gripe sessions.
Forgive us for all of the time we've spent on self-pity and
inviting others to our pity parties. Create in us a
winning attitude instead of a whining attitude."
*Bishop Vashti McKenzie, first woman elected as bishop
of the African Methodist Episcopal Church*

At our essence, we are spirit. As originated by philosopher and
priest Pierre Teilhard de   Chardin and popularized by songwriter and producer Donald Lawrence in his song, *Spiritual*, "You're
not a natural being living a spiritual experience/But you're a spiritual being living this natural experience" (Lawrence, 2011). We
have been created, redeemed, and sustained by a loving God, and
our highest form of worship is to remain connected to our Source.
Worship is really showing God's "worth-ship;" acknowledging the
all-powerful, all-knowing, and ever-present nature of our God, who
is truly worthy of our praise. To be sure, God is not dependent on our

praise and worship. Scripture notes that if we do not give God the praise that is due God, the rocks will cry out to give the glory that we creatures owe God (Luke 19:40). Nevertheless, God delights in *our* acknowledgement of who God is, as well as our appreciation for what God does. This is the God whom our spirits long for, the God who desires true intimacy with us.

What does intimacy with God look like? Traditionally, any time that we intentionally dedicate to spending in God's presence with minimal distractions provides an excellent foundation for intimacy with the Divine. Sometimes we call this intimate time "a devotional," "quiet time," "personal worship," or "solitude." As is true for all other relationships, building a relationship with God requires focused time, investment, and commitment. We do best when we are intentional about preserving time in our schedules for God. For some, the best time to connect with God is the first thing in the morning, while the home is still quiet and before the world starts percolating with its incessant requests and distractions. Morning time can also be ideal because it allows God to set the tone for your day, both emotionally and practically. Walking into your day with your most elevated attitude and with a game plan outlining specific, God-directed strategies is when you often feel your most powerful.

But let's say that you're not a morning person, or you have to be at work at "0-dark thirty," or you regularly experience disruptions to your morning routine. Perhaps you can commune with God during your morning break, or at your lunch break. Maybe nighttime works best for you, after your home gets quiet (i.e., after you've turned off your phone, TV, tablet, and other devices), or after everyone else has gone to bed. Some say that they can hear God best when they are commuting, perhaps through the use of Scripture recordings, your favorite radio evangelist, soul-stirring gospel music, or pure, sweet silence in your car. The means of getting connected to God is not nearly as important as the end—reveling in God's presence.

Traditionally, devotional time has included Scripture study and prayer. But knowing how to connect with Scripture is not always obvious. If you're newer to the faith, the sheer volume of the Bible can be overwhelming. Although the word "genesis" means first things, beginning with the book of Genesis and taking in the early history of the people of Israel through multiple generations as they traveled across new territories can leave you feeling like *you're* in the wilderness! So, for new students of the Bible, or even for seasoned saints who want to make a more intentional journey through Scripture, I recommend beginning with the Psalms. The book of Psalms is not only Israel's historic songbook, but it also accurately reflects the range of thoughts and feelings experienced by all of the psalmists, the best known of whom was King David. Their lyrical outpourings, preserved for the ages by a process called canonization, help us to connect with our humanity across time, space, and culture. It's often helpful to begin with a study Bible that provides background and explanation of the Scriptures, and a contemporary translation that you can understand. It can also be helpful to invest in a parallel Bible, which allows you to visually cross-reference several translations at once. Many also find it helpful to use a devotional guide, such as "Our Daily Bread" or one that can be electronically delivered from a host of web resources. See Appendix E for a sample of recommendations.

Another intimate form of connection with God is prayer. Prayer is virtually universal, since prayer is communication with God. We know that prayer is important because we see in Scripture how often God's people, and even God's Son Jesus, used prayer regularly to commune with God. If the thought of praying to God intimidates you, you are not alone. Some persons find it helpful to conceptualize prayer using a formulaic approach. The acronym **ACTS**—*A*doration, *C*onfession, *T*hanksgiving, and *S*upplication—reminds us of the major components of prayer. This ordering of prayer's components reminds us to come before God's throne of grace with an attitude of **adoration** simply for who God is, apart from what God can do for us. This is not your standard prim-and-proper, church-girl adoration. Think of how much you adore little babies, chocolate, or your favorite actor, and then multiply that excitement times 100!

Confession allows us to ask forgiveness for all offenses against God and humankind, no matter how "big" or "small," and to receive God's purging and God's assurance that God has thrown those sins into the sea of forgetfulness. Although some denominations and churches include a period of confession in their liturgy or worship service, there is nothing like one-on-one time with God to render a personal confession of our transgressions and to experience God's release from judgment for ourselves. Confession is most freeing when we are willing to be specific with God. Confession allows us to see our weaknesses juxtaposed with God's strength and cleansing power.

Thanksgiving is very important for the maintenance of a balanced perspective, especially when we are enduring the storms of life. Even in our secular society, gratitude is recognized both anecdotally and empirically as a source of peace and joy when we can tap into it. In Christianity, however, gratitude is grounded in the God who makes all blessings possible. Additionally, thanksgiving helps us demonstrate to God our recognition of our everyday, "manna-and-quail" blessings (see the 16th chapter of Exodus). We can thank God often for the "big" blessings of "life, health, and a reasonable amount of strength," and we can use mindfulness often to help us be grateful for the "little" blessings that occur moment by moment, such as a gentle breeze, an encouraging phone call from a friend, a smile from a stranger, or clean water to drink. Scripture leads us to "give thanks in all circumstances, for this is God's will for you in Christ Jesus" (I Thessalonians 6:18).

Supplication is a concept that refers to our prayers for our own needs and the needs of others. We present our petitions to God and solicit God for protection, provision, promotion, healing, comfort, guidance, and all other things that only God can supply. Sometimes prayers of supplication are easier to offer up for others, because sometimes in our own desperation, all we can say is "Help, Jesus!" At all times, but especially in these times, we know that we have an Intercessor who is praying on our behalf for our deepest needs and concerns. From my reading of the Gospels and the Bible as a whole, I believe that God desires for us to pray with specificity and to make our requests known to God. As we commit our way to God and trust in God, God will give us the desires of our hearts (Psalm 37:4). In humility, however, we must always remember to pray for God's will, rather than our own, to be done.

One final note: In my own prayer journey, I have found it immensely helpful to add one more step to the ACTS formula. **Listening** is a crucial component of communication, and it should be no different for our most intimate relationship with God. If you add an "L" for Listening to the ACTS formula, you get "ACTS-L," which sounds like "axle." (Think of this axle as that which keeps your prayer wheel turning!) Once we've shared our adoration, confession, thanksgiving, and supplication, we want to allow a space in our prayers for God to speak back to us. As you engage this final step, remember that God speaks in various ways. Sometimes God may speak with a still, small voice in a manner that resonates with our intuition, when we just "know" the right thing to do or say. At other times, God may speak through a dream, vision, or an image. Every now and then, God may even speak with an audible voice. Many times, however, we may feel that God is not speaking at all. If this is your experience, don't stop listening. Continue to sit in a silence for a few moments after you have expressed the contents of your heart. You may find that you become more acquainted with God's voice over time. Write down what you experience in those moments, and watch for ways that God may speak through others who you may encounter in your day. More than a few sisters can testify that they've received a powerful word of confirmation from a stranger! Your prayer life will become stronger as you participate in the mutual exchange of sharing and listening.

 Listen to Recording #9, "Keepin' It 100 Prayer"

Chapter Eleven

Journaling, Meditation, and Other Spiritual Disciplines

*"Learn to be quiet enough to hear the genuine with yourself
so that you can hear it in others."*
Marian Wright Edelman, activist for the rights of the disadvantaged
and president and founder of the Children's Defense Fund

Beyond the most common spiritual disciplines of Scripture study and prayer, there are many other means of connecting to God (e.g., Foster, 1978; Thompson, 1995). **Traditional journaling** is a method of recording your thoughts and feelings about the events of your life. Some women use journaling as a way to chronicle daily or weekly events, whereas others may use journals to record their prayers and God's responses to their prayers. When I encourage my clients to journal, I understand that while it is a powerful way to increase insight through connection with God, it is also a spiritual practice that takes some getting used to. For that reason, it's important to be flexible when you're adding journaling to your routine. For example, journaling can be prose or poetry; fluid text or bullet points; hand-written, typed, audio-recorded, or video-recorded; and daily, weekly, monthly, or somewhere in between. Journaling can be so powerful because it allows the thoughts, even the ruminations, that have been swirling about in our minds to take a more tangible form when expressed, which creates a very liberating effect. One example of journaling is prayer journaling.

In order to further build your relationship with God, I recommend the use of **prayer journaling**. Pick up a convenient composition book from the dollar store, find a fancy decorated journal with an inspirational message on its cover, or use anything that excites you. Use this journal for one or more of the following purposes:

1. As often as you can, chronicle the happenings of your life from the perspective that God is accompanying you on your journey. God sees your mountains as well as your valleys, and has promised to be present with you all the way. Write down your life events as a way of acknowledging that God's purpose is being realized through you every day, through every magnificent and mundane event.

2. Write down your specific prayer requests, both for yourself and for others. No matter how insignificant or outlandish your prayer requests may seem to others, God honors every desire. It has been said that God's responses are "Yes," "No," "Later," and "I have something better in mind for you" (Comer, 2012). Even more important than writing down your requests is writing down God's responses to your requests, no matter how long it may seem to take. Your own personal record of God's faithfulness in your life and in the lives of your loved ones can be a powerful and hopeful touchstone as you encounter challenges in the future.

3. As you are listening for God in your devotional time, or even as you hear God's voice at unexpected times in your day, record what God shares with you. Perhaps you occasionally hear God's

voice in a clear and unmistakable way. Maybe God confirms something previously shared with you through a conversation with a friend, or even a stranger. Or maybe God speaks to you through everyday sounds or images. Even if you don't understand the significance of what is shared, write it down. God may give you more clarity later.

4. Keep track of the grace in your life. In my prayer journal, given to me by one of my "prayer warriors," I keep a list of Grace I Give ("GIG") and Grace I Receive ("GIR"). The list of GIG keeps me accountable for being gracious to others on a daily basis. I may extend grace through a smile, a donation given to a stranger in need, a word of encouragement, or even an angry response swallowed. The list of GIR reminds me that God's principles are true: we reap what we sow (Galatians 6:7). I delight in receiving a word of advice from a mentor, a slice of cake from a church mother, a hug from an old friend, or a heartfelt compliment, especially from a stranger. In today's terms, we use the language of "karma:" that what goes around comes around. I deliberately sow grace because it pleases God and shows God's image in my life. I also realize that a natural by-product of sowing is reaping, and because I am in need of grace, I share grace with others, and reap the harvest God has promised. According to gospel songwriter Doris Akers (1957), "You can't beat God giving, no matter how you try!"

Meditation is another form of intimacy with God. Because many of us raised in traditional Christian worship settings may not have grown up with exposure to meditation, we may initially harbor suspicions about the practice of meditation. We may think of persons engaged in rituals with peculiar finger positions chanting mantras that we do not understand, particularly if the practice emerges from an unfamiliar Eastern religion such as Buddhism. However, we often are unaware of the significant history of meditation going back to the early days of Christianity. Back then, some men and women who were committed disciples of Jesus would retreat to the desert, not to withdraw permanently from the world, but to find a quiet place with God (Earle, 2007). Contemporary meditation, then, continues the tradition of stillness before God, even in the midst of a busy and chaotic world.

One popular form of Christian meditation is the **Jesus Prayer.** This prayer, also referred to as the prayer of the heart, dates back to use in the Orthodox Church as far back as the 5th century. Although early formulations of the Jesus Prayer include the more formal statement, "Lord Jesus Christ, Son of God, have mercy on me, a sinner," more recent formulations simply state, "Lord, have mercy." Its recitation is often coordinated with the heartbeat and the breath to harmonize body and spirit. As you breathe in (inhalation), recite mentally or verbally, "Lord" as you consider God's infinite love, power, and forgiveness. As you breathe out (exhalation), recite "Have mercy," and experience the release of all negative thoughts, feelings, and behaviors that separate you from God. Practice this exercise for 5-10 minutes whenever you need a deeper connection with God.

 Listen to Recording #8 for a more detailed experience of the Jesus Prayer.

In order to meditate, it is important to retreat to a quiet place. While you may prefer a prayer closet, shrine, altar, or other place of worship or devotion in your home, recognize that in a pinch, your car or a bathroom stall at work will suffice. Close your eyes and sit still for at least 5-10 minutes. In Christian forms of meditation, it is often helpful to think of a Christian principle, such as God's love or forgiveness, or a relevant Scripture to repeat over and over again in your mind. Your mind becomes focused on God's truth, and your body relaxes as well. If you find that your mind wanders from its focus, nonjudgmentally bring it back to your original focus. Many find meditation to be more difficult than they first imagined. It requires a level of concentration that is fleeting in our current rushed society where distractions abound. However, just like most other skills, meditation becomes easier with practice. Meditation practice is associated with lower heart and respiratory rates, decreased blood pressure over time, and several indicators of psychological well-being (Morse et al., 1977).

 Listen to Recording #10, "Balance Meditation," for one example of how to engage a meditation practice.

Fasting is another spiritual discipline. It is the practice of abstaining from a substance or product that you normally consume for the purpose of spiritual connection. Traditionally, early practitioners of our faith viewed fasting as abstinence from food, either a total fast, or a partial fast, often for a period of several hours to several days or weeks. Often we are most acutely aware of the body's craving and the mind's preoccupation for food during the first few hours or days of the fast. We recognize how easily we take for granted the privilege of eating and our typically quick access to food. During fasting, we can also observe just how saturated our culture has become with images of food throughout all types of media and discourse, often with food that is good *to* us but not necessarily good *for* us. The hunger pangs and emotional longing for gustatory satisfaction are a reminder of our craving for God's substance to deeply satisfy our every need and to bolster our every weakness.

True fasting, as discussed in Isaiah 58, is not about fasting to demonstrate spiritual superiority; instead, fasting is about adopting an humble posture before our Creator to reflect on a spiritual need, a family situation, a community crisis, or other issue over which we wish to see God's movement:

> Is not this the kind of fasting I have chosen:
> to loose the chains of injustice
>   and untie the cords of the yoke,
> to set the oppressed free
>   and break every yoke?
> Is it not to share your food with the hungry

and to provide the poor wanderer with shelter—
when you see the naked, to clothe them,
    and not to turn away from your own flesh and blood?
Then your light will break forth like the dawn,
    and your healing will quickly appear;
then your righteousness will go before you,
    and the glory of the LORD will be your rear guard.
Then you will call, and the LORD will answer;
    you will cry for help, and he will say: Here am I...
You will be like a well-watered garden,
like a spring whose waters never fail

(Isaiah 58: 6-11; emphasis added)

As you can see from this passage of Scripture, fasting extends well beyond our concerns and crises to the work that God is accomplishing in God's kingdom. Fasting addresses local to global injustices, including problems in the criminal justice system, food insecurity, and homelessness. Notice here that God is present when we need help, and that God's presence keeps us and our communities blossoming.

In more contemporary times, fasting has also incorporated abstinence from television, phones, social media, and other incessant distractions. Several of my clients have found great success in taking a break from Facebook and other similar platforms, or even in taking a break from a relationship that has become all-consuming. In this world of constant connectivity, however, it is advisable to alert your friends or followers ahead of time that you are taking this break as a form of self-care, so that they will neither be excessively concerned about your absence, nor personalize your absence as a sign of trouble in that relationship. (Of course, if there *is* trouble in that relationship, you will want to communicate your concerns assertively rather than passively. See the section on assertiveness in Chapter 20.)

Silence is another spiritual practice that can yield great benefits. In a world where voices, music, phone notifications, and noise constantly surround us, practicing silence is a radical form of listening for the sounds and voices that really matter. In silence, we can better clarify the voices in our head, which are occasionally in conflict with each other. Like the iconic angel and devil images often portrayed as sitting on our shoulders and whispering their various influences, our minds often harbor clashing ideas of right and wrong decisions and behaviors. We often struggle to discern what is God's voice and what is the voice of the enemy. Moreover, we are typically fighting our own worries, fears, doubts, skepticism, and mistrust. Silence can help us sort out these weights and tune in to the voice that truly counts: the still, small voice of the Lover of our souls. In the midst of his sense of persecution and experience of depression, the Prophet Elijah sought the LORD:

> The LORD said, "Go out and stand on the mountain in the presence of the LORD, for the LORD is about to pass by." Then a great and powerful wind tore the mountains apart and shattered the rocks before the LORD, but the LORD was not in the wind. After the wind there was an earthquake, but the LORD was not in the earthquake. After the earthquake came a fire, but the LORD was not in the fire. And after the fire came a gentle whisper.
>
> (1 Kings 19: 9b-12)

Following his fantastic miracle of calling down God's fire before prophets of Baal, Elijah might have expected God's voice to come to him in a similarly extraordinary way. However, God did not come in the wind, the earthquake, or the fire: God came in a gentle whisper, the soft voice that we can only hear in silence.

The spiritual discipline of **solitude** is a practice that, on the surface, may not offer much appeal, particularly if you display more extroverted tendencies. Solitude requires that we spend time by ourselves. We may view solitude as terribly akin to loneliness, a state that we may be motivated to avoid at all costs. However, removing ourselves from others may be one of the best ways to draw closer to God.

As we practice solitude, we become more dependent on and satisfied with God's presence. No, God is not tangibly supportive in the ways that we desire other loved ones to be. God does not manifest directly through a hug, a stroke on the hand, or a pat on the back (although some anecdotally report having these experiences). However, as you mature in your faith, you will grow accustomed to the power and comfort of God's intangible presence, the presence that is best learned in solitude. Our Christian forebears often retreated to the desert, but we may not have to venture very far to find solitude. Perhaps for one person, it's a walk on a trail or parkway, or in the nearby woods. For another person, it may be a ride in your car to no place in particular, just you and God. For yet another of us, we just need a "trip" to our bathtub to soak, relax, and listen. You may have already been practicing solitude without knowing it!

Silence and solitude often go together, but can also be practiced separately. One word of caution: There is a meaningful difference between solitude and isolation. In solitude, we withdraw to hear the voice of God and to be strengthened for the journey ahead. Whether it takes a few hours or a few weeks, we have usually intentioned to observe a defined period of solitude to grow stronger spiritually and emotionally. We return to our routines refreshed and "ready for the world."

Isolation, however, often occurs as a symptom of depression. Depression is associated with disruptions in our social connections. When experiencing the symptoms of depression, relationships can become so complicated that we tell ourselves that we're better off without those relationships. We don't want to be bothered, even by well-meaning loved ones. Isolation can reveal a cycle of withdrawal from relationships, prolonged loneliness, confusion about what is happening in our lives, frustration that others are not reaching out as we wish they would, further withdrawal, and so on. We may look up and realize that days, weeks, or months have gone by without significant human interaction. (Going through the motions at work doesn't count.) If it becomes increasingly difficult to reconnect in a meaningful way, we may be struggling with depression and may need professional assistance.

While not specifically prescribed in many of our traditional church settings, **movement** can often reflect a spiritual practice in and of itself. Practices such as yoga, tai chi, qigong, liturgical dance, and praise dance (i.e., "shouting") can all be practiced as forms of devotion to God. Unfortunately, our Christian culture has sometimes taken a dim view of bodily practices for several reasons. For centuries, we have often misunderstood the body and its functions as sources of evil. The seven deadly sins, especially gluttony and lust, bring to mind the godless uses of the body. To add insult to injury, we have often confused references to the "flesh" in the King James Version of the Bible as references to the physical body. After all, Jesus Himself said to His disciples, "The Spirit gives life; the flesh counts for nothing." (John 6:63a) However, the term "flesh" (here, the Greek term *sarx*) is more properly translated as the sinful nature, that which is opposed to God. When Scripture is referring to the physical body, it more often uses the Greek term *soma*, the living or dead body, and the metaphorical notion of believers united in one body, that is, the idea that Christian believers are the eyes, ears, hands, and feet of Christ. Thus, we can embrace our bodies as good, as our bodily movements as reflections of God's glory. Whether you direct your church's dance ministry, lead a Zumba group at the gym, or like to move in the privacy of your own home, claim the energy you display through movement as worship of and connection with the God who made it all possible.

Worship and fellowship are corporate spiritual disciplines, meaning they involve the body of Christ. Participating in worship allows us to express our recognition of God's eternal worth, and our willingness to lay aside our temporal concerns to do so. Engagement in worship connects us with the sacraments, or ordinances (depending on your denominational persuasion), of baptism, Holy Communion (the LORD's Supper or the Eucharist), and celebrations of confirmations/baby dedications and weddings. Fellowship is an important by-product of gathering together for worship, as Scripture reminds us in Hebrews 10:25, for the purposes of encouraging each other. Livestreaming a church service has its place, yet face-to-face and heart-to-heart interactions with our brothers and sisters are vital components of our spiritual formation. As we become more consistent in our practice of spiritual disciplines, we are empowered to turn our thoughts toward how we can best serve the body of Christ. We will now discuss God-ordained service through the use of our spiritual gifts.

Chapter Twelve

Stirring Up Your Spiritual Gifts

"What are your spiritual gifts?" Often when I ask clients about this, many of them stare blankly at me, as though I've asked them to explain the relevance of calculus for our daily lives. Sadly, we typically are not aware that God has not only created us "fearfully and wonderfully," but also that God has empowered us mightily for God's work through spiritual gifts. Whereas spiritual disciplines are the practices that we develop in our lives to remain vitally connected to the True Vine, spiritual gifts are those talents and abilities that we are given by God for the upbuilding of God's kingdom on the earth. Spiritual gifts take on a spiritual and practical significance when God gives us supernatural power to accomplish our purpose, and in so doing, bless the world. As much as we'd like to, we cannot bargain for the gift(s) that we like; our gifting is God's choosing. I believe that although every human is endowed with natural gifts and talents, spiritual gifts are designed and given expressly for the building up of God's kingdom in the earth. Examine how the Amplified Bible describes the role of the prophetic gift within the body of Christ:

> But [on the other hand] the one who prophesies speaks to people for edification [to promote their spiritual growth]

and [speaks words of] encouragement [to uphold and
advise them concerning the matters of God] and [speaks
words of] consolation [to compassionately comfort them.
(1 Corinthians 14:3)

Does this mean that spiritual gifts are only for the Church, the people
of God, or only to be used at "the church house," that is, within the
four walls of the church building? By no means! Wherever we go as
women of God, God's Spirit and spiritual gifts enable us to make a
tangible and lasting difference in that setting.

Spiritual gifts are discussed in a few different places in Scripture.
The most significant discussion of spiritual gifts occurs in 1 Corinthians 12: 8-10, 28-30. The list below reveals these spiritual gifts:

- Administration
- Apostleship
- Discernment
- Evangelism
- Exhortation
- Faith
- Giving
- Healing
- Helps
- Knowledge
- Leadership
- Mercy
- Miracles
- Missionary
- Pastor/shepherding
- Prophecy
- Service
- Teaching
- Speaking and interpreting
  tongues
- Wisdom

Additionally, there are many other contemporary formulations that
include gifts such as craftsmanship, hospitality, intercession, and
music/worship.

There are a number of ways to discover your spiritual gift(s). One
way is to take any of a number of spiritual gift inventories that are
available on the Internet (see Appendix F for links to several inventories.) A good inventory will include most, if not all, of the gifts
listed in Scripture as well as those from the broader contemporary

lists. The inventory will assess each gift with multiple questions, and will provide you with a description of each gift. Additionally, you can pray for God to give you guidance and discernment about which gift(s) belong to you. Moreover, you can receive wise counsel from the people of God that know you and have insight into your spiritual gifts. Your pastor, Sunday School or Bible study teacher, a trustworthy elder, or a particularly spiritual brother or sister in Christ can gently and candidly share their observations of where your gifts lie. Once you discover your pattern of gifting, you can also pray for specific guidance in the ways that you can share your gifts with the body of Christ and beyond. One client gifted in the area of mercy, skilled in knitting, and compassionate toward elders was able to translate her gifts into a ministry of knitting blankets for elders at a nearby assisted living facility. Another client with extensive experience in hip-hop dance was able to utilize her gifts in coordinate a dance ministry for teens at her church. Which of your gifts is waiting for public expression?

Part Four

Blossoming in Body

The role of the body in this life is unmistakably important. Our bodies allow us to navigate our physical environments, participate in all sorts of physical activities, regulate all of our systems through our amazing brains, all while distinguishing us from others' bodies through the natural boundaries of our skin. Yet we don't always recognize the tremendous asset we have in the human body. Each of us receives exactly one body. Thankfully, modern science and technological advances have helped us recover from all sorts of physical injuries and setbacks; however, a body replacement is simply not available. This chapter is written to help us understand more deeply how God gave us a body that God intended to be as sacred as a temple for God's worship. Our bodies allow us to express ourselves as salt and light in the world and help us to inspire others to deeper spiritual connection. Lest we become overly spiritual, however, there are health-promoting practices that permit us to continue serving God in practical ways in this earthly kingdom. With this balanced view of our bodies, we can take more seriously the opportunities to pursue a healthy presentation of our bodies, healthy relationships with our bodies, and healthy fitness, eating, and sleep practices.

Chapter Thirteen

Beauty & Hair

**"I want you to understand that your first duty is to humanity.
I want others to look at us and see that we care
not just about ourselves but about others."**
*Madame C. J. Walker, entrepreneur in beauty, philanthropist,
and first female self-made millionaire in the U.S.*

"Beauty is only skin deep." What does this mean? For some, it means that the traditional markers of beauty—attractiveness, facial symmetry, a smooth, even complexion, a beautiful smile, a well-maintained figure—do not necessarily correspond to one's strength of character. A Nigerian proverb states: "If there is character, ugliness becomes beauty; if there is none, beauty becomes ugliness." A strong character, that is, one possessing love, integrity, compassion, faith, consistency, generosity, wisdom, and courage, is developed over time in the crucible of life. These inner characteristics, unlike external indicators of beauty, not only stand the test of time, but like fine wine, grow richer with the passing years.

So, what happens when we redefine beauty in the context of a community where we have been told in no uncertain terms that we fall short, to varying degrees, of the traditional standards of beauty—light eyes, white skin, straight hair, a thin frame, slender facial features? Can we still maintain, or even gain, a radical sense of self, and group pride? When we see few, if any, flattering portrayals of ourselves in the media, can we still observe the preponderance of tanning salons, collagen-injected lips, and all manner of derrière enhancements as forms of secret flattery and not-so-subtle indicators of the desire for our unique signs of beauty? Does God even care about how we perceive our beauty?

Of course God does! As we struggle against cultural denials of our beauty, let us remember that true beauty resonates from the inside out. It exudes as confidence in who God has created us to be. After all, Black women are a fully legitimate part of creation made in the *Imago Dei*, that is, in the image of God. Can you replace the innumerable representations from childhood now intractably implanted in your mind of the "Jesus of Norway" (i.e., straight blonde hair and blue eyes) with the "Jesus of Nazareth" whose Scripturally-referenced bronze skin tone and woolly hair (Rev. 1:14-15) looks a lot more like ours? Can you accept that the image of God is not just a philosophical assertion, or a mere commentary on our constantly evolving, righteous character? Much more than those transient ideas, Scripture affirms over and over again that we "favor" or resemble God! Have you ever noticed how fascinating it is to observe the resemblances between human beings and their family members? Physical traits, mannerisms, language patterns, even styles of laughter are shared across generations. Very few Biblical figures, such as Moses and Hagar, have seen God and survived the encounter, so we can't render a physical description of the Living God. The best that each culture can do is to assert its own traits onto the Living God. Why not us?

Therefore, we boldly choose to represent our divine essence. To be sure, beauty is worth the investment to put our best selves forward. Whether you wear a full face of make-up or prefer the simplicity of a natural look, it's important to be conscious of how you're presenting yourself to the public. Also, consistent hygiene is a basic necessity, particularly if we are seeking to promote social connections. Yes, it takes a few extra moments to put your personal best "face" forward, yet your image is often how people remember you. Whether it's your gap, your moles or freckles, how you carry yourself, your special birthmark, or the shape of your 'fro, your marks of beauty make you distinctly you!

At the same time, there is a word of caution for those of us who are tempted by the dominant cultural narrative that says what we have is not enough (or too much), and that we require a significant expenditure of time and money on cosmetics, plastic surgery, body parts, or hair and other accessories with which the good Lord didn't endow us at birth. Wal-Mart-sized beauty stores sell us wares that seem to be able to deliver on the promise of greater attractiveness, which in our minds often equates with more love and attention, but many sisters can testify to the fact that even a beauty shopping spree doesn't necessarily aid us in reaching those goals.

From my perspective, God doesn't have any problems with some extra shine, sparkle, ombre, or intense color—we just want to have a clear enough mind to evaluate critically what our look accomplishes. We can tell how deeply we are invested in these tools by how we respond in their absence. If we are willing to alter our social calendars or forego special events because we feel inadequate without the supports of our beauty tools, we might be too reliant on projecting an image that is not based in reality. If we can only imagine utter embarrassment, rejection, incapacitation, or some other form of devastation if we do not use such beauty tools, we might be too dependent on our beauty aids.

Without attention to this process of increasing reliance on the external tools, we might be shifting more and more emphasis onto the most superficial aspects of ourselves, when we really want to be expanding the inner beauty that never passes away.

Hair

"… I want to talk about natural black hair, and how it's not just hair. I mean, I'm interested in hair in sort of a very aesthetic way, just the beauty of hair, but also in a political way: what it says, what it means."
*Chimamanda Ngozi Adichie, Nigerian author
and recipient of a MacArthur Genius Grant*

Contrary to popular belief, *all* of our hair is good hair. After all, hair is a part of the inheritance that each human receives from our Creator. And how versatile our hair can be! Depending on your taste, it can be "fried, dyed, laid to the side," relaxed, braided, blown out, Jheri-curled, finger-waved, twisted, flat-ironed, layered, shaved, wet-set, straw-set, locked, cornrowed, coiled, cropped, wigged, weaved, or any other creative way we can think to express our true essence.

For much of our existence in America, our minds were colonized by our oppressors, and our hair followed. For a while, we bought into the notion that straighter was better, and we hid our kinks in shame. "Good hair" was determined by having a "fine grade of hair," hair with looser rather than tighter curls, and hair cascading down a sister's back. What does it mean, however, for us to value and purchase the hair of others to the point that we deny the value of our own God-given hair? One of the most poignant, albeit tragic, moments of comedian Chris Rock's documentary, *Good Hair* (Rock, HBO Productions, & Stinson, 2009), is when Rock contrasts the "value" of the best-selling Indian hair with the "value" of kinky hair, which no shop owner is willing to purchase.

So, it behooves us to appreciate what God has already given us. As we've already acknowledged, our styles can range the gamut from one moment to another. Rather than judging another sister for how she chooses to style her hair, we can rejoice in the sheer possibilities afforded to us. Our hair allows us the ultimate form of self-expression. It has been said that you should watch out for a woman who changes her hair, because she is preparing to set the world on fire! No matter where your transition takes you, accept what you have and reflect God's glory!

Chapter Fourteen

Body Awareness

"I found the Negro, and always the blackest Negro, being made
the butt of all jokes, particularly black women..."
Zora Neale Hurston, anthropologist and author of
Their Eyes Were Watching God

As Black women, we sometimes have complicated relationships
with our own bodies. Historically, there was a time in the
not-too-distant past when our bodies were not our own; rather, our
bodies were subject to the whims, economic goals, and sexual desires
of the slaveholder. Our bodies endured the profound hardships of
"can see to can't see" (i.e., from dawn to dusk) work in fields, whip-
pings and beatings, sexual assault, multiple pregnancies during hard
manual labor in extreme weather conditions with little to no prenatal
support, exploitation through wet nursing, medical experimentation
without anesthesia, and transitions from one plantation to another.

These traumas took their toll emotionally as well as physically. While
slavery officially ended over 150 years ago, our psyches are still dealing with its effects psychologically. According to social scientist and

trauma expert Joy DeGruy (2005), U.S. Blacks have long been traumatized by several events, from the Middle Passage to lynchings to redlining. In her formulation, "multigenerational trauma together with continued oppression and absence of opportunity to access the benefits available in the society leads to Post Traumatic Slave Syndrome (PTSS)." The psychic impact of PTSS affects how we view and use our bodies. We have more control over our bodies, yet many of us often feel even now that our bodies are not our own, particularly if we are involved with controlling or abusive partners.

One of the most obvious threats to our bodies is what we regard as physical or medical illness. Black women are more likely to be managing chronic and life-threatening conditions, including obesity (57%), hypertension (45%), cancer (19%), diabetes (10%), and stroke (3%); American Cancer Society, 2016 (Centers for Disease Control and Prevention, 2014). In the midst of these disease threats, we sometimes lose sight of other more pernicious dangers to our bodies. One very real hazard to our bodies occurs in the form of sexual assault. Sexual assault or sexual violence is any unwanted sexual contact that includes molestation, incest, rape, and date rape. Sadly, many Black women are first exposed to sexual violence as children. Community studies reveal that 34-65 percent of Black women are survivors of childhood sexual abuse (West & Johnson, 2013). Our bodies are misused for the sexual pleasure of someone else, often a family member or "friend of the family." Such abuse can range from one isolated episode to a recurring pattern that can last for years, even into adulthood. Commercial sexual exploitation of children (CSEC), closely related to sex trafficking, is defined as "crimes of a sexual nature committed against juvenile victims for financial or other economic reasons (Greenbaum & James, 2015). Some of us have suffered in silence, sworn to secrecy by our perpetrator. Others of us have dared to tell another, and perhaps have gained support, protection, and relief from our abuse. Unfortunately, when some divulge this secret, we have been accused of lying, "asking for it," and have even been rejected, sometimes by our own mothers or other close family members. A few others have formally filed charges against the perpetrators, and have experienced or are waiting for justice to be served. This legal path, however, is fraught with challenges of going public and being subject to judgment and commentary, having to testify repeatedly about a very painful episode, and dealing with the possibility that, after all that trouble, the perpetrator may not be found guilty.

No matter where we are in this process of disclosure, the effects of sexual assault on the mind are indelible. Sexual assault can leave us feeling dirty, worthless, ruined, and unlovable. It affects our daily functioning, our relationships, our self-perception, and our motivation to pursue the purpose that God has given our lives. Particularly when undisclosed, sexual assault can also have a devastating effect on our physical health, including unplanned pregnancy, sexually transmitted infections (STIs), and gynecological disorders (Campbell, 2002). In terms of mental health, sexual assault is most closely related to chronic depression and posttraumatic stress disorder (PTSD). Several research studies also indicate that childhood trauma is associated with chronic illness in adulthood (Mock & Arai, 2010). Additionally, sexual assault can contribute to our sense of shame regarding our bodies and hinder our physical, emotional, and sexual intimacy, even in a loving relationship.

Another threat to our bodies, not to mention our minds, souls, and spirits, is domestic violence. Domestic violence is defined by the verbal, emotional, physical, financial, spiritual, and/or sexual misuse and abuse of our bodies. These behaviors are intended to assert power and control over the victim. Every nine seconds, another woman in the U.S. is subjected to physical abuse (Partnership against Domestic Violence, 2017). While 39 percent of women first experience domestic violence between the ages of 18 and 24, 22 percent of young women between the ages of 11 and 17, 7 percent of women between ages 35-44, and 3 percent of women aged 45 and older also become exposed to domestic violence for the first time. Although there are pastors who have preached that women should remain in a marriage even when they are being battered, we now understand that God does not call us to withstand abuse. Even when we know that we must exit the relationship, however, it takes much courage, the right timing, and sufficient resources to leave successfully. Most states or regions have domestic shelters, crisis response centers, or other havens where women can seek consultation and refuge. See Appendix G for a list of these resources.

Whether desired or not, pregnancy is a bodily experience that requires several adjustments over the nine months of gestation, although premature birth is more common among Black women. During pregnancy, we yield our bodies to the demands of the life growing inside of us. There are foods of which we eat more or less than usual, horse-sized prenatal vitamins to swallow, lifestyle changes to commit to (especially if we were partial to drinking or smoking), fetal kicks, turns, and other gestures to endure. We submit to greater vigilance for any medical conditions such as gestational diabetes or tendencies toward hypertension, and who can forget the sleepless nights when finding a comfortable sleeping position becomes a lost cause! After the birth of that beautiful child, our bodies then surrender to the vicissitudes of the baby's sleeping schedule and the choice of early (and not-so-early) challenges of breastfeeding and expressing your breast milk. Developmental science demonstrates that it takes the average infant up to a year to realize that his mother is a separate entity from him, rather than an extension of his own body. And even as your child matures, there are still needs for physical presence and affection.

In addition to the physical challenges faced by our bodies, there are also psychological factors that affect how we relate to our bodies. For example, Black women often see a lack of affirmation of our bodies in the media, and even further, the negative portrayals of our bodies. Because our bodies do not often conform to the mainstream images of rail-thin forms with straight blonde hair and blue eyes, our thicker, darker bodies, tightly curled hair, and fuller facial features are seen as abnormal or even deficient. I almost jumped out of my skin when I beheld for the first time the movie poster for Disney's *Queen of*

Katwe. Not since some of the blaxploitation films of the 1970s (think Pam Grier) had I seen our naturally kinky hair portrayed on a major movie poster for consumption by the mainstream public. Not surprisingly, this film lost money at the box office, despite its uplifting portrayal of a real-life Ugandan girl who became an international chess champion. Still, public exposure to uncommon images is an important step toward acceptance, and people of every hue can benefit from more of this exposure.

Another complicated facet of our physical bodies is the color of the skin we're in. Positively, Black women of all hues are now more likely than a generation ago to be seen on some magazine covers, TV shows, and films. Although our roles still gravitate toward women in supporting, subservient roles (think Aunt Jemima), or in roles depicting questionable moral character (e.g., prostitutes and drug fiends), the fact that we have more creative control in directing and producing roles means that we now are able to present ourselves to the world in a more accurate and appealing light. These more recent portrayals of Black womanhood have an immeasurably positive effect on the generations that come behind us, not only because they present more realistic options to our daughters and our sons for who they can be, who they can marry, and who they can raise, but also because those images send unconscious affirmation of who they are and how they look.

Even as we have received Biblical affirmation of our darker skin (e.g., King Solomon's lovely and dark beloved) and of our worth ("I have loved you with an everlasting love"—Jeremiah 31:3), it is helpful in our natural and daily occurrences to find affirmation in our broader world, and especially in our own communities and families. It's more than a cliché to *practice* loving the skin that we're in. Sadly, whether we'd like to admit it, skin color continues to play a significant role in our communities, specifically when it comes to determining one's attractiveness or worth. Just think of the saying that so easily rolled off many lips in our families: "If you're white, you're alright, if you're brown, stick around; but if you're black, get back," from the song written and performed by Big Bill Broonzy (Broonzy, 1951). In self-preservation mode, darker-skinned people retort, "The darker the berry, the sweeter the juice" and "Black don't crack."

As if we didn't have enough battling to do between the races, we're also dealing with an intra-racial battle that has raged for centuries— it's called colorism. While we can see that distinctions were made in skin color even back during Biblical times and across cultures (Chua, 2001; Kruszelnicki, 2001; Welsing, 1991), colorism was elevated to a fine art during slavery in the U.S. (Bennett & White, 1975). Enslaved persons who were darker-skinned were often relegated to field work (which reinforced their darker skin), while those of lighter hues (most often the progeny of the slaveholder) were often given work inside of the "Big House." The physical labor required in the fields was seen as inferior to the work conducted indoors, so the lighter-skinned enslaved persons were typically perceived by others (and perhaps eventually, themselves) as "better" than the darker-skinned enslaved persons. In this instance, the strategy of "divide and conquer," whether by default or by design, was effective in entrenching infighting based on skin tone deep within our culture. Even when we know that there are no inherent differences between us that can be ascribed to skin color, we still pass on this false pecking order from generation to generation. The resentment felt by darker-skinned people has created a backlash, such that Blacks who have fairer skin have been accused of not being "black enough." As a result, people on both ends of the color spectrum are teased, criticized, and even traumatized because they are "too light/bright" or "too dark." The media only contribute further to the problem, in that standards of beauty are almost always associated with white or light skin. Several clients have disclosed (some with tears) in the privacy of my therapy office how painful an issue skin color has been in their lives.

In the face of colorism that has persisted over many generations, how do we begin to heal this rift? First, we have to re-condition our minds to see the beauty in ourselves that is denied by the broader culture. Challenge yourself to find attraction to hues that White people, your neighbors, and perhaps even your grandmother may have taught you to disdain. Second, we must advocate for people of all hues and not allow others to insult any color in the spectrum. Although others often use "light" humor to scorn another's skin color, when we are in the presence of such intra-racial microagressions, we can gently but firmly disagree with the offender and affirm the person being insulted, as well as her skin color. Third, we can prevent the contamination of another generation by vocalizing around our young people the beauty and value of all shades at every opportunity. In the presence of your children, for example, compliment a sister on her beauty whose skin color is at most risk for rejection. Just because we may have been brainwashed with colorism doesn't mean that we can't become more conscious and adjust the standards of beauty for the next generation.

Chapter Fifteen

Optimizing Our Physical Health and Fitness

"Health is a human right, not a privilege to be purchased."
*Shirley Chisholm, first Black woman elected to U.S. Congress,
and first Black and first woman to run for the
Democratic Party's presidential nomination*

"Your health is your wealth." This saying is never truer than when we've experienced a threat to our health. Perhaps you've received a diagnosis of a life-threatening illness, which has shifted your perspective on the value of life. Maybe you've lived vicariously through another person's struggle, which has helped you to appreciate your own life and "reasonable amount of health and strength," as our elders often say. Or it's possible that you have been through a temporary health inconvenience, such as a severe bout of the flu or a sprained ankle and have realized anew just how much each of the "small" parts of our body actually perform. And of course, health is not only about the condition of our physical body. There is tremendous interplay between our physical health and psychological health. Being diagnosed with a chronic illness, for example, can lead to depression if you are unsure of what the future holds, or if you lack support to help you cope with this illness. The reverse can also be true. If you experience the chronic effects of an untreated anxiety disorder, for example, the less-than-adaptive ways you deal with worry and stress can place the body in overdrive and lead to such physical consequences as hypertension, heart disease, breast cancer, and premature aging (Clark et al., 1999; Geronimus et. al, 2010). So, paying attention to maintaining or improving our health is of utmost importance. Having annual physicals and suggested screenings (e.g., mammograms, colonoscopies, vision and dental exams) are important maintenance tools. Giving prompt attention to a symptom that doesn't feel or look right and doesn't resolve in an expected amount of time can also be a life-saving move.

In addition to the significant roles of nutritious eating and consistent sleep routines, exercise plays a crucial role in the quality of our health. Scripture acknowledges that "physical training is of some value," even as it places greater emphasis on developing godliness (I Timothy 4:8). The Physical Activity Guidelines for Americans (United States Department of Health and Human Services, 2008) has recommended that every adult engage in a minimum of 150 minutes of moderate aerobic activity per week. Additionally, stretching is important for building flexibility, which is especially important as we age, to prevent falls. Strength training is important for maintaining muscle mass, which naturally decreases with age unless we intervene. Strength training can also contribute to weight loss (U.S. Department of Health and Human Services, 2008). Depending on your current physical condition, you may need to make certain modifications to your exercise regimen. Nevertheless, there is a fitness routine appropriate for every age and every stage. Consult a personal trainer for a customized plan and ongoing support for the routines that work best for your body.

Chapter Sixteen

Seeking the Right Amount of Sleep

> "I like to embrace natural beauty. I try to get at least
> eight hours of sleep, drinking a lot of water and exercising."
> *Tia Mowry, actor, model, and author*

O ver the span of our lives, we have such an interesting relationship with sleep. When we were younger and were required
to take naps, we often fought them. We didn't want to miss one
moment of the action going on in the world around us. Now, ironically, there's not a Black woman I know who wouldn't give up a
material possession to get a twenty-minute power nap! Sleep is so
vitally important for our physical, mental, and emotional functioning, yet it can be so elusive because of all the demands that we take
on. We often don't realize how much a good night's sleep enables
us to feel calm, think clearly, and facilitate our body's full execution
of important processes (e.g., cellular repair, metabolism, hormone
function). Conversely, poor sleep quality can contribute to fatigue,
irritability, mental fogginess, and weaknesses in judgment.

How much sleep do we actually need? Research varies, but most empirical work suggests that adult women need between seven and nine hours of sleep, on average. There is a deep chasm between what is recommended and what is actually achieved, however. Data collected by the Centers for Disease Control and Prevention (CDC) between 1985 and 2012 revealed a national increase in the number of adults reporting six or less hours of sleep from 38.6 million to 70.1 million, which they declare as a public health epidemic (Watson, et al., 2015). Your individual need for sleep may depend on several factors, including genetic inheritance and your personal constitution, so you will need to pay attention to how much sleep maximizes your performance. Be careful, though, that you haven't talked yourself into insufficient sleep. We might actually say out loud, "I only need five hours of sleep," or some other number that seems superhuman. It may be true that you've learned how to survive on five hours of sleep, but it is unlikely that a pattern of five hours per night allows you to truly blossom in mind, body, soul, and spirit.

"In vain you rise early and stay up late, toiling for food to eat— for [God] grants sleep to those [God] loves" (Psalm 127:2). In this verse, sleep is recognized as a gift from God, an indication of God's provision. Yet, we do often find ourselves "burning the candle at both ends." We may be staying up late and getting up early to tend to household chores, work on reports, answer e-mails, or take care of our loved ones. At other times, however, we are missing out on sleep because we are seeking entertainment. Once we start binge-watching missed episodes of our favorite TV show, we can't stop watching until we're fully caught up. Or maybe we're surfing channels and we run across a favorite movie or a marathon that pulls us in. Perhaps we have a favorite game we like to play on our phones or gaming systems. The Lord knows that we work hard, and "numbing out" every now and then is a welcome relief. However, we want to be cautious of entering a cycle where our leisure time begins regularly to take over our sleeping time.

For those whose "second-shift-at-home" job can easily stretch into

the wee hours of the morning, how do we put housework, job responsibilities, and entertainment down and begin making the transition
toward sleep? The key is to develop and sustain a ritual for sleep.
For some of us, we're so tired at the end of the day that our ritual is
fairly brief—a few words of nighttime prayer are swiftly followed by
our drifting into la-la land. For others of us, getting to sleep doesn't
happen so quickly. Any nighttime routines including bathing, teeth
brushing, and dressing for bed best happen earlier in the evening,
before you become too tired to perform them. As far as your sleeping
garments go, choose items that are comfortable, like fluffy pajamas,
which give you something to look forward to wearing. If intimacy
with your mate is sometimes a part of your nighttime routine, wear
garments that are attractive (or nothing at all), garments that reveal
your desire for your mate and your investment in enhancing your
total connection.

In order to begin the body's transition into restful sleep, consider
taking a warm bath or playing some relaxing music. (Lullabies aren't
just for babies!) Furthermore, sleep experts recommend that we
incorporate a soothing drink into our ritual to prepare for sleep, perhaps warm milk or chamomile tea, as these beverages send signals
to the body that it is time to calm down for rest. A herbal remedy
that works for many to enhance sleep is melatonin, a hormone that
naturally occurs in the body. Unlike other over-the-counter or prescribed sleep aids, melatonin is not habit-forming, making it a more
appealing remedy for many.

After employing these interventions, should you find yourself still
having difficulty getting or staying asleep, you may be dealing with
insomnia. Some of us have heard our ancestors say that when you
wake up in the middle of the night, the Lord is trying to talk to you.
Many advise that you should have the spirit of Samuel, saying "Speak,
for your servant is listening" (1 Sam 3:10b). Prayer, especially the listening portion of prayer, and journaling can be important activities
for those times when you wake up in the middle of the night. Resist
the temptation to engage in stimulating activities, such as watching

TV, checking email, eating, or playing games. Those "solutions" can often aggravate the problem, making it even harder for you to return to sleep. Persistent insomnia may signal that you are struggling with depression or another mental disorder. Seek professional help to prevent many of the long-term effects of chronic sleep deprivation. Complete the Sleep Log in Appendix H to establish a baseline measure of the quantity and quality of your sleep, then use it to track your improvements.

 Listen to Recording #11, "Restful Meditation"

Chapter Seventeen

Emotional Eating:
When Eating Hurts So Good

"Don't block your blessings. Don't let doubt stop you
from getting where you want to be."
*Jennifer Hudson, recording artist, actor, and
spokesperson for Weight Watchers*

Have you ever had a day when you "woke up on the wrong side
of the bed," and things got worse from there? Perhaps your
supervisor publicly confronted you at work about your job performance, or maybe you found out that a chronically ill loved one had
taken a turn for the worse. Worse yet, you might have had a major
argument with your significant other that seemed to threaten the
very foundation of your relationship. Under these or other stressful
circumstances, it would be very tempting to turn to your favorite
foods to nurse your wounds. Because food delights the taste buds,

dissipates our hunger, is more accessible than ever, and often carries positive memories, we often experience food as a faithful friend. However, if we begin to recognize in ourselves a patterned tendency to turn to food for comfort, we may be developing an unhealthy relationship to food that is often described as "emotional eating" or "stress eating."

Far beyond pursuing nutrients, we may be seeking a temporary solution for long-standing emotional and/or spiritual issues. Sometimes instead of talking it out, we're eating out! Quite frankly, at other times we prefer a literal fullness to a more abstract "fullness" of God. Thus, emotional eating often carries a hefty price tag that not only evades psychological healing, but when left unchecked contributes to physical and financial self-destruction. Research demonstrates that almost 50 percent of people with eating disorders also meet diagnostic criteria for depression. Additionally, around 65 percent of people with binge eating disorder are obese, and are at a higher risk for developing hypertension and diabetes. Black women are becoming increasingly susceptible to disordered eating (Flowers, Levesque, & Fischer, 2012).

Even if you don't have enough of the symptoms of commonly known eating disorders to be diagnosed with anorexia nervosa or bulimia nervosa, you may have several of the symptoms of disordered eating. In the African American community, we are more likely to move from "normal weight" to "overweight" to "obesity," even when our "big bones" and cultural preferences for "full figures" are taken into account. According to the Centers for Disease Control and Prevention (CDC), about 80 percent of African American women and 22 percent of African American girls are overweight or obese (CDC, 2016). If we don't correct our negative patterns with food, we can leave a legacy of compromised health and unhealthy examples for our families.

So, what do you do if you find yourself on the slippery slope of emotional eating? Well, the first step in any problem-solving task is to adequately define the problem. It will be very helpful to explore the extent of any unhealthy relationship you may have with food. Keep a daily log of your eating behavior as well as the thoughts and feelings that accompany such behavior. Once you establish a clear baseline, your journey and destination become easier to identify.

There are many ways to begin logging your eating behavior. Some approaches involve tracking your eating habits using the latest technological advances, including apps (such as MyFitnessPal, Google Fit, Fooducate, and 7-Minute Workout) or sleep- and activity-tracking wearable equipment (such as the Fitbit, Garmin Forerunner, or Apple Watch Nike+). Other approaches require little to no technology at all. For example, you might keep a comprehensive written diary of the foods and beverages you consume to track the frequency, caloric intake, and nutritional profiles of your meals and snacks (see Appendix I for an example of a food diary). You could also keep an audio or video recording of the items you consumed, and consult with a handbook or dietitian to calculate calories and nutrition. It doesn't matter how you collect the data, but the data are important for telling an accurate story of your level of vulnerability to emotional eating. Establishing your baseline demonstrates a good starting place for effective thinking as well as effective praying for the presence of mind to create positive dietary changes.

Once you recognize the extent to which emotional eating is a challenge, you can then begin to strategize about how to reduce negative eating behavior. Incorporating strategy is a significant way of combining practical knowledge and wisdom to produce positive physical outcomes. First, investigate whether you currently display any positive eating behaviors that you can slowly but surely expand. For example, are you a fairly consistent breakfast eater? If so, pat yourself on the back, as diet experts say that breakfast is the most important meal of the day. Now you can build upon this foundation. Slowly add the consistency of lunch, which is another oft-ignored meal. Schedule a specific time slot on your calendar of at least 15- 30 minutes away from your work tasks that is dedicated to enjoying a healthy lunch. Few of us miss dinner, yet we typically find ourselves eating well into the late night, which flies in the face of recommendations to eat dinner early in the evening. Because we often have competing evening activities such as late hours at the office, children's school or sports activities, or church and civic meetings, we may postpone dinner until these events conclude. However, it may be beneficial to "pack dinner" the same way we may "pack lunch" so that this important meal gives us energy into the night without too many late-night calories. Additionally, don't forget about snacks! In order to keep our glucose (blood sugar) levels even, experts say we should eat about every two to three hours. Snacks packed with protein, and fiber in particular, can sustain our energy until the next meal. Consult with a registered dietician or nutritionist to tailor your food intake to your health status as well as your dietary needs and preferences.

All of these recommendations for improving our bodies through self-respect, safe relationships, fitness, sleep, and nutrition are offered to help us achieve overall wellness. We will examine next how to blossom in the soul realm.

Part Five

Blossoming In Soul

In this section, we discuss the elements of the soul—our emotions, our relationships, and self-care, as well as how we use our money and time. We begin with emotions, for our emotions often form the basis for how we relate to all other facets of the soul. We then explore our relationships with our selves and surroundings, our husbands and children, our extended family members, our community members and events, and even our relationships with the deceased. Finally, we examine our relationships with our money and time, and discover how to blossom at higher levels through the use of these commodities.

Chapter Eighteen

Feelings

"It's time for your feelings to catch up with your faith.
Don't worry about how you feel. Rest in what you know
God's word says about you. Meditate in it. Rest in it."
*Erica Campbell, award-winning gospel recording artist
and radio host of "Get Up!"*

Although we sometimes carry ourselves above our emotional experiences, Black women indeed have feelings. Our society has trained us to think of feelings as "good" or "bad," with the latter being avoided at all costs. We have concluded that the Christian journey shapes us toward the positive feelings such as happiness, excitement, hope, and joy, and away from the negative feelings such as anger, sadness, jealousy, and fear. The reality, however, is that all feelings are a part of the human experience. The book of Psalms, in particular, demonstrates not only the breadth and depth of our emotional experiences, but also God's presence with us through our emotional experiences.

Rather than judging our feelings, we can use our feelings as a way of better understanding ourselves, our values, and our perspectives.

For example, if Kenya becomes angry when her husband does not give her flowers for their anniversary, she could focus her energies on trying to understand his behavior. On the other hand, Kenya could also look within to understand why his oversight triggered her anger. She may learn from examining her anger that she is, in fact, hurt if she assumes that flowers equal love, and that no flowers equals no love. Alternatively, Kenya may discover through examining her anger that she has always assumed that her husband knew how important flowers were to her, but has never actually communicated the importance of flowers to her husband. In either case, Kenya's reflection on her feelings, rather than merely the experience of her feelings, allows for deeper insight and a course of action. She can now more clearly communicate with her husband based on her enhanced self-understanding of her feelings.

As we become aware of our feelings, it is also important for us to express them. Depending on where and with whom we experience our feelings, we may have to delay full expression, particularly if the feelings are intense. However, we do not want to get into the habit of denying or suppressing our feelings, because they do not disappear; they only resurface in another situation or through our bodies. If we regularly experience strong emotions, we will also do well to learn skills of emotion regulation. Although anger management is perhaps the best known model for regulating emotion, we also must become adept at managing sadness, shame, disappointment, and other emotions. Your mental health professional can help you learn and implement these skills in your daily life.

In addition to reflecting on, expressing, and regulating our feelings, we can enhance our mood by participating in enriching events. Visit my website at *drtonyaarmstrong.com/blossominghope* to secure a list of "111 Blossoming Tools" that can be used for life enrichment, even in small yet important ways. Many of these tools are low- to no-cost activities that you can do on your own, in case others are not available. Research shows that increasing positive events in your life can increase positive emotions, accumulate positive experiences, and can refocus our time and energies on building positive rather than negative experiences (Linehan, 2015). Strive to incorporate at least one Blossoming Tool per day, planning ahead when possible. Be mindful during your experience, focusing on any pleasure your experience and detaching from worry as much as possible.

In a culture where Black women are expected to always put the needs of others ahead of our own, it's important to continue this conversation with the radical notion of self-care, which sometimes requires that we allow ourselves to receive support and nurturing from others.

Chapter Nineteen

Self-Care and Surroundings

"If I didn't define myself for myself, I would be crunched
into other people's fantasies for me and eaten alive."
Audre Lorde, poet and feminist

Taking Care of the Golden Goose

According to Aesop's Fable entitled "The Goose that Laid the
Golden Eggs" (Jones, 1912)," a farmer and his wife were delighted
to discover that their goose had begun laying golden eggs, but only
one at a time. In an attempt to increase the goose's productivity by
getting to its source of golden eggs, they killed the goose and found
that they'd lost all hope of any further profit from the goose. Similarly, in an effort to maximize our own productivity, we sometimes
shoot ourselves in the foot by demanding more of ourselves than is
healthy or compassionate. Rather than burning ourselves out, we do
much better to turn our attention and efforts toward self-care.

"Self-help" and "self-care" are two terms that are used liberally across media platforms to remind us of the importance of attending to our needs, strengths, weaknesses, and opportunities for growth. Endless books, TV shows, podcasts, blogs, and support groups have focused on the global epidemic of stress and lowered well-being, and various means by which we can aspire to return to our earlier days of glory, or even better, soar to new heights of blossoming. Isn't it ironic, though, that the impulses of our individualistic society have convinced us that the path to healing is best traveled and achieved on our own, by the "self" referred to in "self-help"? With the emphasis on the "self," we might be led to believe that we are responsible for our own successes, much like the Horatio Alger myth of pulling ourselves up by our own bootstraps, that is, through our own merit and sheer force of will. Many see this myth as the prototype of the American Dream, so to question it may seem countercultural. Yet the notion of self-redemption is certainly countercultural to the gospel of Christ: "For it is by grace you have been saved, through faith—and this is not from yourselves, it is the gift of God— not by works, so that no one can boast" (Ephesians 2: 8,9). God has freely given us the gift of redemption through God's Son, Jesus Christ. No amount of hard work or "perfect" behavior can come close to earning redemption. God created us, God redeemed us, and God is our help.

Consider also the central Christian concept of God's people being members of one body. That means we belong to each other. We not only help each other, but even more significantly, have responsibility for each other's well-being. Sadly, I am witnessing a trend, particularly in faith community circles, where we are reluctant to ask for help or receive help from our brothers and sisters in Christ. This trend seems to encompass physical/medical, emotional, financial, social, and spiritual troubles. Only in desperation do we reach out, often when the eviction has been scheduled, a grim prognosis has been rendered, or the marital separation has already occurred. It's not impossible, but much more difficult for healing to occur once extreme circumstances have been reached.

In all fairness, it is important to note that perhaps there has been a societal swing toward self-care because, in the not-too-distant past, there has been an exploitation of the notion of caring for each other, especially when some members of the community read that as "You take care of me as much as possible, and I'll return the favor...eventually." This struggle to remain true to the tenets of our faith, to love God, one another, and ourselves has particularly plagued Black Christian women. In our context, loving another person is often translated into providing physical presence, hands-on care, domestic support, and administrative assistance for our ailing family and community members. As your circumstances permit, your ability to supply loving care and attention are truly blessings to the circle surrounding that loved one, and a likely reflection of God's grace in your life. Loving one another, however, can unfortunately be translated into taking on significant financial burdens of family and friends, allowing others to intrude upon your personal space for seemingly endless periods, and/or enabling behaviors like addictions that do not lead to the greater well-being of that person so enabled. Often, it can be difficult to discern where love ends and enabling begins. Knowing where and when to draw the line, and how to establish firm boundaries (e.g., Cloud & Townsend, 1992), requires a growing relationship with God and consultation with wise confidantes.

The Word of God also provides guidance in this area. In the Apostle Paul's letter to the church at Galatia, he tells the members of that body to "carry each other's burdens and in this way you will fulfill the law of Christ" (Galatians 6:2). This passage reveals to us that carrying the burdens of others is not optional, or temporary, or specific to our favorites—it is a Scriptural mandate! (This passage also teaches us that it is Scriptural for us to allow others to carry our burdens.) Yes, sisters, burden bearing is a part of our Christian journey.

Nevertheless, if you keep reading that Galatians passage in the King James Version of the Bible, you will see just a few verses later that the Apostle Paul says, "each one should carry their own burden." (verse 5) Huh?? Well, our English language doesn't translate very well the nuances of the Greek, in which the passage was written. In the Greek, the term "burden" in verse 2 is represented by the Greek word *baros*, which refers to weight, heaviness, or trouble. This burden of which Paul speaks is something that is cumbersome and troublesome to the mind and spirit. It's a burden that is virtually impossible to carry on one's own without significant damage to the soul. Examples in our contemporary lives include grief and loss, domestic and community violence, infidelity, unplanned pregnancy, abortion, emotional, physical, and sexual abuse, and traumatic experiences, all of which can contribute to shame.

The term "burden" in verse 5, on the other hand, refers to something quite different: *phortion*, which refers to the freight routinely carried by a ship during its daily schedule. *Phortion* also refers to the obligations placed on us by Christ, in contrast to the impossibly oppressive rites required by the Pharisees during Biblical times. By comparison, this burden, although a hassle, is much lighter than the weighty burdens of life. These burdens have more to do with our daily obligations, including working under typical circumstances, chores, child rearing, and church and civic responsibilities.

This Galatians passage teaches us that in our daily lives, we are to carry each other's heavy burdens of crisis and suffering, because these burdens can be debilitating to face on one's own. On the other hand, if we are regularly carrying someone else's daily burden (or "load" in the NIV), we are doing them *and* ourselves a disservice. Unfortunately, we tend to get this backwards: We are willing to pay the car note of an able-bodied, right-minded individual for years, but we flee from situations of offering support to the grieving, or to the victim of a crime, or to another sister carrying the weight of a loved one's deployment or incarceration. May God grant us grace to re-order our priorities.

Because of the very existence of the daily burdens or loads that we carry, we need individual and communal forms of care to nurture us toward wholeness. Sometimes the term "self-care" is the most appropriate term to use because it refers to activities that we initiate and/or perform on our own. I sometimes indulge myself by curling up with a book, watching a movie, or playing my favorite smartphone game.

At other times, I remind myself to engage in a few moments of deep breathing, stretching, or yoga poses to rebalance myself. Other types of activities that are considered "self-care" often require the involvement of other people to make them happen, and are more appropriately thought of as communitarian care. For example, one of my favorite treats is receiving a massage. Although I could use my mechanical, over-the-shoulders shiatsu massager or sit in a massage chair at the mall, I prefer the hands of my gentle and attentive husband or a competent professional trained in the art and science of massage. I am dependent upon his availability, or her expertise, to provide a stress-reducing and pleasurable experience, and I rely on the atmosphere to be calming, fragrant, and warm. In other cases, like when my group of therapist-friends takes a quarterly trip to the spa, I am dependent not only on the massage staff at the spa, but in some cases I am dependent on the coordinator of the group to help the appointment to "magically" appear on my calendar. Even further, I am dependent on my office manager to make sure that I am free of client appointments on spa day. I am dependent on my children's teachers to faithfully educate and supervise them while I'm gone. And I am dependent on my husband to compensate for the loss of revenue that occurs when I am out of the office. So, you see that "self-care" sometimes only happens in the context of an intricate web of communal support.

Even more examples could be shared from the practical perspective of ways that we are dependent upon our family members, friends, and community to take care of us when we don't have the means to arrange such care for ourselves. For instance, your greatest "self-care" moment of the week may involve having support to take a walk through the leaf-changing beauty of your neighborhood on a golden fall afternoon while a loved one volunteers to watch your child when a babysitter is out of your budget. At other times, communitarian care occurs when a girlfriend drops by with a pot of soup when you're under the weather, or when a cousin calls to check on you following surgery.

To be sure, communitarian care doesn't always happen. People, including Christians, don't always follow through as they say that

they will. "Just let me know if there's anything I can do to help."
and "Now that your loved one is gone, I'll be there for you" are just
two of the oft-quoted phrases, when unfulfilled, that are disappoint-
ing many times over. Our culture has reinforced the importance of
speaking in clichés, even when the person has no intention of following through. And even when we have the best intentions, life
happens and we "all fall short of the glory of God" (Romans 3:23).
The pace of life has become so maddening that sometimes our bestie
or our "ace boon coon" isn't there when we reach out to her. Even
when we know the Word to say that Jesus is a friend that sticks
closer than any brother, one who will never leave us nor forsake us,
we still find comfort in the presence of flesh and blood. This prefer-
ence is a part of our human essence, and its absence when we most
desire it leaves us feeling neglected, or downright rejected. In these
instances, we may have a God encounter as a last resort.

Yet how often is assistance made available and we stop short of
receiving it? What happens when someone calls and we don't return
the call? Or we take the call using our best phone voice to mask the
pain we feel? Shame and mistrust can rear their ugly heads. After
all, we've been hurt in relationships before. Friends and family
members have betrayed confidences, even when sworn to secrecy.
But sometimes our fear is the true culprit. What if someone asks
us how we're doing in an area of struggle, and even though they've
never betrayed us before, we somehow find it hard to swallow our
pride and make ourselves vulnerable in that conversation? When
the Word indicates that God will supply all our needs according to
God's glorious riches (Philippians 4:19), God also means the emotional ones. In a very human way, we've missed our opportunity to
share that burden, to have someone listen to us vent; to have someone else interceding on our behalf; someone else who could supply
wisdom to help extricate us from our mess. Another opportunity
lost…Yet God is a God who continually gives more opportunities,
especially as we show ourselves to be good stewards.

While God desires us to be connected to other believers, God makes

God's self available to us for all of our cares and concerns:

"Cast your cares on the LORD and he will sustain you; he will never let the righteous be shaken" (Psalm 55:22).

"Cast all your anxiety on him because he cares for you" (1 Peter 5:7).

Or consider the assurances of the refrain of the hymn "God Cares" (Martin, 1904):

God will take care of you
Thro' every day, o'er all the way
He will take care of you
God will take care of you

Over and over again, God shows to us that God is the lover of our souls. What would happen if we *truly* entrusted ourselves to God's care and keeping? How might being rooted and grounded in God's TLC (tender loving care) provide the best antidote for our stress? Self-care and communitarian care in this context might be engaged for the purposes of blossoming, and not just for crisis management. Receiving the gracious and continuous offer of God's care just might enable us to provide the kind of deep, nurturing, effective, but not depleting care that is in keeping with the law of Christ.

Taking a Long View of Career and Professional Development

> **"The essence of America—that which really unites us—**
> **is not ethnicity, or nationality or religion—it is an idea—**
> **and what an idea it is: That you can come from humble**
> **circumstances and do great things."**
> *Condoleezza Rice, first Black woman to serve as U.S. Secretary of State*

(Some of us do not desire a career, and exist in circumstances that afford this privilege. For those of us who desire a

career, or for those of us who don't want to work but are
required by our circumstances to work for the time being,
this section is for us.)

One powerful form of self-care that promotes our future blossoming
is education. Earning your training and/or degree(s) can be a very
important step toward building a solid financial future and moving
toward the effective execution of God's purpose in your life. It's not
usually the final step, however, because of the licensure and/or certifications needed to demonstrate your competence in your industry.
Again, you may feel that you've already "put in your time" by completing school. This is where we as a culture of sisters need a paradigm
shift, that is, a new way of thinking about our career and professional
development over the long haul. Instead of imagining your college or
vocational training as a relatively short, discrete period of time that
prepares you for landing a job that makes you "all set" for life, consider your career path as a continually evolving journey rife with new
opportunities (and new crises) at every turn.

Becoming certified and/or licensed signals to the world, and to
employers in particular, that you are invested in honing your craft,
whatever it may be. Yes, a considerable amount of time and money
may be required in studying, applying for, and taking your licensure
or certification exam. However, given the doors that certification and
licensure open in terms of available jobs and salary increases, think
of the process as an investment in your future. As a self-employed
beauty representative, for example, you would have to pay enrollment
fees, monthly membership fees, and purchase a reasonable amount
of inventory to have on hand. You trust that your investment is not
in vain, and that you will eventually receive a good return on your
investment. Although more abstract, the same principle is at work
with pursuing your credentials.

So, what if you believe that you don't test well? It is true that the
path to most certification and licensure is through the successful
completion of a standardized test under controlled conditions, as in

a live, proctored testing environment, or in a tightly controlled electronic environment. Multiple research studies support the idea that standardized tests are not often normed with Black or female groups, so assessment developers don't necessarily design the tests with our learning styles in mind. Until such time that licensing and certification boards grant an alternative path to the end goal, however, we must learn how play the game until we have the power to change it.

Perhaps you've taken your exam more than once, or several times, and have even come very close to passing, but not quite close enough. My advice to you is to find the best test preparation program you can afford, saving your funds for a period of time if necessary. Understand that for many fields, certification or licensure exams are not necessarily measuring how well you understand the foundations of your discipline. Instead, they are often measuring how well you understand the test itself and how effectively you can answer the questions in the mode in which they are delivered. That's why ordering test materials from the test developer who administers the test is often wise. Take this period of preparation seriously, and understand that it may take a period of weeks or months to truly grasp the information. Getting "in the zone" may require you to temporarily cut back or cut out some of your favorite activities, such as TV watching, reading for pleasure, attending sporting or social events, hanging out on the weekends, or traveling.

Another idea is to enroll in a test preparation course. The better programs usually meet for a series of meetings rather than just one intensive training. Meet in person if at all possible, or combine an ongoing, in-person study group of like-minded people with a webinar experience. Take as many practice exams as you can! And don't stop there: once you take a practice exam, examine your scores to see how you fared overall, as well as where your particular strengths and weaknesses lie. This feedback can then shape the way you study for subsequent practice exams leading up to the official exam.

Once you obtain your certification or licensure, you can become even more stable in your career. But don't rest on your laurels: God will continue to "enlarge your territory," or expand your capacity. Even though I have been in my current career as a psychologist for twenty years, I have watched God bring amazing opportunities and challenges through my work as a minister, entrepreneur, clinical supervisor, faculty member, department dean, trainer, motivational speaker, gospel recording artist, board member, association president, and author. And God's not finished yet!

Managing Our Homes

> "Sometimes you've got to let everything go—purge yourself.
> If you are unhappy with anything, whatever is bringing you
> down—GET RID OF IT! Because you'll find that when you're
> free, your true creativity, your true self comes out."
> *Tina Turner, dancer, actor, and Queen of Rock and Roll*

"Home is where the heart is." Given our diversity as Black women, it stands to reason that we have different visceral responses to the term "home." "Home" may remind us of the household(s) or community/ ies of our youth. Home may be a place of welcome, love, comfort, refuge, and repose. Alternatively, home may signal all of the tasks and responsibilities waiting for us to perform. Or home may be where we lay our heads for a brief time between all of our moving and shaking. If we live alone, home can be a place of escape and solitude, or a place of loneliness and excessive quietness. If we've fallen upon hard times, home may be elusive, and may bring to mind a tight space divided with other family members, a shelter shared with strangers, or worse, a transient set of locations on the streets or in the woods.

Given our different walks of life, perhaps we should be asking ourselves what we desire home to be, and to pray for the energy, creativity, and resources to make it what we desire. This is especially true if we share our household with others. Prayerfully, we begin with the basics—places for preparing and eating food, sleeping, and maintaining our personal hygiene. Now think about what makes these basics come to life—comfortable furniture, entertainment, music, laughter, and décor, including pictures and other mementos of our family and friends. To elevate to a higher place, consider the tasteful use of color and the principles of *feng shui*, the Chinese art of arranging the space in our homes to maximize harmony and energy in our environments.

Maintaining a household can be a welcome rhythm in our lives, or a challenging prospect, especially if we agree with the saying that "a woman's work is never done." Because household tasks can multiply quickly, we will do well to cultivate the division of labor in our homes. As much as possible, share chores with your husband or significant other, particularly if you both work outside of the home. As they mature, train your children to assume increasing responsibility for their own room(s), then other spaces in your home. Even if you have housekeeping support, develop good habits of upkeep in between visits. If you are a clutterbug, a packrat, or a hoarder, you may require additional support from family, friends, or a professional to fend against crippling disorganization.

Meal Preparation

> **"Women are dominating the charts, and women are doing it for themselves. We're kicking butt and taking no prisoners."**
> *Patti LaBelle, award-winning recording artist,*
> *author, and culinary expert*

In this age of fast food restaurants proliferating on every corner, it has never been so easy to meet your or your family's needs for sustenance…or so difficult to find nutritious options. It is undeniable that the current pace of our lives makes it increasingly impossible to provide healthy, home-cooked meals every night of the week. Between our church and civic commitments, our children's extracurricular activities, and our desire for personal development through networking or hobbies, the family meal around the table is becoming a relic of the past. Yet because home is the place where we have the most control over the quality and nutrition of the ingredients used and how food is prepared, there is value in providing this gift to our family. Additionally, cooking at home saves significant money compared to eating/taking out, and sitting around the table making eye contact and sharing stories can serve as the basis of positive family memories for decades to come.

How, then, can we place more of an emphasis on sharing meals at home? First, take an honest assessment of your current situation. Does your teen have basketball practice three days per week, plus games on the weekend? Maybe you can begin with a commitment to cooking two days per week. Next, create a meal plan. Few home-related activities are more anxiety provoking than figuring out, in rush-hour traffic, what to prepare for dinner. Before the busyness of the week gets underway, ask yourself what dishes will you prepare? What ingredients will you need? When will you need to go grocery shopping so that you will have the ingredients you need, without compromising freshness of the food? Keep your planning simple, remembering any food preferences or dietary restrictions of your family members. Once you establish a rhythm of preparing a few basic dishes enjoyed by your family, you can slowly begin to incorporate new recipes into your repertoire. Seek out old family recipes, choose from the cookbooks galore at your local bookstore, order dinner kits online, and/or search the Internet for a myriad of recipe websites, some of which include step-by-step, how-to videos. Lastly, share the fun of cooking and cleaning! Invite your spouse and children to contribute to the family with their cooking skills. Although instruction can slow you down on the front end, teaching your daughters and sons how to cook skillfully will pay dividends in the long run! Perhaps meal preparation will be more manageable if you establish rules around who cooks and who cleans up after a meal. Post a schedule on the refrigerator as a reminder, if needed. Most importantly, whether eating by yourself or with others, enjoy meals as nourishment, pleasure, and a tangible reminder of God's provision.

Chapter Twenty

Relationships

Family

"I didn't grow up in one of those restrictive Christian
households where you couldn't do this or that.
We were brought up with a great collection of good morals
and good values, but we also had fun. We'd go to church
on Sunday, but then have ice cream, roller skate
or play in the park afterwards."
*Yolanda Adams, award-winning gospel vocalist and
host of the "Yolanda Adams Morning Show"*

Who's in your family? Black families have always been inclusive, partly as a survival mechanism, and partly because of our love and the value we place on family (Boyd-Franklin, 2003). In our mainstream American culture, family is traditionally defined as the nuclear family, that is, typically one or two parents and their biological children. In our Black experience, however, our households are often multigenerational, often including three or more generations of family members. Often, members of our households include a matriarch, and sometimes a patriarch, with child(ren) and grandchild(ren). Thus, in this scenario, cousins are commonly raised as siblings. Our rich history has often included informal adoption of other family members or non-family members, particularly under dire circumstances. Every now and then, these young people are formally adopted.

Our families also quite often include people known as "fictive kin." This term was originally used by anthropologists to describe those persons are not related to us by blood nor marriage, yet we "claim" one another as "Mama," "Pop," "Sis," "Auntie," "Uncle," "Cuz," or some other term of endearment. Perhaps you remember Ja'Net DuBois's character, "Willona" from the popular 70's sitcom, *Good Times*. Willona was not related to the Evans family, but in nearly every episode, her character was woven into the plot of the story. And it's the same today with those "play" family members we have. They are the family members that we choose, perhaps your "brother from another mother." In other instances, women who are unable or unwilling to birth children can still create families through foster care, adoption, or other informal means of taking in a child under their wings. Even when biology fails us, freedom of choice allows us to create family. These "other mothers" (Collins, 2000) have been vital to our survival as a race.

More and more, families of the 21st century are blended families, or families comprised of children from a previous relationship. In blended families, children may be the product of the new union, a previous divorce, a widowed parent and the deceased parent, a previous common-law relationship, a casual sexual encounter, and/or in some cases, an extramarital affair (think of the play/film *Fences*). Although shows like "The Brady Bunch" and "Modern Family" have popularized the notion of blended families, the reality is that blended

families have many challenges to work through. These include unrealistic expectations of the marriage or of the new family, a perception that stepchildren are being treated unequally by the stepparent, a lack of involvement or potential conflict between the stepparent and the stepchildren, and underestimating the bond between biological parent and children (Deal, 2014). Although a fairy tale existence is tempting to dream about, blended families can expect to take a few years for their new family configuration to stabilize. Connection to other blended families, bonds with harmonious extended family members, and regular interaction with church or broader community supports are important coping resources to incorporate into family life (Tyler and Tyler, 2012).

Relationship Building Blocks

"If you're having fun, that's when the best memories are built."
Simone Biles, Olympic gold medalist and the most decorated American gymnast (17 medals and counting)

In order for any family to share meaningful relationships with each other, there are certain principles that must govern. The Apostle Paul wrote about family relationships in what are referred to in theological circles as "Household Codes" (Ephesians 5:21-33; Colossians 3:18-22, 4:1; 1 Peter 3:1-7). These codes, or rules, were not a novel Christian concept; rather, they were a reflection of the broader Greco-Roman household codes of the times out of which Christianity first emerged. The household codes provided instruction about how members of the household related to each other. These guidelines gave details about how husbands, wives, children, and household workers were to relate to each other. Under these codes, a clear hierarchy was established with husbands as rulers of the women, children, and enslaved persons in the household.

While we can derive wisdom from the household codes, they can also be problematic because of the ways that husband-wife relationships are repeatedly compared to the master-slave relationship (Evans, 2012). The hierarchical submission articulated in these passages is being recast, even by the Apostle Paul, as *mutual submission*. Paul shows how Christianity is distinctive from the Greco-Roman worldview of that time by the way Christians *love* each other. Paul's countercultural assertion was that in Christ, there was "neither Jew nor Gentile, neither slave nor free, nor is there male and female, for you are all one in Christ Jesus." So, although we usually examine the notion of marital submission beginning in Ephesians 5:22, the 21st verse reminds us to submit to one another out of reverence for Christ. Does this mean that wives should disregard the call to submission? Not at all! Rather, we do well to remember that Jesus Christ has ushered in a new standard of respect and servanthood toward others, particularly our husbands. Jesus's standards for right relationships with each other include trust, harmony, honor and respect, clear and timely communication, compromise, emotional expressiveness, rules/structure, and affection and love. These principles are timeless building blocks for building strong relationships.

Trust is one of the most foundational elements in any relationship, particularly in families. Trust is your heartfelt sense that another person will do what they say they will do. In the earliest relationship between parent and child, trust is not spoken so much as demonstrated. Parents demonstrate to their infant through basic behaviors such as feeding, clothing, protecting, and soothing that they are reliable and consistent. As infants move toward toddlerhood and begin to explore more and more of the world around them, their ability to trust the ground under their crawling knees and cruising feet is connected to the trust they have experienced up to that point. Within developmental psychology, there is a classic demonstration of this trust in an exercise called The Strange Situation, developed by Mary Ainsworth in 1969 and informed in part by her field work in Kampala, Uganda (Ainsworth, 1967). Usually conducted in laboratory settings, this exercise observes how an infant will respond under variations of parental and stranger presence and absence. The infant's degree of comfort or distress reveals something about the quality of attachment, or closeness, between parent and child. According to Ainsworth's theory, the stronger the attachment between parent and child, the more secure the child will be, even in the presence of a stranger. Needless to say, this quality of attachment has implications far beyond toddlerhood in terms of the child's sense of trust in subsequent relationships.

As family relationships encounter new challenges, each family member hopefully learns that trust is earned, not given. If trust is ever breached, it can take significant work for that trust to be earned again, yet it happens in most relationships. Also, trust is vital for the development of intimacy. The higher the level of trust that exists between two or more parties in a relationship, the more ideal the conditions for growing intimacy there.

The stronger the trust in a relationship, the safer each person feels in expressing her emotions. Emotional expressiveness is a practice of sharing your innermost thoughts and feelings with someone you trust. We don't always practice this concept because it requires a certain level of vulnerability; however, its benefits are numerous. Not only does it help to name our emotional experience(s), but naming those experiences can assist us in avoiding more negative emotions and their attendant behaviors that can threaten our relationships, such as anger, anxiety, and jealousy (Baucom & Epstein, 1990). To be effective in expressing our emotions, consider the use of a brief "X-Y-Z" statement: "When you do Behavior X in Situation Y, I feel Z." This formula reminds us to own and express our emotion in a manner that specifically names the other person's behavior in a specific situation. We also want to include any authentic, positive feedback in our exchange. When using this formula, it is important to remember that we are stating our feelings subjectively, as we feel them, rather than as objective truth. The positivity of our feedback, the brevity of the statement, and the specificity of one situation (rather than piling on offenses from the last several months or years) maximizes the chances that the other person can hear and receive what we are sharing. Receiving is not the same as agreeing with us, but it does increase the possibility of greater empathy in the relationship, which can lead to more harmony.

Harmony is the relational quality demonstrating that even in our differences of personality and preferences, we are still able to get along with each other. We may not like the tendencies of the other people in our family, but in the grand scheme of things, we recognize that we are able to tolerate them and they are able to tolerate us. As we mature, we are even able to accept others for who they are as we learn how to honor and respect them. We can cultivate more respect for our family members if we can learn to not judge them from our vantage point, but to peer over their shoulder to see the world as they see the world. Rather than insisting that a sister, mother, or daughter see and experience situations as we see and experience them, we affirm that her viewpoint is valid and we honor her, *even if we disagree with her decisions.* To honor someone means to see her as a child of God and to treat her accordingly. To respect someone means to humbly make room for the other person's way and to give her the benefit of the doubt.

Learning clear and timely **communication** requires practice to develop this vital skill, yet can yield great dividends in family life. Communication is about the content conveyed through speech and language, yet is also about the soft skills such as volume, tone, pitch, facial expressions, body language, and other nonverbal gestures. Have you ever witnessed a commercial or a real-life scenario where two people are using the exact same words, yet end up with very different meanings based on how they express those words? Well, the same thing happens in our households all the time. Proverbs 25:11 says, "A word spoken at the right time is like fruit of gold set in silver." (New Life Version) Thus, we will do well to consider how to maximize the reception of our communication.

In your household, you may need to experiment with which *mode of communication* works best for each of your family members. Does your spouse prefer to keep up with family business through spread-sheets or email? Does your teenager respond best to text messages? Perhaps your play sister prefers to catch up face to face. Also, consider the *timing* of your message. Does the recipient of your communication need some down time when returning home from work or school before you introduce a weighty subject? Might you be interrupting an important event, such as a football game or a favorite TV show? Is the person possibly "hangry" (i.e., hungry and angry), suggesting that a conversation might go better after a meal? Employ alternative forms of communication to maximize the effectiveness of your message, whether it's a mundane reminder about chores, or a meaningful reinforcement of your family's values.

Recreation. Look at that word carefully and you'll discover that it calls us into activities so important that they foster "re-creation," or making ourselves new again. Busy Black women often don't prioritize recreation because it often doesn't seem to be associated with any particular or measurable outcome. However, our husbands, children, and other enlightened sisters might convince us otherwise. Recreation comes in all shapes and sizes, so there's bound to be a version that is accessible to you and your family. Some families like to have fun being active in sports (playing or spectating), hiking, walking the beach, or other ways of taking in the beauty of God's creation. Other families like to use vacation or staycation as opportunities to see and experience new or familiar activities. Although getting time off from work can be a challenge for some wage earners, almost everyone can squeeze out some family time for board games right at home. However you recreate together, you can increase the bonds of attachment and good feelings toward each other, release feel-good endorphins, share laughter, build common experiences, and experience enjoyment!

In order to maintain order and stability in the home, it is important for everyone in the family to understand the **rules** of engagement. Rules that are overly harsh and rigid can be discouraging and break the spirit of one or more family members. The Amplified version of Ephesians 6:4 says, "Fathers [and mothers], do not provoke your children to anger [do not exasperate them to the point of resentment with demands that are trivial or unreasonable or humiliating or abusive; nor by showing favoritism or indifference to any of them], but bring them up [tenderly, with lovingkindness] in the discipline and instruction of the LORD." At the same time, Scripture is replete with indications that discipline is not only appropriate, but also necessary: "Discipline your children, for in that there is hope; do not be a willing party to their death" (Proverbs 19:18). Helping our children to understand and comply with the structure of the household, then, is one of the most life-saving contributions we can make to their futures. Families, and even parents, differ from each other with regard to how much order and organization is needed around cleanliness of personal and shared spaces, meal times, bedtimes and waking times, how and when homework is completed and/or reviewed, whether allowance or other earning opportunities are provided, the degree of participation in church and other extracurricular activities, and other priorities. Despite parental variability, it is important for parents to find a compromise to clearly communicate household standards to their children, standards by which parents themselves are also abiding.

Compromise is another necessary ingredient in any healthy relationship. In a situation where each party would ideally get her own way, compromise is a gesture of humility that signals that you are willing to give up something that you desire in order to gain something else that you want. The second chapter of Paul's letter to the church at Philippi instructs believers to imitate Christ's humility:

Do nothing out of selfish ambition or vain conceit. Rather, in humility value others above yourselves, not looking to your own interests but each of you to the interests of the others. In your relationships with one another, have the same mindset as Christ Jesus:

Who, being in very nature God,
did not consider equality with God something

to be used to his own advantage;
rather, he made himself nothing
by taking the very nature of a servant,
being made in human likeness.
And being found in appearance as a man,
he humbled himself
by becoming obedient to death—
even death on a cross.

(Philippians 2:3-8)

When we might otherwise be inclined to assert the right to have our way based on intelligence, seniority, logic, or credentials, the example of Jesus Christ reminds us to yield by looking to the interests of others. You will often find that although you may be giving up something you want now, in the long run you will gain more through the trust and richness of a relationship that results from making mutual concessions. (If you find, on the other hand, that you tend to be the only person in the relationship making concessions, it may be time to examine the need for balance in that relationship or to re-evaluate the relationship's importance in your life.)

Because the potential is always present for humans to maliciously or inadvertently take advantage of another human being, it is important to mention the power of **assertiveness**. We can relate to one another in one of three major ways. First, we can passively relate to others by constantly deferring to them and placing their needs or wants first. Second, we can aggressively relate to others by using any means necessary, even violence, to ensure that our needs or wants are met, without regard for the needs of anyone else. Third, we can relate to others assertively, being attentive to the needs or wants of others *without losing sight of our own needs or wants* (Koch & Haugk, 1992).

We have often been taught, or have interpreted, that Christians, especially Christian women, are to engage the world primarily with a passive approach; after all, wasn't Jesus meek and mild? Actually, the gospel accounts are full of examples of Jesus operating assertively with his family, his disciples, and even his detractors. Once we understand that the gospel encourages us to balance the needs and wants of others with our own, we can better handle our feelings and relationships. The key is to know the difference between your core values, around which you should not compromise, and the other issues of life, where compromise is acceptable. For example, if you strongly believe that your destiny is to be equally yoked with another Christian, you will not seriously consider marrying someone outside of your faith. However, you may be more willing to compromise around relatively less important matters such as whether your children will attend Vacation Bible School versus a sports camp.

Affection and love are important for all relationships. Let us remember that God first loved us, and that in Christ, we are all called to love others as a sign of belonging in the vine. Recall God's definition of agape, or unconditional love:

> Love is patient, love is kind. It does not envy, it does not boast, it is not proud. It does not dishonor others, it is not self-seeking, it is not easily angered, it keeps no record of wrongs. Love does not delight in evil but rejoices with the truth. It always protects, always trusts, always hopes, always perseveres. Love never fails.
>
> (1 Corinthians 13: 4-8a)

Showing God's love is a lofty goal that requires a lifetime of effort, so how do we translate these pearls of wisdom into concrete, loving actions? Relationship expert and associate pastor Gary Chapman (2015) has identified five primary ways that couples, singles, children, and teens prefer to be loved. These "love languages" include *Words of Affirmation* (e.g., receiving positive words of encouragement); *Quality Time* (e.g., receiving one's time and active attention); *Gifts* (e.g., receiving a heartfelt, material token of affection); *Physical Touch* (e.g., receiving gentle hugs, kisses, and other affectionate touches); and *Acts of Service* (e.g., receiving care as demonstrated through the completion of tasks or projects). Although it is relatively easy to love someone from the vantage point of our own love language, it is often much more challenging to love another based on her or his love language. Thus, it takes practice to love others the way they want to be loved. Using the love languages also requires some trial-and-error attempts at successful loving. You may be on the right track to using affirming words, for example, but you may need to refine which words are most suitable for your loved one. Don't be discouraged by the work involved, however: based on God's law of sowing and reaping (Galatians 6:7), the efforts you place in showing love and affection to the best of your ability will come back to you, even if not from the person toward whom you direct them.

Parenting

"We have to teach our boys the rules of equality and respect, so that as they grow up, gender equality becomes a natural way of life. And we have to teach our girls that they can reach as high as humanly possible."
Beyoncé, best-selling female music artist most nominated in the history of the Grammy Award (22 won to date)

Whether you are a biological mother or a mother who has gained the title by virtue of the nurturing you provide to young people in your family or community, mothering can be one of the most fulfilling roles in which you can ever engage. It can also be one of the toughest. Molding and shaping a little one to become a responsible, caring, and God-fearing adult is truly a massive undertaking, especially in the context of a culture that does not always look favorably on Black children. For some of us, we sought out motherhood. We prayed for pregnancy, counted days until ovulation, and even took pills and shots in order for blessed conception to occur. For others of us, motherhood sought us out. Due to fleeting circumstances of quick romance or trauma, ignorance about the true facts of the birds and the bees, or imperfect medical procedures or advice ("I thought my tubes were tied!" or "Due to your condition, you'll never conceive."), you may have discovered you were pregnant when you least expected it. Regardless, we find ourselves on the path of motherhood. The task can be even more challenging when you are in it with few, if any, supports.

Raising children effectively requires energy, wisdom, social support, and money! We thank God for the fathers who are "ride-or-die" dads, and the dads who, although physically absent, make a concerted effort to play a consistent role in their children's lives. Some fathers are physically present but psychologically absent. Other fathers are absent altogether and removed from the major events of their children's lives. Positively, some dads make child support payments, whereas other fathers have never even acknowledged paternity. Their children may live for years with the pain of this rejection unless another caring adult helps these children to understand that their worth is independent from the absence of the father.

After we've prayed over our children, we still have a significant responsibility that remains in our court. After all, Scripture indicates that we are to "train up a child in the way that he should go, and when he is old, he will not depart from it" (Proverbs 22:6). I also like the way the Amplified Bible puts it: "Train up a child in the way he should go [teaching him to seek God's wisdom and will for his abilities and talents], Even when he is old he will not depart from it." This emphasis on the *child's* abilities and talents suggests that one-sized parenting does not fit all; we must know our children well enough to raise them in a manner that reflects an understanding of their learning styles, personalities, and gifts. We have to lovingly instill quality education, Christ-centered values, God-honoring habits, and a reasonable example of discipleship in order to reap the benefits of a God-fearing, joyful, and productive citizen who gives back to his/her community.

Notwithstanding the individual differences that each child brings to the table, what do our children and youth need from us? They need affirmation of who they are, inside and out. They need to know that they are created by God as good, no matter their hue, hair texture, or facial features, and no matter what others have said about their physical appearance or their personhood. (If you have family members who, for whatever reason, send a different message, it is your job to respectfully but firmly run interference to stop such damaging messages, even if those messages are said "in jest." If those family members don't honor your request, your job is to limit exposure to those individuals and messages.) Do what is reasonably possible to enhance your child's presentation, providing resources and encouragement for good grooming, a clean and neat appearance, and stylish clothing, improvising with homemade creativity as necessary. I would recommend investing in brand-name clothing only to the extent that you are able to invest an equal or greater amount into your child's savings fund.

Mothering requires constant training around Christ-centered values and standards. Mothering also requires discipline. Depending on how you were reared, you may find yourself repeating the forms of discipline under which you were raised, or you may choose to take a different or more effective path. "Spare the rod and spoil the child." That's what the Bible says, right? Well, not exactly. Proverbs 13:24 actually states, "Whoever spares the rod hates their children, but the one who loves their children is careful to discipline them." The "rod" is often interpreted as referring to corporal punishment, and there may be distinct instances in which you choose to spank your child to teach an immediate, life-saving lesson. However, before you quickly defend your right to spank your child, give some thought to our historical connection to whipping and other forms of violence used to control enslaved persons. Think about whether you intend to convey to your child the message that spanking is the only form of discipline that he will respond to. Consider other approaches for teaching your child right from wrong. Time-out involves removing your child from all stimulating activity (including your attention) for an age-appropriate, prescribed period of time, such as one minute per year of age (e.g., 5 minutes for a 5-year-old). Younger children experience absence from more favorable or fun conditions, and older children experience that absence along with the cognitive ability to reflect on how to make better choices in the future.

Removal of privileges is an approach that takes away a child's access to activities such as playing with their toys, watching television or movies, using their phones or tablets, hanging out at the mall with their friends, or any other experience they enjoy. (If a parent reports that her child gets confused about rights versus privileges, I half-jokingly point her to guidelines from the law or the local Department of Social Services regarding the basic necessities of life that the government requires of parents—food, clothing, and shelter. This is a low bar, yet it helps to demonstrate how young people often develop a sense of entitlement to things that are not required for them to blossom.)

If you utilize this approach of removing privileges, be sure to clarify for your child what the offense(s) is/are, which privilege(s) will be removed, and for how long those privileges will be removed. If you don't clarify the period of the removal, you run the risk of increasing your child's exasperation and decreasing their motivation for demonstrating positive change in their behaviors. Remember that we as parents have a Scriptural mandate ourselves: "Fathers [and mothers], do not exasperate your children; instead, bring them up in the training and instruction of the LORD" (Ephesians 6:4). When it comes to discipline, much of the empirical research has found that authoritative parenting tends to be the most effective for children. Authoritative parenting combines a clear presentation of parental authority with a loving approach to parenting. Other forms of parenting classified as authoritarian (i.e., demanding and punishing), neglectful (i.e., detached and unresponsive), and permissive-indulgent (i.e., responsive with few demands and avoidant of confrontation) are less likely to support children in a solid understanding of the positive consequences of prosocial behaviors and the negative consequences of misbehaviors (Baumrind, 1991).

In addition to learning Christian values and discipline, Black children of today also need to be well grounded in their cultural history. In this post-Civil Rights Movement age, and even in the midst of the Black Lives Matter Movement, it seems that our children run the risk of knowing less about their history than generations that have come before them. Black History Month is still observed every February, but chances are, your child's school is not offering a complete picture of our rich heritage. Even many of our churches, long known for having Black History bees or oratorical contests featuring speeches from some of our greatest leaders, have faded away from these previously rigorous programs. So, the onus of the responsibility for teaching our children about our great history falls on us as parents. Every day is a good day for a Black history moment! For example, The *Tom Joyner Morning Show* is a highly accessible medium that does a great job of highlighting the wonderful achievements of our ancestors from all walks of life. When our children continually hear of great accomplishments achieved often with so few resources, they grow confident in what they can accomplish.

As they develop self- and cultural-confidence, our children and youth do best with an understanding of the realities of being Black. We must lovingly teach them that others may harbor or demonstrate negative perceptions and behaviors toward them through no fault of their own. In response, they must understand how to behave in a way that minimizes suspicions and challenges. While we may possess the long-term vision of a level playing field where inequities no longer exist, acting responsibly as a Black person, especially in America, often means finding *healthy* ways to cope with unfairness on a daily basis. Helping our children to develop an internal locus of control, in which they focus on exercising power over the things they *can* control, is vital.

While we're training our children, we also serve them well when we deliver a healthy dose of financial literacy. Children's brains are like sponges, especially during the formative years between birth to five years of age. Whatever they are exposed to, for better or for worse, is understood as "normal" to them. If you model actions that demonstrate budgeting, saving, investing, and wise spending, hope-fully they will do the same as they begin to accrue their own funds from allowance, birthdays and holidays, and other gifts. Young people can even begin to generate their own income. Child labor laws notwithstanding, there are plenty of tasks that children and youth can perform in order to earn money. Babysitting, newspaper delivery, lawn care, and working in the family business are a few of the traditional jobs that even children can begin to perform. In some states, children as young as age fourteen can work in fast food or retail jobs. And children who have particular interests or passions in areas such technology or the arts can invent moneymaking oppor-tunities for themselves, especially with some guidance from their "village" of supporters.

Many parents have wondered how a child's financial increase should be managed. In ancient cultures, and even in our fairly recent agricul-tural past, children have contributed to the family livelihood through their labor, often in the fields. In fact, historians have noted that some parents intentionally produced large families, in part, to facilitate assistance with the cumbersome demands of farm work, and later, factory work (Trattner, 1970). Children quickly gained an implicit understanding that their contributions were a requisite aspect of the family's livelihood. Since the end of the era of the Civil Rights Movement, however, many of us have noticed a change in the level of responsibility assigned to children. Because our work as a society was evolving from an agricultural and manufacturing employment base to technological and knowledge-centered employment, there were decreasing demands for children's manual labor. Moreover, many middle- to upper-class African Americans tended to shield their children from harsh labor, often moving into more affluent neigh-borhoods and larger houses, providing cars, educational opportunities, vacations, and other amenities that integration now afforded them. So, work is sometimes viewed as a distraction from the priorities of edu-cational, cultural, and athletic opportunities. Yes, childhood is fleeting, and no child or adolescent should have to work at the expense of achieving his or her personal best. At the same time, ask yourself if your young person might have some extra time in his/her schedule, time that might otherwise be spent on binge TV watching, engaging social media, playing video games all hours of the night, or sleeping late. Repurposing that extra time toward productive work can generate revenue toward college savings, summer camps, benevolence, and/or to offset the cost of premium goods (such as the name-brand sneakers that you may not buy for yourself)! Young people can be taught at an early age to integrate a measure of self-discipline into their lives that includes a path toward generating income. After all, children grow into adults who have ongoing financial responsibilities and need good money management skills. Why not allow them to start honing their skills sooner rather than later? Knowledge is power!

Single Parenting

"Talk about your negative experiences with the father, with your girlfriends. Not with your children. And bite your tongue when it comes to diminishing, denying, dismissing, name-calling."
Iyanla Vanzant, attorney, author, and host of "Iyanla: Fix My Life"

The task of parenting is challenging enough with two involved parents; however, it is truly a gargantuan task as a single mother. Although some of us enter this circumstance willingly, many more of us do not set out to become single moms. Being responsible for the total well-being of a vulnerable, often defenseless, human being can seem overwhelming. To be engaged in the tasks of providing food, lodging, clothing, emotional and environmental security with little to no support is even more difficult. We know that legions of women before us and around us have done it, but how do we raise the healthiest children possible?

1. Be proactive about growing your child's village. An African proverb, profound well before then-First Lady Hilary Clinton popularized it, informs us that it takes a village to raise a child. Every son and every daughter benefits from exposure to positive

male authority figures, whether an extended family member, coach, pastor, or other friend of the family. Many of us can attest to our experience of realizing that men have a view of the world that is different from our own. This fresh perspective on life helps our children to be well rounded as they develop their own viewpoints. Of course, we also want our children to be nurtured (and occasionally, straightened out) by a group of trusted "mothers," "aunties," "godsisters," "play cousins," and other members who make up the village.

2. Stay focused on the positive experiences you are offering your child rather than worrying about what you may not be able to offer. As you continue to blossom as a human being, your capacity to offer even more attention, praise, presence, and material support can grow.

3. Keep your expectations realistic. There are only 24 hours in one day, and you can only be in one place at a time. You and your child(ren) may need to have a discussion about which activities are the greatest priorities in your lives.

4. Identify your supports and ask for help when needed. Resist the Strongblackwoman's attitude of invincibility and show vulnerability when you or your child(ren) have a need that causes great challenge for you to meet.

5. Be willing to receive help when it is offered. Even if you don't ask for help when you need it, be humble enough to receive it when it is offered. Although you may initially be ashamed or offended at someone's perception that you need help, don't allow pride to go before destruction, or a haughty spirit before a fall (Proverbs 16:18).

6. Recognize the possible benefits of your situation. One client who had been raised by a single mother commented that relative to many of her peers raised in a traditional two-parent home,

she felt stronger in her female identity. She elaborated by noting that unlike some of her female peers whose fathers had traditional mindsets about what girls could and could not accomplish, she was not receiving messages that placed limits on what she should or could achieve as a female.

7. Keep your child's needs at the forefront of your mind, but not to the detriment of your own needs. Granted, the typical single mother often has less privilege around getting her needs met than her partnered counterpart; still, single mothers cannot simply ignore their needs during the two decades or more of active parenting. Make room for the village to support not only your child, but also to support you.

With these practical tips, single mothers can raise healthy children, minimize the impact of a destructive society, and maintain their psychological well-being in the process. Don't postpone your own blossoming waiting for your children to grow up!

Raising Our Sons

> **"Until the killing of black men, black mothers' sons, becomes as important to the rest of the country as the killing of a white mother's son, we who believe in freedom cannot rest until this happens."**
> *Ella Baker, civil rights activist and founder of the Student Non-Violent Coordinating Committee (SNCC)*

Raising a son is an endeavor that is fraught with joy and challenge. Boys are often desired because they are viewed as the defender of the family and will carry on the family name (although more and more women are doing the same in contemporary times). We ascribe vision, courage, and strength to men, but the character required to manifest those traits is made, not born. In our society of educational tracking, racial profiling, school-to-prison pipelines, and life-or-death encounters with law enforcement officials, as well as a dash of everyday racial discrimination thrown in for good measure, our sons keep us on our knees. Even if we have the resources to send them to the best schools, engage them in the best sports teams, and support them with quality Christian education at the most dynamic church in town, we cannot create in them immunity to the dangers of being Black and male in America. We can, however, cover them with the blood of Jesus to protect them mind, body, soul, and spirit wherever they may go.

Our sons also need reinforcement of their internal qualities, even as they are still works in progress. No matter how dynamic their Youth Pastor or Sunday School teacher may be, *you* tell them early of God's love and of Jesus's ultimate sacrifice for their sins. Show them their worth through Christ's atoning work, and remind them that they and their lives belong to God. Teach your son about the fruit of the Spirit (Galatians 5:22-23), and impress upon him that the LORD seeks to cultivate all of these fruits in the lives of every Christian. Help him to know that his character is affirmed by his Creator, no matter how it may be the target of questions, suspicion, or attack. Model for him the power of a prayer and a worshipful lifestyle. Articulate that holiness and purity are not just for females!

From a practical standpoint, it is important that you equip your son with the life skills that he needs to survive on his own. In addition to the tasks that he is developing along traditional gender roles (e.g., taking out the trash and mowing the lawn), teach your son such survival skills as cooking, cleaning and disinfecting the home, setting the table, and keeping household items organized. Help him understand that these skills will make important contributions to his own household, whether he becomes a confirmed bachelor or a husband and father raising his own children. (Your future daughter-in-law will thank you for his good training, as more and more households of the future will be more egalitarian in the division of household labor.)

One final note on mothers and sons: Black women, especially single

mothers, sometimes run the risk of becoming overinvolved, or enmeshed, in their son's lives. Sometimes this occurs as an outgrowth of the mother's loneliness and desire for male companionship. These psychological needs are important to acknowledge and address, but don't place your son in the precarious position of fulfilling a need for which he was not created. Also, beware of telling your son, or allowing someone else to tell him, that he is the "man of the house." The importance of taking on age-appropriate household responsibilities is undeniable. As boys mature into manhood, they should take on more and more tasks to contribute to the family's functioning. But unloading the dishwasher and bearing the psychological weight of ensuring the well-being of everyone in the household are two very different things. The parent/s is/are in charge of the household, allowing the children to continue developing into full adulthood at a thorough, rather than premature, pace.

Raising Our Daughters

**"The true worth of a race must be measured
by the character of its womanhood."**
*Mary McLeod Bethune, social activist, and co-founder and
president of Bethune-Cookman School (now University)*

Both the Bible and psychological theory discuss the importance of mothers and older women being models and mentors to younger women. Socialization is the process by which human beings and other members of the animal kingdom learn ethics and behavior. For better or worse, others are watching us and following our example. This is particularly true of our daughters. As mothers of girls, we should give deliberate thought to the attitude and behavior that we would like to see in our daughters, and then make sure that our comportment, that is, the way we carry ourselves, lines up with this vision. Scripture provides us with these characteristics, such as gentle, gracious, and wise. We can also learn about bold leadership from women in Scripture such as Deborah, the judge who led the defeat of Sisera and his Canaanite army, thereby ushering in forty years of peace during her leadership of Israel. Or Esther, who helped to avert the genocide of the Jews. Perhaps she was like the wise woman from Abel, who, although she was not named in 2 Samuel chapter 20, stood up against the injustices of her day and prevented attack from Joab's army.

Think to yourself: What kind of woman do you desire your daughter to be? Then ask yourself, "What will be required to get her from here to there?" What skills will she need to develop? Does she need to secure any particular educational opportunities? What community, national, or global organizations can support her dreams? How can she fully embrace her own identity in God? The power of a strong faith community cannot be overestimated. Bringing up your daughter in a family of faith will equip her with a firm grasp of the Gospel of Jesus Christ, and the stories of hope and deliverance that ground our faith. Connecting her with the care and prayers of Bible study, Sunday School, Youth Church, and other ministry leaders, volunteers, and other brothers and sisters in Christ can surround her with the concrete love and support meant to characterize our Christian relationships. Teaching her to know, love, and trust God for herself, and to "approach the throne of grace with confidence, to receive help in [her] time of need"—priceless!

Sometimes we can inadvertently (if not intentionally) reinforce the gap that exists between our religious and spiritual ideals and the way that we actually live our lives. When Scripture says, "Be perfect, even as Your Father in heaven is perfect," this passage is not referring to a Pharisaical obsession with faultlessness. Rather, the emphasis here is on striving toward maturity in our walk with God. Therefore, help your daughter to focus not on "being perfect," but on presenting her best self to God, knowing that God accepts us with open arms even as we fall short. This means taking seriously the Word of God as it applies to our daily thoughts and behaviors. If we've read about looking out for the interests of others during the Sunday School lesson, then we embody this attitude in our relationships Monday through

Saturday. If Sunday's sermon reminds us that the body is a temple of the Holy Spirit, then our decisions about what to put in our bodies, how to maintain the fitness of our bodies, and who we allow to access our bodies will hopefully show consistency with theological ideals.

Alongside this crucial spiritual foundation, there are some other seeds that you will want to plant and cultivate in your daughter. First, you can aim to develop in her a strong sense of self. The more she knows about the histories of her family, her community, her church, and her faith, the better grounded she will be for navigating the sometimes choppy waters of adult life. Help her to understand the challenges that lie at the intersections of her race, gender, and class, and to rise to the occasion of facing these challenges without succumbing to the façades of the Strongblackwoman. Allowing her options in her decisions and giving her some leeway to chart her own course (e.g., hairstyle, clothing, extracurricular activities) can give her self-respect, confidence in her decision-making skills, and the development of a strong voice that can speak the truth in love to power. Be careful about creating excessive concern about what other people will think about her choices because too much of this concern can be paralyzing.

Teach your daughter how to honor her own beauty, first by affirming her beauty yourself. Let her know through lesson and example that God has created us beautiful in our own right, and that cosmetics, conversion of the hair beyond its natural state, designer clothing, and other traditional accoutrements of beauty and fashion are optional, not mandatory. Take her to events such as cultural fairs, women's conferences, and natural food demonstrations that reinforce her femininity and teach skills for optimal care of the Black body, both inside and out.

Another vital skill set is teaching your daughter how to establish and maintain appropriate boundaries in all of her relationships. Show her that a woman is to be respected by husbands, other males in the family and the broader community, friends, and even strangers, remembering that it is our responsibility to teach others how to treat us. Boundaries consist of understanding where our responsibilities and preferences stop and another person's responsibilities and preferences begin. Help your daughter know that she has the privilege of making known her preferences, and as she matures into womanhood, drawing her own lines of what is and is not acceptable. This includes everything from how she prefers to be addressed, how and when others can contact her, whether and by whom she wants to be touched, and when she is available to give her time and attention to others. Because incidences of exploitation as well as verbal, emotional, physical, and sexual abuse are so high in our communities, the sooner we teach our daughters the value of saying "No," the better. If such exploitation or abuse does unfortunately occur, you will want to have created an accepting, non-blaming atmosphere that allows your daughter to confide in you so that you can assist her in getting the help that she needs.

Friendships

"The success of every woman should be the inspiration to another. We should raise each other up. Make sure you're very courageous: be strong, be extremely kind, and above all be humble."
Serena Williams, tennis star and holder of 39 Grand Slam titles

Much has been said, rapped, and written about friends. A traditional saying encourages, "Make new friends and keep the old/One is silver and the other gold."

In the mid-80s, Dionne Warwick, Stevie Wonder, Gladys Knight, and Elton John crooned, "Keep smiling, keep shining/Knowing you can always count on me, for sure/That's what friends are for/In good times and bad times/I'll be on your side forever more/That's what friends are for." (Bacharach & Sager, 1985) Across time and cultures, most people agree that friendships are important. Friends are those people with whom we share a mutual fondness, similar interests, and overlapping worldviews. Friendships are for everyone, not just extroverts. Whereas extroverts usually have a large circle of friends that recharges them, introverts need friends, too, but are usually content with just a handful of friends to balance their desire to spend time alone. Whether we met in preschool, playing sports, or last year on the job, friends encourage and support us, accompany us on this journey called life, go the extra mile, and make us smile!

But not everyone makes and keeps friends so easily. Sometimes friendships do not stand the test of time. The hip-hop group Whodini once asked "Friends, how many of us have them? Ones we can depend on?" (Hutchins & Smith, 1984). Perhaps a disagreement or misunderstanding brings undue pressure on a friendship, and one or both parties decides that the friendship is not worth preserving. Or maybe through extended separation over time or distance, friends become vaguely known acquaintances. After a few of these experiences, we may find ourselves reluctant to create new friendships. After all, they do require an investment of time, sustained effort, and trust. Based on our prior life experiences, trust may be a rare commodity, especially in situations where trust has been breached. Sometimes we choose to go it alone, protecting our hearts from further damage, but we often forget that God created us to be social beings, vitally connected to each other.

The image of the body of Christ (1 Corinthians 12: 12-27) demonstrates that we belong to each other and that we need each other to function properly. Friends supply the social support, moral support, and practical support that we need to thrive in a challenging world. We also should not lose sight of the fact that friendships allow us to give deeply of ourselves in a way that can have a profound impact on our friends and their lives for many years to come.

Okay, let's be honest: Maybe we don't have the best track record when it comes to choosing friends. Perhaps in our younger years, we were inclined to compromise our time, needs, desires, even values for the sake of maintaining a friendship. Friends weren't always as good to us as we were to them. Maybe we even got in trouble, potentially deep trouble, for the sake of a so-called friend who didn't appreciate us, or even kicked us to the curb when we no longer benefitted her. "Once bitten, twice shy," the saying goes. Instead of amending the way we make friends, we might decide to steer clear of all possible friendships. This choice, however, is a recipe for loneliness, resentment, and an overall poorer quality of life.

In order to establish quality friendships, you must "show yourself friendly." The next time you're around strangers in a social situation, pay attention to those who appear friendly (e.g., making eye contact, smiling, turning toward you). Allow yourself to engage in "small talk," even if it feels a bit superficial to you. Discuss the weather, sports, or light-hearted current events (i.e., avoiding topics like the political climate or your views on the latest televangelist scandal). Through casual conversation, find out if the other person has anything in common with you, such as geographical location, community activities, the experience of being a parent, or the like. If there is sufficient overlap, you two may decide by the end of the conversation that it would be worth staying in touch, or getting together again soon for coffee, tea, or a meal. At this juncture, it is very important to preserve boundaries, even (or especially) when you feel excited about the blossoming of a friendship. Occasionally, people who have not experienced meaningful friendships for a long time become quite excited at the prospect of a new friend and become overzealous in their level of disclosure (i.e., telling all their business). Just because someone shows herself friendly does not necessarily mean that you should tell all. Instead, allow time to reveal whether this person is truly trustworthy. Does she demonstrate respect for you as a person, and a well-developed sense of confidentiality? Does she avoid telling you other people's business? Does she also make herself vulnerable as your friendship develops over time? Can she observe and abide by the boundaries you establish? If you can answer these questions affirmatively, you may be on your way to developing a strong friendship. Strong friendships will stand the test of time. "Perfume and incense bring joy to the heart, and the pleasantness of a friend springs from their heartfelt advice" (Proverbs 27:9).

Dating

"We all have to let go of the Prince Charming complex and realize he doesn't necessarily exist in the package we assume he'll come in."
Gabrielle Union, award-winning actor and advocate
for assault survivors

One topic that has dominated women's thoughts, conversations, time, and energy is romantic relationships. We're either trying to find a relationship, trying to survive a relationship, or trying to get out of a relationship. Some of our struggle reflects the reality that each woman is one imperfect human being (no matter how saved, sanctified, and filled with the Holy Ghost she may be), attempting to create a deeply meaningful and loving relationship with another imperfect human being. Often, we're seeking a romantic relationship to heal some other relationship wounds from our past. Perhaps we were neglected or abandoned by a father, so we subconsciously seek someone who can serve as a father figure and fill the voids of childhood. Or maybe we felt unloved and ignored in general and desire the constant attention and companionship of a man who can finally validate our humanity. When we enter into a prospective relationship with these emotional needs and expectations, we are already creating an insatiable dynamic, one that is impossible to fully sustain.

In our 21st century society, as we have become more and more obsessed with the self and how others can meet our needs and wants, a true, loving relationship does not deny the needs of the self, but is very concerned with how to deeply love the other. Love often requires the sacrifice of time, money, energy, and even will. We must be careful, however, to judge whether in the midst of our sacrifices, we are being loved in return, or merely exploited. Some men, possessing their own wounds, are nonetheless skilled in presenting themselves artfully, speaking eloquently and persuasively, and behaving charmingly—for a while. However, if these characteristics are not connected to his essence, he cannot sustain them, and may even blame you when things fall apart. Marriage is designed to be collaborative, and while each couple negotiates among themselves the particulars of their roles and responsibilities, both should share in constructing a strong and positive life together.

Sometimes our judgment of whether a man is truly God's gift to us is clouded by sex. The advent of birth control and women's rights have given Christians, along with the rest of society, the "freedom" to engage in sex with little to no consideration of the moral consequences of our actions. God views sex outside of marriage, be it fornication, adultery, sexual intercourse, oral sex, anal sex, or mutual masturbation, as something we should not only resist, but flee:

> Flee from sexual immorality. All other sins a person commits are outside the body, but whoever sins sexually, sins against their own body. Do you not know that your bodies are temples of the Holy Spirit, who is in you, whom you have received from God? You are not your own; you were bought at a price. Therefore honor God with your bodies.
>
> (1 Corinthians 6: 18-20)

It seems unreasonable, we argue in this day and age, for anyone to take seriously the call to sexual purity, particularly in what appears to be a long-term, committed relationship. Because of our society's emphasis on individual rights and the illusion of being self-possessed, we often forget God's declaration that we were bought with a great price, that is, the precious blood of Jesus Christ. We forget that God, as Our Creator, knows us and our bodies best, and seeks to preserve the special gift of sex for marriage alone.

Putting aside the moral implications of our sexuality, there are social and relational consequences to engaging in sex with a man who is not your husband. Endless numbers of women can testify to how their relationships changed for the worse when sex was added into the equation. Some of the change possibly has to do with the woman's greater sense of connection to the man (although sex rarely equates to love in casual encounters). At the same time that the woman is feeling more deeply attached to the man, the man may feel less connected, especially if he feels that he has won the "prize" or the "cookie." He may reason that he has achieved this feat and is off to explore the next challenge. The woman may interpret the man's behavior as a personal rejection and internalize the reasons for his distance: "I'm not pretty, smart, sexy, fun, _____ enough" or "I'm too fat, boring, dark, insecure, _____." Particularly if she has a history of rejection from her father, this rejection from her lover deepens her wounded self-image. The use of sex to obtain love ironically results in the woman's lowered sense of self-worth.

What about when a woman's engagement in sex has been against her will? Unfortunately, incest, rape, and other forms of sexual assault are all too common in our society, and the effects of such acts some-times live on much longer than they should through generational secrets. Such abuse often begins in childhood, during the vulnerable time when virtually all children blame themselves for anything that goes wrong. Young girls often keep secrets of sexual abuse for years (many into adulthood, if they ever reveal them) due to threats of harm to themselves or other family members, or fears that they won't be believed. Sometimes family members create an environment of forced secrecy that frightens children from ever disclosing sexual abuse. In other families, delayed disclosure results in the blaming of the victim for creating emotional division in the household, or even physical separation if a social services entity becomes involved and the abuse is substantiated. Sadly, too many mothers and daughters' relationships have been severed when a mother chooses to "stand by her man" rather than to believe and support her daughter. In those cases, much spiritual and psychological healing is needed for the mother's insecurities, the daughter's rejection, and the fissures and divided loyalties that result throughout the rest of the nuclear and extended families.

So what about the ways by which the social and economic realities of current Black America complicate dating and marriage? Terms such as "shortage" and "missing" often come up in discussions about why it is so difficult for a good Black woman to find a good Black man. Statistical data have been quoted, sometimes erroneously, about the reasons for the gap. The increasing rates of openly gay and bisexual men, men who date outside of their race, detention/incarceration, and premature deaths are all significant factors contributing to why many Black women find romantic relationships with Black men elusive. And sometimes we are less than satisfied with the Black men who remain. After all, we do have our standards! Some of us remember our mothers telling us about the importance of the BMW—"Black Man Working." And oftentimes, mere employment won't do. We need a husband whose profession makes us look good and supplies us with a comfortable, if not extravagant, living. Of course, we want him to have a certain swag, be well-educated, really handsome—no—fine, built like Adonis or Dwayne "The Rock" Johnson, well spoken, funny, and sensitive to our needs. It is appropriate for us to establish high standards for our life mate, because we know that God exhibits standards of excellence for us. At the same time, we sometimes establish unrealistically high expectations that, if the truth be told, we ourselves cannot meet. How often do we find ourselves asking God for discernment about who God sends our way, rather than insisting on who *we* think is best? Even further, are we willing to ask other difficult questions, such as "Is it God's will for me to marry?" Although it is not a popularly accepted concept, there are some individuals who are chosen for a life of celibacy, so that they may more robustly give themselves to the Lord's service. Another hard question is, "Is God providing for me to marry outside of my race?" Interracial marriage was illegal for the vast majority of our country's existence, and Black women are the least likely of all groups to marry non-Blacks. Still, there is a growing number of Black women who have found fulfilling marriages to men of other races.

As Christians, it only makes sense to discuss long-term romantic relationships on the path to marriage. God designed marriage as the illustration of Christ's love for the church, the body of believers who await Christ's return. Scripture teaches us that God emphasizes the importance of a husband loving his wife and sacrificing himself for her. The wife, in turn, is to respect her husband and surrender to his leadership (Ephesians 5: 21-33). The notion of submission has been an oft-abused concept that, at its extreme, has resigned women to abusive treatment and demonized women who refuse to remain in marriages that are destructive to their physical and emotional well-being. However, if we use even contemporary, secular examples of submission, we recognize the importance of leadership and follow-ship in virtually every successful enterprise. Teams follow coaches; workers follow managers who follow executives; sorority members follow basilei; congregations follow pastors. In a day and age when we as women are less dependent than ever on husbands for economic viability, our marriages can truly be founded on a commitment of love rather than dependency.

Marriage

"That we arrived at fifty years together is due as much to luck as to love, and a talent for knowing, when we stumble, where to fall, and how to get up again."
Ruby Dee, award-winning actor, social activist, and wife of Ossie Davis

If we are given the gift of marriage, we need the will and the skill to keep that marriage healthy, as much as it is in our power. There are some fundamentals that every relationship needs: consistent and effective communication; the provision and enjoyment of emotional, physical, and sexual intimacy; commitment to identifying and implementing reasonable money management strategies; skills in conflict resolution; and healthy interactions with other family members (whether children or extended family members). Although cliché, the idea that opposites attract is true in many marriages, and what is sometimes an appealing trait earlier in a relationship can become a source of great frustration. Keep this reality in mind as we explore these important facets of marriage.

As discussed earlier, **communication** occurs at both content and process levels. The pace of lives today means that marriage and family issues require almost constant communication about the "business" of the family-who is picking up whom and when, what's for dinner, and why the grocery bill is higher than usual. Having reciprocal communication helps all of these transactions flow more smoothly. What gets lost in the hustle and bustle, at times, is communication about emotional matters—what it felt like to get passed over for the job promotion yet again, how distressing it can be to observe your mother's declining health, or how Junior is responding to his negative consequences for not completing his chores. These latter matters are extremely important in our hearts, but it's not always easy to find the time or the courage to discuss them. Couples must create and protect space for meaningful communication to happen.

Since marital communication is so vital, and because your husband may have different communication preferences, it can be easy to experience confusion in your communication. Anticipate the possibility of confusion and rely on your knowledge of your mate. A key element of marriage is knowing your husband as well as knowing yourself. Some aspects of your husband, you learned right away, perhaps even from the first date. Even if he is someone who communicates less content, or less often than you'd prefer, you know a lot about him from observation of his nonverbal expressions (e.g., tone, pitch, and volume of voice, facial expressions, posture) and from past experiences. You know how he is likely to respond to novelty, routine, conflict, and crisis, and as you develop in your own wisdom, you learn how to interact with him to maximize the harmony in your relationship, as well as a positive outcome in each situation. Your husband, like you, is constantly evolving, and part of the richness of marriage is continuing to learn new things about your husband.

Emotional, physical, and sexual intimacy is another central component of any strong marriage. Maintaining trust is one of the most important factors in emotional intimacy. While Physical Touch is one of the five love languages discussed earlier (Chapman, 2015), it is not a high priority for every individual. Still, affection is important to incorporate in most marriages. Holding hands, hugging, kissing, and gentle touches and strokes, when shared in a meaningful rather than perfunctory, "going through the motions" manner, can greatly influence the relational dynamic and contribute to emotional intimacy. Sometimes touch, rather than words, can literally smooth things over in your relationship. Also, physical affection can build a helpful foundation for sexual intimacy. Our partners don't always understand the need for foreplay, or how foreplay often begins long before you move to the bed (or wherever). It is often incumbent upon us, often for years, not only to gently remind our spouses to provide foreplay, but to provide ample instruction in what constitutes effective foreplay. If you were raised to be shy about discussing sexual matters with anyone, God has liberated you to have these discussions with your husband! Again, sometimes you can show a partner something better than you can tell him. Then there are the classic differences in preferred frequency. In the spirit of mutual sacrifice, talk with your spouse about creating a mutual compromise. After all, Scripture reminds us that under the marriage covenant, our bodies belong to each other, and that we should not abstain from sexual relations for too long (1 Corinthians 7:1-5). Although some women consider sex with their husbands as more of an obligation than a privilege, pray and act in a direction that affords you and your husband as much mutual pleasure as possible, as God intended.

While spouses will often differ in their views of and behavior around **money**, perhaps the most important component in a couple's ability to effectively manage their money is to discuss their money matters. Unfortunately, it is far too easy for couples to avoid conversations about finances, even if maintained separately, until a financial emergency brings everything to an often shocking and demoralizing reality. I encourage my clients to think practically about what works for them. Some couples maintain a joint account and have an agreement about how to handle individual purchases. Other couples maintain separate accounts and have an agreement about who pays which bills. Still other couples have a hybrid approach to their money. In all cases, I recommend that a couple establish a transparent budget that allows the other person to be aware of the overall financial picture. Such an agreement allows for much more psychological freedom as each partner can think holistically about how their spending, saving, and investing behavior affects their spouse and the rest of the household. If you find yourself sneaking purchases into the house, you may be taking away from not only the bank account, but from the relational trust in your marriage. If it's hard to control your spending, see Chapter 21.

Believe it or not, even Christian couples have conflict and need **conflict-resolution** skills. Although this should not come as a surprise to those who have observed their share of conflict in Bible stories, we often have a fantasy that our marriage will be conflict-free, and that anything less is an indictment of our walk with Jesus. Drs. John and Julie Gottman, seasoned marital researchers and practitioners, describe the "The Four Horsemen of the Apocalypse," or four behaviors within marriage that best predict a couple's likelihood of divorcing (Gottman, 1989). Those behaviors are criticism, or complaining about aspects of your spouse's personality; defensiveness, or protecting yourself through righteous indignation or by portraying yourself as the victim; contempt, or speaking to your spouse from a superior position; and stonewalling, or withdrawing emotionally from interacting with your spouse. They also propose antidotes to these behaviors to help minimize conflict and strengthen marriage. Criticism can be replaced with sharing your own feelings using an "I-statement" followed by expressing a positive need. For example, you might say, "I am feeling unappreciated. Can you tell me something you appreciate about me?" Defensiveness can be replaced by accepting responsibility for some portion of the problem. Instead of contempt, you can build an atmosphere of appreciation and respect with your spouse and describe your own feelings and needs (e.g., "I am feeling lonely. I need for us to spend some time together").

Finally, the best antidote for stonewalling is to soothe yourself so that you can remain engaged over the long haul with your husband. Here, you might listen to some of your favorite music or go outside for some fresh air.

Keep in mind that all of these skills require practice and patience over a long period of time to help your marriage blossom. Even seasoned Christian marriages will continue to manage significant ups and downs, yet your commitment to each other and to God can yield much mutual fulfillment.

When Marriage Does Not Work Out

> "I always believed that when you follow your heart or your gut, when you really follow the things that feel great to you, you can never lose, because settling is the worst feeling in the world."
> *Rihanna, producer, philanthropist and best-selling digital artist of all time*

Sometimes, despite our best attempts, marriage does not work out. Perhaps you are unexpectedly widowed through a terminal illness or a sudden death. Maybe the love of your life walks out on you to pursue another relationship, or you come to the painful conclusion that you can no longer tolerate living life with the person your husband has become. It's amazing how so many people outside of your relationship can have such strong opinions about how you should or should not handle your situation. At the end of the day, however, how you manage the end of your relationship is between you and God. We've read Scripture about how women, especially in Biblical times, often did not fare well following the death of their husbands. However, women of today are typically much less financially dependent on their husbands, or more likely to have some provisions through life insurance, savings, or other assets to rebound after becoming widowed. We're also aware of Scriptures indicating that God hates divorce, and that the person who divorces and marries again commits adultery (Malachi 2:16; Matthew 5:32). Whether we are on the initiating or receiving end of divorce, it is a painful decision fraught with concerns about its impact on our children and in-laws, our financial picture, our relationships with others (especially other couples), our reputation, and our psychological well-being. Still, recognize that divorce may be the lesser of two evils, especially if physical, emotional, or sexual violence was a part of the picture. Additionally, be comforted by the fact that God is a forgiving God, and will bring new life, whether you remain divorced or marry again with important lessons learned from your previous relationships.

What if you haven't married at all? In spite of all of your good efforts praying and fasting, maintaining your appearance, keeping yourself active in networking arenas, placing yourself on online dating sites, and following up with leads from Auntie Matchmaker, you still may not receive a husband. This reality has been one of the most frustrating situations that my clients, on the whole, have had to manage. Recognize that this situation is neither an indictment of your faith nor a punishment for past transgressions. You may yet marry later in life, but even if you never marry, resist the idea that something is wrong with you. Those who do not marry often have greater availability to fulfill the purposes of God in their lives (1 Corinthians 7:34). Rather than giving in to the temptation to be *bitter* about your situation, ask God for the strength to be *better* through your situation. Focus on making the best of the relationships you *do* have.

Extended Family Dynamics

"Be strong, be fearless, be beautiful. And believe that anything is possible when you have the right people there to support you."
Misty Copeland, ballerina and first Black woman to be promoted as principal dancer of the American Ballet Theatre

Family is the most important institution that God has created. God told Adam and Eve to be fruitful and multiply, and the world has been obedient to that command ever since! Families occupy such significant roles for multiple reasons: (1) family provides the context in which we are enculturated, or taught about the standards of the family's culture, including ethics, customs, traditions, faith, "home training," and other practices; (2) family supports us practically in the provision of shelter, food, clothing, transportation, and other tangible needs; (3) and family gives us the encouragement, confidence, sense of belonging, and security that are needed to ground us emotionally. When our family ties are biological, we also receive a genetic inheritance from our forebears that determines our physical attributes (e.g., skin, eye, and hair color; facial features, body type) as well as our physiological and constitutional tendencies toward health or disease (e.g., high metabolism or hypertension).

Ideally, then, biological and fictive family serves these important functions of tangible provision of our physical, spiritual, and emotional needs. Unlike friends, who may come and go, family is supposed to be with you for the duration. The concept that "blood is thicker than water" implies that it is family who will last through your ups and downs. However, the actual saying states, "The blood of the covenant is thicker than the water of the womb," suggesting that sometimes our family relationships can disappoint us. Sometimes family members flake out from the very beginning of your life. Even if you survived fetushood, you might have been emotionally aborted. Your life and its value may have been questioned from conception. Perhaps a parent caved under pressure from a grandparent or society's dictates insisting that you be carried to term (an instance of valuing "life" for all of the wrong reasons), but your parent(s) felt ambivalence about you entering the world and turning their world inside out. Or maybe your parents were polar opposites around the news of your conception. Whether you were the product of rape, incest, fornication, adultery, or an "accident" between parents who "thought they were finished," family members' reactions to news of your conception or birth may have been mixed, or at the very least, complicated. One very common response under these complex circumstances is for the parent(s) to "check out" mentally or physically. So many of my clients are still dealing with, even in adulthood, the impact of an absent father, or in some cases, an absent mother. One client told the story of being left at the police station as a baby by a mother who'd been abandoned by her lover and apparently felt that she couldn't handle the pressure of raising a child. Another client shared that her mother raised her, but was always mean to her, and once said to her during an especially heated argument that she wished she'd followed her "first mind" and aborted her. With the foundations of life being erected by parents or caregivers who hold these attitudes, life's trajectory seems hopeless from the start.

Not all of us have these shaky beginnings, yet we may still have our share of family struggles. Some of us were raised in households where our parents and guardians were less than nurturing. They may have been neglectful, expressed harsh attitudes, used excessive physical discipline (all in the name of avoiding "sparing the rod and spoiling the child"), or may have spoken to us in demeaning ways. We may have even endured emotional, physical, and/or sexual abuse, through such means as harsh parenting, excessive physical punishment, lack of recognition of our strengths or potential, co-dependence, or over-dependence. With these early burdens, it may be difficult for us to imagine how we can create anything different for the next generation. This is where we align ourselves with loving role models, find a healthy church family, pursue books or videos to educate ourselves about parenting, and connect ourselves with a child therapist with expertise in parenting skills.

For those of us who have healthy relationships with our extended family members and in-laws, we can enjoy fellowshipping with them and exposing our children to their positive examples. Because of Scriptural guidance to "leave and to cleave," however, we should be sure not to allow influence that interferes with the functioning of our now primary household. For the sake of harmony, this delicate balance is worth striving for.

Mentoring

> "Never underestimate the power of dreams and the influence
> of the human spirit. We are all the same in this notion:
> The potential for greatness lives within each of us."
> *Wilma Rudolph, educator, coach, and record-setting*
> *Olympian in track and field*

Above virtually all else, Black women specialize in giving back to our communities. We often make career, educational, and family decisions based on whether those opportunities will help or hinder our chances of making a positive contribution to those around us. One way that we can give back is by becoming a mentor. A mentor (or "jegna," if you prefer) is defined as a counselor or guide who is wise, nurturing, and trustworthy. We can serve as mentors in a variety of ways. Some mentees (i.e., those who receive our mentoring) can benefit from our business acumen as they climb the career ladder. Other mentees are looking for guidance in navigating educational institutions, civic organizations, and church life. Additionally, many around us need hands-on advice for becoming a better wife and/ or mother. So, isn't a reflection on mentoring unnecessary? Aren't we already doing all we can to uplift the race, and for the advancement of Black women in particular? This section is written out of my growing awareness that although we are often working hard to support others with our wisdom and knowledge, we aren't always working smart. Perhaps there are ways that we can become more effective and efficient with the ways that we provide mentoring.

One important facet of mentoring is having the right mindset toward that activity. "Freely you have received, freely give." It is a natural part of our heritage as Black women of Christian faith for us to understand what it means to give generously. We often think of such giving in financial terms. This not only means to give tithes and offerings to the church where we attend or hold our membership, but to also give to those in need, including our family and friends. We are also called to give back to our educational institutions, civic organizations, and local-to-global causes that we care about. However, once we've done all that giving from our bank accounts and investments, we're not done giving. The greater challenge in this super busy day and age is to give of ourselves, namely, our time. With all the demands in our lives, time is a deeply precious commodity. It is precisely for that reason that giving something so precious is a sign of deep love and affection.

Am I suggesting that mentoring requires a significant portion of every workday, or that mentoring should become a part-time job? Not at all! Sometimes mentoring works best when we can effectively incorporate mentoring activities into our regular schedule. Perhaps there is a place in your schedule for powering up at your favorite coffee house or breaking bread over a business lunch. Why not reserve a certain number of times or hours per month on your calendar that you might be willing to offer to someone requesting mentorship, whether she uses that language or not? Or better yet, why not pray that God would direct you to someone that could benefit from your listening ear, wisdom, and practical advice? Even one to two hours per month offered consistently over time can leave a sizable legacy.

Chances are, as you continue to perfect your craft, you will receive more and more requests for mentoring. At times, these requests may seem burdensome. In the same way that you set aside money for particular purposes, however, you can earmark your time for building mentoring relationships. Here are some key strategies for successful mentoring:

1. Prior to meeting your mentee for the first time, ask questions to help her clarify what she is looking for in the mentoring relationship. This clarity will help both of you use your time most efficiently.

2. Listen carefully with all of your senses to the context of your mentee. What is her story? What experiences does she bring to the table related to her goals? What strengths and weaknesses will help or hinder her pursuits?

3. By the close of your time together, help your mentee develop an action plan. What is her next goal, and what resources and strategies have you identified together that will help her achieve it? This step is vital because it articulates the active engagement of the mentee with the goods that you have already provided.

4. Communicate the extent of your availability to your mentee so that she knows what to expect and what not to expect. Balance compassion with practicality. Perhaps you are open to answering brief e-mails as she runs into stumbling blocks while executing her action plan. Maybe you are willing to respond to a quick phone call on the way to work in the mornings. It is probably wise to establish the expectation that the next face-to-face meeting can occur after your mentee has completed or made significant progress on her action plan.

5. If you find yourself inundated with mentoring requests, consider innovative methods for offering group mentoring. Perhaps you can reserve a space in your office or at a local restaurant for a monthly or bimonthly get-together where you not only share your wisdom, but allow for the cross-pollination of creative ideas from multiple sharp minds, like iron sharpening iron (Proverbs 27:17)! Some friends who are also mental health professionals and I coordinated a two-hour program called "Choosing the Right Path" at our local Historically Black College and University (HBCU) for students who were interested in the mental health subdisciplines. We advertised the program to faculty across our region and encouraged them to share the news with their students. Our program included refreshments, a panel of experts from each subdiscipline (in this instance, social work, marriage and family therapy, professional counseling, and psychology), subdiscipline-specific breakout sessions, and handouts. Students who attended expressed their gratitude for the program, and we felt gratified with the hope that we had helped those students choose the best path to attain their career goals. In some cases, we have even continued follow-up contact with some of the participants.

6. Keep a list of referrals handy. Mentoring does not always require your direct presence as much as your willingness to direct traffic. Perhaps there is a colleague who is more involved than you in the area of your mentee's interest, and would be willing to field an e-mail from this mentee. Maybe you have some professional organizations that can advance your mentee on her journey. If your mentee needs more emotional support than you can manage, refer her to a mental health professional for those needs. Remember, you can refer someone to additional resources without ending your relationship. It's up to you.

These strategies for mentoring can assist you in extending your time and expertise to many others through healthy boundaries. Sharing your passion for what you do can result in tremendous results for those who sit at your feet, and can also provide refreshing inspiration that reminds you why you do what you do.

Social Activism

> **"If this work can contribute in any way toward proving this, and at the same time arouse the conscience of the American people to a demand for justice to every citizen, and punishment by law for the lawless, I shall feel I have done my race a service."**
> *Ida B. Wells, journalist, newspaper editor, and suffragist*

From our earliest days on U.S. soil to the current day, our Black communities have found it necessary to resist the subtle to egregious forms of marginalization and oppression that contribute to our ongoing suffering and injustice in this land. Depending on our personalities, family and community subcultures, and geographic realities, we reveal diverse preferences for how we engage resistance. For some of us, the best way to blossom in the midst of the systemic "-isms" is to reach success through self-improvement and robust home training. For others of us, we find it vital to connect with community and/or church organizations to press for local to national change, be it through the school board, the city council, or state and federal legislators who create the policies that so deeply impact our communities. Sometimes we are actually calling the Church herself to action (e.g., Roberts-Lewis & Armstrong, 2010). For still others of us, our souls cannot rest until we have marched in the streets, gone to jail (as needed), and have become the literal embodiment of the urgency needed for massive, if not global, reforms.

Wherever you may occupy this continuum, press yourself to take one more step toward making justice a reality for everyone. Sometimes our activism may take the form of voting in all elections, working at the polls, and canvassing neighborhoods door-to-door; however, we can also make a great impact through writing a newspaper editorial, conducting an online campaign, blogging about political, moral, and/or ethical issues, or otherwise raising awareness about a lesser known topic or issue. Becoming socially active around an area of your passion is not only consistent with our Christian ethics, but also necessary for the survival (and ongoing blossoming) of our people. Just like Mary and Martha were busy supporting the establishing and blossoming of the early church, so, too, are well called to be engaged in major movements of our time. The spiritual referring to them seems to be speaking of end times when the archangels descend upon Jerusalem for battle, thus "rocking Jerusalem." However, just like most other spirituals, there is a double entendre, or additional meaning, that calls for action *now*. What locale will you be rocking with your civic engagement? Perhaps your activism will connect with other places of protest over the last few years: Ferguson, Charleston, New York City, Chicago, St. Paul, or Charlottesville. Or maybe your activism will ignite in a lesser-known town, school board, detention facility, mental health/ substance abuse treatment center, or other space where injustice looms. "Ring dem bells!"

 Listen to Recording #12, "Oh Mary, Oh Martha (Rockin' Jerusalem)"

Grief & Loss

"Challenges make you discover things about yourself that you
never really knew. They're what make the instrument stretch,
what make you go beyond the norm."
*Cicely Tyson, model, award-winning actor, and
recipient of the Presidential Medal of Freedom*

Grief and loss are included in this section on relationships because
they are important processes that occur when a loved one is no longer
physically available. Grief is a normal response to the loss of someone or something that we love. A range of emotions may be stirred,
including sadness, anger, disappointment, regret, relief, guilt, and
frustration. Depending on the circumstances of the death, we may
feel that we have not had a chance to say goodbye. In our communities, there is a higher rate of sudden deaths as compared to other
communities. For example, Blacks are more likely than other racial
groups to lose a loved one to community violence (e.g., drive-by
shootings, gang violence, shootings by law enforcement officials)
and relational violence (e.g., domestic abuse). Our life expectancies,
particularly for Black males, are nearly a decade shorter, compared
to our White counterparts. Due to chronic health disparities, we are
more likely to be diagnosed with a more advanced disease, and to die
sooner from those diseases. For all of these reasons, our world may
be turned completely upside down by grief.

In some instances, a loved one is diagnosed with a life-threatening or terminal illness. When this information is shared with the
family, each family member, in her or his own way, enters a period of
anticipatory grief. Even though your loved one is still present with
you, the disease has likely compromised his or her functioning. Thus,
other family members have already begun to step into those roles
of decreased functioning. Moreover, each family member begins to
imagine what life may be like without the dying loved one. These
reflections, while they may be sad, help to generate practical consid-
erations, such as getting one's affairs in order, finishing or supporting

items on a "bucket list," and giving last instructions, wisdom, or other blessings, and saying final goodbyes.

Sadly, many of us are familiar, either directly or indirectly, with a loved one who was aware of a grim prognosis, yet did not share the news for many weeks or months, if at all. If you are ever in the position of receiving a terminal diagnosis, it may be a part of your Strongblackwoman make-up to carry on and to "protect" your loved ones from this news so that you won't "impose" on them. Still, I implore you to reconsider this conclusion. Not only can you benefit immensely from receiving care when you need it most, but you also can allow your family as much time as possible to adjust to the possibility and consequences of your demise.

Because of cultural pressures to be the Strongblackwoman, we may not take the time we need to fully, or even partially, engage the grieving process. We may tell ourselves that we are too busy to grieve. This feels like reality, because if we lose someone close to us, we may find ourselves having to assume the responsibilities of the person who died. For example, if our partner was always responsible for maintaining the household finances, we may have to step into this major gap in order for bills to be paid and investments maintained. Also, we may find that our jobs are less than supportive when it comes to time off from work. In previous times, jobs could give up to two weeks as a standard bereavement leave. These days, some employees can barely get time off to attend the funeral, and then, it must be for a member of the immediate family (a policy that does not take into consideration the value we place on extended family and fictive kin).

We may also tell ourselves that grieving is too painful to confront. Some of us worry that if we ever open the floodgates to our grief, the results could be disastrous. We worry that we may be completely debilitated by our grief, and won't be able to provide important functions to our families, which are even more burdensome due to the loss. So, it can be very easy to find ourselves striving to "get back to normal" and throwing ourselves back into an even busier routine, when the grief actually doesn't go away. In fact, we can store grief for months or years, and eventually find ourselves falling victim to what mental health professionals refer to as complicated or prolonged grief. This type of grief reflects challenges with eating and sleeping, trouble concentrating, difficulties with functioning in our basic roles, and even suicidal thoughts. These challenges often occur as a result of not working through the process of grief for so long that these symptoms have become intense, frequent, and of such long duration that support from a mental health professional is often required.

While sudden and unexpected death can wreak havoc on our emotional lives, disenfranchised grief has its own (and additional) challenges. Disenfranchised grief is grief that generally is not expressed openly due to judgments that a person does not have the right, the role, or the capacity to grieve. There are usually some components of the loss that prevent a public recognition of the grief. For example, a woman dealing with the loss of a loved one who died due to a drive-by shooting, suicide, an abortion, HIV/AIDS, or a drug overdose may be suffering from hidden grief because of her own sense of shame, the shame imposed by her community, or a combination of both factors. Similarly, someone who is bereaved following the death of an extramarital lover, a same-sex partner, or a former spouse who was abusive is much less likely to be recognized for her grief. Unfortunately, human beings, and Christians in particular, may find it difficult to express sympathy or empathy to someone whose circumstances do not neatly fit our (often misinterpreted) theological categories. Alternatively, those of us surrounding a sister suffering from disenfranchised grief may struggle with finding the "right" thing to say. If we're not sure, for example, what to say to the woman who just lost her adolescent son to suicide (since we may be wondering about whether his soul can attain eternal rest), we may become paralyzed and simply say nothing. While we certainly don't want to do damage to another sister in one of her darkest hours, one of the most important gestures we can offer to a grieving person is our presence. Our listening ear is another element of care that displays a profoundly caring practice.

No one is in the position to place a time frame on our grief. At the same time, it's important for us to be honest with ourselves about whether we are working through grief, or simply running from grief. Doing needed grief work can allow us to progress to other lessons and tasks, those activities that are intended for the living. See Appendix J for a list of grief resources.

Chapter Twenty-One

Money

Maximizing Our Earning Potential

"Ignore the glass ceiling and do your work. If you're focusing
on the glass ceiling, focusing on what you don't have,
focusing on the limitations, then you will be limited."
*Ava Duvernay, screenwriter and first Black woman to win the Best
Director Prize at the Sundance Film Festival*

Our Scriptures have much to say about establishing a proper relationship with money.

"The love of money is the root of all evil" (1 Timothy 6:10).

"If you don't work, you don't eat" (2 Thessalonians 3:10).

"Render to Caesar what is Caesar's, and to God, what is
God's" (Matthew 22:21).

"Honor the LORD with your wealth, with the firstfruits of all your crops; then your barns will be filled to overflowing, and your vats will brim over with new wine" (Proverbs 3: 9,10).

"The LORD will open the heavens, the storehouse of his bounty, to send rain on your land in season and to bless all the work of your hands. You will lend to many nations but will borrow from none. The LORD will make you the head, not the tail" (Deuteronomy 28: 12-13a).

"Suppose one of you wants to build a tower. Won't you first sit down and estimate the cost to see if you have enough money to complete it?" (Luke 14:28).

"As Jesus looked up, he saw the rich putting their gifts into the temple treasury. He also saw a poor widow put in two very small copper coins. "Truly I tell you," he said, "this poor widow has put in more than all the others. All these people gave their gifts out of their wealth; but she out of her poverty put in all she had to live on" (Luke 21:1-4).

Sadly, however, many of us Black women, along with many other Americans, are doing just the opposite: We are living beyond our means. Some have even said that debt is the new slavery. We can take decades to pay off money we've borrowed, and pay for our goods and services many, many times over. The ease of accessibility to credit begins for many in their late teens, particularly on university campuses where credit is so freely available. Moreover, student loan debt has grown exponentially and is now a staggering load for many Americans. Because our families are the least likely in America to have generations of inherited wealth, little to no savings for college or starting a business, and parents who are working two to three jobs just to make ends meet, many Black women enter adulthood at a distinct financial disadvantage.

However, transcending these disadvantages and furthering our education and skills through a college degree, vocational training, and/or military experience gives us the opportunity for greater earning power, as well as greater use for God's glorious ends. There used to be a time when a college education was seen as the "extra" credential needed to ensure a comfortable, financial future. These days, however, a college degree is seen as the bare minimum, and in most cases, graduate training is the prerequisite for advancement opportunities in most fields.

If powering through the college experience was extremely difficult for you, thinking about further education is probably the last thing on your mind. However, it may be important to re-assess the difficulties you experienced in college, whether it was last year or three decades ago. Did you graduate from a high school that may not have fully prepared you for the rigors of study at the collegiate level? Maybe you had an undiagnosed learning or other disability that interfered with your success in the classroom. Were you overwhelmed by the freedoms and temptations of college life, with more of the food, parties, alcohol, and cute guys than you could safely handle (and so few curfews, checks, and balances)? Did your financial situation require you to work so many hours that you could not focus on your studies? And were you struggling to pay your tuition, books, housing, and other college essentials, while perhaps also supporting a lifestyle to which you had become accustomed? (After all, many college freshmen already have credit card debt from spending what, at the time, appeared to be "free money.")

Maybe rather than encouraging you to develop the discipline needed for academic success, some of your family members back home may have seemed indifferent to your college struggles, or even actively encouraged you to return home. Chances are, if you made it to college, you may have been one of the greater contributors to your family's economy and/or functioning. You perhaps may have been one of the first to go to college, while other family members did not have a deep understanding of what it takes to perform well academically, emotionally, financially, socially, and spiritually in a college environment.

For any combination of these reasons, many of us were trapped by a low grade-point average (GPA), or even worse, were unable to graduate at all. Using hindsight, however, you can probably discern that any trouble you had in college had less to do with your ability to learn and more to do with the distractions that surrounded you at that time, and perhaps having less support than you needed to thrive. So perhaps thinking about returning to school can be re-examined with fresh eyes and an awareness of the strengths-based factors in your life that can now contribute to your academic success. Pursuing apprenticeship or internship experiences in your chosen field can also give you the training you need to maximize your earning potential.

Growing in Fiscal Responsibility

"Be thankful for what you have; you'll end up having more.
If you concentrate on what you don't have,
you will never, ever have enough."
Oprah Winfrey, media mogul and greatest Black
philanthropist in U.S. history

God promises bountiful blessings to all of God's children who are obedient to God's commands:

"If you fully obey the LORD your God and carefully follow all his commands I give you today, the LORD your God will set you high above all the nations on earth. All these blessings will come on you and accompany you if you obey the LORD your God:

"You will be blessed in the city and blessed in the country.

"The fruit of your womb will be blessed, and the crops of your land and the young of your livestock—the calves of your herds and the lambs of your flocks.

"Your basket and your kneading trough will be blessed.

"You will be blessed when you come in and blessed when you go out.

"The LORD will grant that the enemies who rise up against you will be defeated before you. They will come at you from one direction but flee from you in seven.

"The LORD will send a blessing on your barns and on everything you put your hand to. The LORD your God will bless you in the land he is giving you.

"The LORD will establish you as his holy people, as he promised you on oath, if you keep the commands of the LORD your God and walk in obedience to him. Then all the peoples on earth will see that you are called by the name of the LORD, and they will fear you. The LORD will grant you abundant prosperity—in the fruit of your womb, the young of your livestock and the crops of your ground— in the land he swore to your ancestors to give you.

"The LORD will open the heavens, the storehouse of his bounty, to send rain on your land in season and to bless all the work of your hands. You will lend to many nations but will borrow from none. The LORD will make you the head, not the tail. If you pay attention to the commands of the LORD your God that I give you this day and carefully follow them, you will always be at the top, never at the bottom. Do not turn aside from any of the commands I give you today, to the right or to the left, following other gods and serving them."

(Deuteronomy 28: 1-14)

 Listen to Recording #13, "Trust and Obey"

The extensive nature of God's promises to us are a reminder of what happens when we trust and obey. We not only give God the glory so clearly deserved, but we also have much to gain. Many of these blessings are spiritual blessings, but make no mistake—God is also referring to material abundance in this passage. Financially, God wants us to be lenders, not borrowers! The steps outlined in the previous section provided insight into how we can maximize our earning potential, no matter how much money we make. However, if we are frequently spending more than we earn, we are creating a personal financial disaster that will inevitably affect our family and friends. When we live above our means, we are much less likely to build up any savings, emergency funds, retirement accounts, or other investments. Thus, when the winds of life blow, as they undoubtedly will, we will find ourselves dependent upon others to bail us out. Needing a few more dollars until payday is one thing, but needing to replace a major appliance or attend a funeral of a loved one several states away is a much more urgent and burdensome request. As we have acknowledged in other sections, it is very important for us to learn the skill of interdependence. Family members and friends usually don't mind helping us out when they can afford to do so and perceive that we are doing the best we can. However, if our own negligent behaviors contribute to an emergency that becomes a crisis on their part, then we expose that relationship to the dangers of contention and mistrust.

So, exactly what does taking fiscal responsibility look like? After offering an humble prayer of commitment, you will need to develop or refine your budget. See Appendix K for a sample. Take a good, long look at your income and expenses. Have you accounted for all sources of income, including second or third jobs, alimony and child support, benefit payments, gifts, and pay from your side hustle(s)? Do you make tips or receive bonuses at certain times of the year? For purposes of this financial planning session, resist the urge to not count a certain line of income because you have it earmarked for something else. For example, your "shoe money" could be the very funds needed to help you get out of debt!

After you have fully assessed your income, examine and list all of your expenses. Taking a look at your bank statement, if you have a bank account, is a good place to start. However, if you're someone who tends to spend cash, often without any tracking system in place, many of your actual expenses may be hidden. Many of our major bills are easy to remember, often because they put a sizable dent into our funds: rent or mortgage payment, car note, and utilities.

Don't forget, though, that some expenses occur on a different payment cycle from most of our other bills, such as annual tax payments, bimonthly utility bills, quarterly insurance premiums, or gift expenses. Some of the most impactful expenses are the ones that sneak up on us because we don't realize how often and how much we are spending, say, at fast food drive-throughs or at Starbucks. And although tithing may not be in vogue in the broader culture, we must ask ourselves how often we are both able and willing to honor God with our firstfruits, that is, ten percent of our earnings? The first 10 percent is referred to as "firstfruits" to remind us to show honor to God by trusting God with what we get first, not what is left over in the end. If you are able to automate your tithe payments through bill pay or automatic debit right after payday, you'll probably find quickly that you don't even miss the money. You become accustomed to living on 90 percent, often more efficiently than you used to live off of 100 percent of your income. Psychologically, tithing can provide you with an assurance of pleasing God and making a real difference in the lives touched by your church's ministry.

Once you have calculated your income and expenses, a simple comparison between the two figures will let you know whether you have more money than month, or more month than money. If your money regularly runs out before your pay period ends, you must choose a remedy for your situation. You can either commit to increasing your income, cutting your expenses, or doing a little of both. One of the greatest drains on your budget is debt, so we'll spend some time discussing how to get rid of debt.

Getting Rid of Debt

"In terms of my profession, I'm passionate about financial literacy.
I want to live in a financially literate society. I want kids
to understand the importance of savings and investing.
I want to try to replicate the great savers who came out of
the Depression, the best savers the country has ever seen.
It's crucial that people understand the importance of
financial literacy, because it's actually life saving."
*Mellody Hobson, president of Ariel Investments, one of the largest
Black-owned money management companies in the U.S.*

Most financial experts advise that you first get out of debt before you
can truly begin building wealth. Unfortunately, many of us have debt
spread across several credit cards (and loved ones). Some advise that
after you establish an emergency fund (which can vary from $1,000
to eight months' worth of expenses), you can begin by committing
to discontinue your use of credit cards. Some people even cut up
their credit cards or put them in the freezer. Next, begin paying off
one card at a time. Whether you begin with the credit card with the
smallest balance or the highest interest rate, most financial counselors advise that the best strategy is to roll over payments from one
card to the next smallest/highest until they eventually are all paid
off. If paying off debt has been difficult or next to impossible, it may
be important for you to create another income stream, usually in the
form of a new job with regular and predictable income. The earnings
from this job are best earmarked specifically for debt repayment, or
you'll be tempted to "treat" yourself to one thing after another, until
your debt is merely remaining stagnant or even worse, growing with
your additional indulgences.

A gentle yet firm accountability partner can help keep you on track
with your debt repayment goals. Yes, it is certainly true that "we work
hard for the money" (in memory of singer Donna Summer) and we
deserve to reward ourselves every now and then. Psychologically, we
feel that we have earned some indulgences, and we feel deprived if

we deny ourselves. Yet when our goal is total financial freedom, we cannot allow our rewards to shoot our dreams in the foot! During this part of your journey, it's better to identify rewards that are low to no cost, or to enjoy rewards that result from sacrificing another item in your budget. Once you are liberated from debt, your rewards will be more affordable, more meaningful, and guilt-free!

Another important aspect of obtaining a solid financial footing is in monitoring your spending. Overspending is more of a threat to some than to others. If you equate your worth as a human being with the value assigned to material goods, you are at risk of placing your hard-earned money in a vicious pursuit of false worth that is never truly captured. Sometimes it can be disheartening to discover just how little discretionary income you truly have, that is, the money that is left over after you have accounted for all of your obligations. Not only do you have to consider all of your bills, but even the "small" expenses add up. Imagine how it feels if you are paid on a monthly schedule but have spent most of your earnings before a quarter of the month is over. If you find yourself in this situation frequently, the most eye-opening practice toward resolving this dilemma is to record every transaction, whether you use a written budget or online resources such as Mint.com, blog.readyforzero.com, or budgetpulse.com. You may be surprised to learn that your perception of your spending and your actual spending behavior may vary greatly. Some have even recommended the use of the envelope system, in which you divide your cash into envelopes established for your major spending categories (e.g., utilities, fuel, dining out). Once the cash is gone, it's gone, signaling that it's time to stop spending until more income is available. Although turning to credit cards or payday loans is tempting, the interest rates on these options are often so high that we can be swept away by the storms of mounting debt in a matter of weeks and months. Intellectually, we understand the ills of money mismanagement, yet often find ourselves in financial bondage.

If this describes you, your challenge is not merely increasing your income. Increasing your income would likely be paired with increasing your expenses. You may need to explore your relationship with money and how you think about it. Ask yourself, "What does money represent to me?" Power, survival, security, a necessary evil, freedom, a means of showing love to others, and status are some of the most common associations we make with money. However, if your view of money is distorting your use of money, you may want to seek a therapist with expertise in money issues, such as someone certified in behavioral finance or financial social work. She can help you better understand your relationship with money and redirect your thoughts and behaviors to better align with your financial goals.

Once you've become stable in your budgeting and getting rid of debt, you'll want to give thought to your priorities for saving and investing. Because life happens, you will want to have a "rainy day" or emergency fund that is set aside strictly for emergencies, such as needing a costly car repair or having to pay out of pocket for an expensive prescription. Next, consider your retirement savings. Find a retirement calculator to determine how much money you will need in retirement. Though daunting, that figure will hopefully motivate you toward more regular savings! If you have an employer that offers retirement benefits, take advantage of those benefits, especially if your employer will match contributions—that's free money! As your retirement calculator will readily show you, however, depending on your job's retirement plan and Social Security benefits will not be sufficient. You will likely need to establish a retirement savings account such as an Individual Retirement Account (IRA) through your financial adviser. Taking this step may seem intimidating if you don't have exposure to or experience with financial planning. However, find a representative at your local bank or credit union, a financial adviser, or locate a sisters' investment club to support you through this process. Fear has kept many a sister from not managing her money as wisely as possible, but remember: You have not been given a spirit of fear, but of power, love, and a sound mind (2 Corinthians 1:7)!

If you have children or want to support a child in a significant way, set aside a regular amount for their educational fund, whether for private education, college and graduate school education, or general educational opportunities. Protect their future from as few student loans as possible.

This section ends on a high note, with a restatement of the Black Enterprise Wealth for Life Principles (Black Enterprise, 2010):

1. I will live within my means

2. I will maximize my income potential through education and training

3. I will effectively manage my budget, credit, debt, and tax obligations

4. I will save at least 10 percent of my income

5. I will use homeownership as a foundation for building wealth

6. I will devise an investment plan for my retirement needs and childrens' education

7. I will ensure that my entire family adheres to sensible money management principles

8. I will support the creation and growth of minority-owned businesses

9. I will guarantee my wealth is passed on to future generations through proper insurance and estate planning

10. I will strengthen my community through philanthropy

If our sister Oseola McCarty, Mississippi washerwoman with a sixth-grade education, could leave $150,000 to The University of Southern Mississippi upon her death, what lasting contributions will we make with our money?

Chapter Twenty-Two

Time

Identifying and Maintaining Our Priorities

"Now I don't put things in boxes anymore.
I'm just focusing on right now."
Robin Roberts, entrepreneur and anchor of Good Morning America

How do we know what our priorities truly are? Some say that how we spend our time is reflective of what we value. However, we often give our employers the greatest portion of our time from week to week, even as we may be working toward the goal of financial independence. So, even though our jobs or careers require forty or more hours of our time per week, we benefit when we look at how we use our time when we're not working or sleeping.

Perhaps family activities are a significant priority for you and consume much of your time outside of work. Maybe you are a dedicated worker at your church, often finding yourself at the "churchhouse" or performing church work in the community. Or maybe you have a hobby such as gardening, quilting, or Zumba, and you're committed to daily or weekly periods focused on these activities. If you're a jetsetter, you have time and resources to travel to your favorite destinations, either for pleasure, or for business (with a twist of pleasure)! Whatever your priorities may be, it's important to take stock of them at least once or twice annually. Sometimes our circumstances change, and with those changes, our calendars have either more or less time for these activities. Occasionally our resources change, and we have to assess whether we can afford more or less of an activity or its related fees. It's also possible that our interests may change, perhaps as we discover new adventures to pursue or re-discover old but beloved pastimes.

It's also important to re-visit our priorities because they sometimes shift without our noticing the change. This possibility makes it vitally important for us to be very clear about our values. What or who do you hold in highest esteem? As Christians, we know that our relationship with God is a gift beyond measure, one to nurture on a regular basis. According to the Greatest Commandment (Mark 12:30-31), our loving relationship with God is directly connected to our love for our neighbors and ourselves. Once we have established God as our main priority, we can invest in the power of preparation to engage with our other priorities.

The Power of Preparation

> **"The only thing that separates women of color from anyone else is opportunity."**
> *Viola Davis, the only Black woman to have won the Triple Crown of Acting (Academy, Emmy, and Tony awards)*

"Plan your work and work your plan." This was the constant riff of one of my beloved sisters in graduate school, and how wise she was! As a Christian herself, she was really tapping into the ancient wisdom of the Scriptures as revealed by Jesus when he was teaching his disciples about the cost of following him.

> Suppose one of you wants to build a tower. Won't you first sit down and estimate the cost to see if you have enough money to complete it? For if you lay the foundation and are not able to finish it, everyone who sees it will ridicule you, saying, 'This person began to build and wasn't able to finish.'...In the same way, those of you who do not give up everything you have cannot be my disciples.
>
> (Luke 14:28-30, 33)

Before we jump into any significant task, we must assess not only the financial cost of the endeavor, but also the spiritual, psychological, physical, and social costs involved. What will this task do to our bodies? How will this work affect our relationship with our Creator? In what ways might we have to think, feel, and behave differently as a result of this undertaking? Could this pursuit have an impact on our social connections? Once we have counted those costs and still deem the quest worthy of our energy and efforts, we can establish a plan. In order for us to be well-prepared to work the plan, there are a few tips for us to keep in mind:

1. Find a balance between living mindfully in each moment and keeping a long-term perspective. God may have revealed to you promises about your future, yet the time of their fulfillment may not have come. Think about the twelve years that lapsed between the time when David was anointed King of Israel by Samuel, and when he actually ascended the throne. Sometimes we have to utilize patience and assurance of God's promise to help us live each day to the fullest, even as we await greater things in store for us.

2. Prepare the night before in order to achieve the greatest effectiveness the next day. That includes selecting and preparing your

clothing and accessories for the next day, preparing your lunch and snacks, laying out items that you may need to remember to take with you, and taking care of any chores that may slow you down the next day.

3. Whether preparing for a staff meeting, an exam, or a parent-teacher conference, do your homework! Review any agenda items that have been provided, read carefully though documents, and learn about the person(s) and institution you are meeting with before you arrive. You will place yourself in a much better position to understand the context of the meeting and will present yourself as someone who is taking your role seriously.

Once you become accustomed to consistent habits of preparation, it will only be a matter of time before a great opportunity presents itself, and you will be poised to take advantage of it.

Managing Our Time and Commitments

> **"I live a day at a time. Each day I look for a kernel of excitement.**
> **In the morning, I say: 'What is my exciting thing for today?'**
> **Then, I do the day. Don't ask me about tomorrow."**
> *Barbara Jordan, attorney and first Black woman from*
> *the South elected to the U.S. House of Representatives*

"There just aren't enough hours in the day!"

"A woman's work is never done."

"Yes, I can fit in that extra task in my copious spare time!"

Have you ever uttered one or more of these phrases? Truth be told, we are often greatly frustrated by our finitude, the reality that we are finite beings and time is a fixed commodity. No matter how hard we try, we cannot add more hours to the twenty-four that God so graciously provides. In my daughter's science class, there was a poster of Beyoncé, accompanied by the caption, "Both you and Beyoncé have twenty-four hours per day." Like Beyoncé, we may be working our hardest to cram in as much as possible in our waking hours, and we may even be compromising our sleep to do so. But as my grandfather used to say, "You can't stay up with the owls and get up with the chickens." Burning the proverbial candle at both ends can result in negative health consequences, decreased judgment in decision-making, and less joy. (Recall how incredible you felt the last time you had a good night's sleep, and you'll know the joy I'm talking about!)

So, with the mile-long to-do list, how do we get it all in? Well, first, we must consult God to determine whether the items on our list are directly related to God's purpose AND meant to occur in the time frame we have designed. Stephen Covey, world-renowned author of *The Seven Habits of Highly Effective People* (1989) draws a distinction between the urgent things of life that command our attention, such as picking up our children from school, taking a loved one to a string of doctors' appointments, or making dinner, and the important things, such as establishing a retirement savings plan and acknowledging the birthdays, anniversaries, or other special days of your loved ones. Important tasks align with your values, but if they are not accomplished, you don't usually experience the same immediate, negative consequences that you experience when you don't accomplish urgent tasks. Here are a few significant questions to ask yourself about how you are spending your time:

1. Am I neglecting my spiritual connection to God?

2. Am I neglecting the physical needs of any of my loved ones?

3. Am I neglecting the emotional needs of any of my loved ones?

4. Am I neglecting my passions, dreams, or purpose more often than not?

5. Am I working harder on someone's behalf than they are working for themselves?

6. Do I need to say "No" to any activities in which I am joylessly involved?

7. Am I able to handle the repercussions of saying "No"?

Once you've answered these questions with clarity, you can identify places in your daily or weekly schedule where you may need to do some re-aligning of priorities. When you're clear on your priorities, you are better positioned to make the most of your time through sound time management practices. Here are some tips I've shared with my clients about maximizing the use of time:

1. Be mindful that time is a gift from God. The next moment, let alone the next day, is not promised to us. We can only commit to doing the best we can with the time-limited parameters that we have. We cannot assume that contingencies will not alter our plans—we, or family members, may experience illness, natural disasters can occur, job crises happen, inspiration can be lost. But take heart—God measures time differently from us. Unlike our limited, chronological time of *chronos*, God's time is called *kairos*, where on one hand time seems to stand still, and in an instant everything changes and much is accomplished. If you've ever had the experience of having an extremely productive period, you were likely in *kairos*, moving in God's time.

2. If you don't already know your most productive time of the day, experiment with accomplishing your tasks at different times of the day until you find the time period where you are most in the groove. Perhaps you are a morning person who can best flow before the rest of the world (especially your household) wakes up. Or maybe you can tap into your highest and most focused energy after your home becomes quiet at night. One client shared with me that she shifts into high gear at 5 pm!

3. Consider what, if any, inspiration you need to get or keep you going. Have you laid a solid spiritual foundation before getting started? Observing your devotional time or whispering a prayer of praise and petition for faithful progress on your task can align your spirit with God's Spirit and help you to be a more grateful recipient of God's grace and discernment in the midst of your task. Also reflect on whether you have a favorite set of affirmations, sermons, or motivational talks that can serve as a catalyst for your drive toward productivity.

4. Make sure your physical conditions are conducive to making the most of your time. Does your lighting set the proper mood, with just the right amount of energy or tranquility? Is the temperature optimized for your greatest focus and comfort? Might a fragranced candle set the right atmosphere for concentrated work? Is music a help or a hindrance for the kind of work you are setting out to do? Do you need to bring your own music to maximize your experience? If your work requires significant concentration, music with lots of lyrics may be distracting. Perhaps instrumental music in your favorite genre(s) would be more fitting.

5. For some of us, it is effective to set about a task and remain in place until the task is done. But because many of us have to press toward our goals "between the cracks," scheduling an important activity and preserving the time in the face of other possible distractions is of utmost importance. Even with the "small cracks of time" that you have, create a plan for how you hope to use that period of time. Even better, write it down for some self-accountability. This practice will help you stay focused on your goal for that period of time.

6. "Let us throw off everything that hinders" (Hebrews 12: 1b)— especially when time is excessively spent on social media! If you have a penchant for checking your phone or social media every few minutes, you will want to be intentional about laying those

distractions aside for a longer period of time than you are usually accustomed. However, your social media experiences can serve as an intermittent reward to which you can treat yourself between significant chunks of work. The Pomodoro Technique (*http:// cirillocompany.de/pages/pomodoro-technique/*) is one example of a way to structure your work to maximize your focus, minimize your distractions, and reward yourself with shorter breaks, followed by a longer break after a couple of hours of work.

7. If you are working on a long-term project, set aside a certain amount of time to devote to that project on a regular basis. If it's not feasible to reserve a few minutes daily for your task, consider establishing at least 20-30 minutes several days a week. It may seem that your small window is inconsequential, but those little bits of time can accumulate into something beautiful!

8. Engage one or more accountability partners to help keep you on track with your goals. In addition to sharing their goals with me, my clients are encouraged to identify friendly, yet firm, supports who can help ensure that they are putting in time on their goals. Of course, just putting in the time in and of itself does not guarantee results. But there is a blessing in moving forward, in season and out of season, under sunny or rainy conditions, to form the habits of success. Just as Moses continued to show up before Pharoah and be rejected over and over again, and just as Moses was commanded by God to move forward toward the raging Red Sea, we sisters are called to display both consistency and obedience in the use of our time as well as our treasure, talents, and temples.

9. If you regularly encounter challenges with maintaining focus or concentration on your tasks, you may have an attentional disorder. These challenges can greatly hamper the quantity and quality of your academic, job-related, or family responsibilities. Consider whether you may be a good candidate for a psychological evaluation to determine whether you meet criteria for

Attention-Deficit/Hyperactivity Disorder (ADHD). Receiving this diagnosis is not an indictment of your value as God's creature. The diagnosis of ADHD can lead you to pharmacological treatments that can support understimulated portions of your brain. ADHD is also recognized by most educational institutions and some workplaces as a disability that allows for modifications to your work load or deadlines through accommodations such as extra time for assignments and examinations, separate seating to accomplish tasks, and assistance with securing notes or recordings of lecture material. Having this assistance can make a significant difference in your quality of life.

Young Sister, Time is On Your Side!

"Struggle is a never-ending process. Freedom is never really won, you earn it and win it in every generation."
Coretta Scott King, singer, author, and the First Lady of the Civil Rights Movement

To be young, Black, and beautiful! If you are coming of age during this time in history, you hold possibilities unparalleled by any other generation. You have before you examples of Black women who have broken the glass ceiling, Black women who have competed in their various arenas of excellence and have emerged as globally recognized leaders. Think of the contributions of Bishop Vashti McKenzie, Condoleezza Rice, Oprah, Beyoncé, Michelle Obama, Shonda Rimes, and Dr. Maya Angelou, for starters. You are standing on the shoulders of your elders and your ancestors who have made endless sacrifices and concessions so that each generation can stand higher, sometimes in microscopic increments, and sometimes in leaps and bounds. God's promise to God's people to be the head and not the tail is not just reserved for White male property owners!

Despite your bright and promising future, however, you may have legitimate doubts and fears about how to get from where you sit today to the fulfillment of your dreams. As you embark upon your journey into adulthood, you'll have some days when you find that things aren't quite what they were cracked up to be when you were on the outside looking in. Although you have probably "escaped" the dominion of your parents, the freedom to choose where and when to be is now somewhat hampered by your obligations to your professors, your boss, and/or your financial obligations. Even when you think that you have completed your education, you may quickly realize the limitations of what you're able to accomplish in your job, or even in your own entrepreneurial dreams, without additional formal preparation or experience. In this age when America has seen her first Black president, racism, classism, and sexism are indeed still alive and well in the workplace. Despite your stellar performance, pleasant demeanor, and well-suited skills, you are still more likely than others in your work setting to be passed over for a promotion. You may still hear from your supervisor, much like your mother and grandmothers before you, that you are "not quite ready" to assume a position of leadership, yet somehow you are well qualified to train those who will eventually supervise you.

Given these dynamics, it is certainly true that your best protection against career stagnation is the best preparation that your money and time can afford you. Similar tips have been mentioned in earlier sections of this book, but they take on special relevance given the accessibility of resources at this stage of your development. Because credentials (e.g., degrees, licenses, certifications) can be so important across both public and private sectors, pursue these credentials, whether they are for the benefit of your employer or your dreams. Don't go it alone. Find other like-minded people in your shared industry (yes, think outside of the box) who are also invested in their professional development. Keep each other informed about books, webinars, networking events, and other resources that can teach you how to refine your craft. Do your research and join the best professional organization in your area. Social media platforms that allow connection with other industry professionals are good networking tools, but nothing beats a firm handshake and face-to-face conversation with someone who shares your passion, is a little farther down the career path you're pursuing, and just might be inspired by the twinkle in your eye to give you some assistance. Don't underestimate the aroma of Christ (2 Corinthians 2:15) in your interactions!

If you have a dream of starting your own business, first make sure that your craft is one that you're passionate about, because during difficult times, your passion may be all that is sustaining you. Continue to work at your craft, formally investing in your professional development through workshops, conferences, and networking events. Don't forget, however, the importance of informal preparation through reading, podcasts, and meaningful connections with persons in your field. Even when you have completed advanced education, you will often find that many programs fall short of preparing you for operating your business in the real world. Everyone needs a mentor, someone who has gone down your chosen path a few (or many) steps ahead of you and knows the lay of the land. Mentors can be hard to find, yet don't be discouraged. Use your networks and professional affiliations to identify someone whose expertise you admire. If possible, have one of your contacts make a warm introduction, either in person or virtually.

If your potential mentor responds favorably, be precise in making your request. Are you looking for feedback on a personal statement for a graduate school application? Are you hoping to learn about the forecasted opportunities in your field so you can choose wisely? Do you need a proven strategy for marketing to your target population? Do your homework before your meeting. Learn as much as you can about this mentor and her company. Prepare your questions ahead of time so that the meeting will run as efficiently as possible. Follow the lead of your mentor to determine whether it is permissible to share any of your personal details. Finally, humbly inquire about whether this person is willing to make herself available for any follow-up contact. By simply meeting with you, she has already made an important contribution to your career/business development. However, if she is willing to avail herself on even an infrequent basis, that gift can be transformative for you. Although you may feel most comfortable with a sister, keep in mind that mentors come in all shapes, colors, ages, and sizes. The very mentors who seem most ill-suited to guide you may be the very ones who expose you to new resources and newer ways of thinking.

In fact, envision yourself growing through the influence of a mosaic of mentors across your career. Maybe one person will be vital for assisting you with getting into graduate school, another will be crucial in helping you land your career-launching job, yet another will advise you in establishing critical business operations, and a fourth mentor may show you the ropes of bringing together your board of directors. All of that may be a bit much to bite off at one time, but rest in the fact that you don't have to figure it all out now. In fact, gospel music lyrics often remind us that "While you're trying to figure it out, God has already worked it out!" Trust that the God who created you is the same God who will lead you every step of the way.

Aging Gracefully

> **"I really don't think life is about the I-could-have-beens.**
> **Life is only about the I-tried-to-do. I don't mind the failure**
> **but I can't imagine that I'd forgive myself if I didn't try."**
> *Nikki Giovanni, poet and leading author in the Black Arts Movement*

"Black don't crack!" This oft-repeated assurance repeated by legions of Black women communicates that we don't have to worry about the appearance of wrinkles as we age. How might we account for the fact, however, that many Black women are showing concerns about aging, as evidenced by the amount of money we spend on anti-aging products? Also, the hair coloring industry is faring just fine, as many women cover their gray hair for decades, perhaps until "death do us part" from hair color. If you've lived long enough, you begin to notice that there are many indicators of our mortality all around us. We begin to experience aches and pains, some of which may be mitigated by our fitness routines, but others that may be difficult to avoid alto-gether. When we gather with family or old friends, we notice how much the little ones are becoming teens or young adults. We notice that our elders look older and perhaps move a bit more slowly, and we realize that they, too, recognize that *we* are aging. We may also begin to have experiences with the public that bring our aging front and center. Perhaps the grocery bagger asks more regularly if we need help getting our bags to the car. Maybe people, not much younger than we are, start calling us "Ma'am" (especially in the South) when we aren't used to hearing this title. As you visit your primary care provider for annual physicals, you notice that there are more screening tests that are now required at regular intervals. Whatever your indicators may be, coming to terms with your own mortality may be humbling, or even downright intimidating. You may be wondering, "Will I ever achieve my life goals?" "Do I have enough money to retire?" "What will my quality of life be like?" "Who will take care of me?" "Will anyone remember me when I'm gone?"

Because of our Christian faith, we have the assurance of a heavenly home after we leave this earth, one where we will be rewarded for all of our toil and good works on this side of Jordan. However, many agree that while we all want to go to heaven, few of us are in any hurry to get there. So how do we reconcile God's promises of an eternal reward with societal pressures to stay as young as possible and to avoid death for as long as possible?

Although there exist some substantive differences in psychological theories that explain human development, a casual observer will note that almost all of them reveal a progression toward maturity through the various stages of life. Despite our common assumption that we arrive at full maturity once we meet the standard age of majority, 18 years of age, we continue to develop across the life span. Because of our mainstream U.S. culture's orientation toward being young, turning even 25 or 30 evokes for some an existential crisis. Yet there is much to be gained and experienced, not feared, as we continue to blossom.

One of my favorite developmental theories is that of Erik Erikson, a 20th-century German-born American psychologist. Although he did not include Black children or women in his empirical research studies, Erikson's theories were influenced by his collaborator and wife, Joan. Unlike other theorists of the day, the Eriksons (Erikson & Erickson, 1998) understood that we as human beings continue to evolve until the day we die. As we approach the end of life, they explained, we encounter the developmental stage of "Ego Integrity versus Despair." At this stage, we look back over our lives and evaluate the extent to which we have met our life goals, and whether we have developed wisdom as our lives come to a close. If we are conscientious, we may give frequent thought to these goals and the grand purpose that God has given to our lives. When God assures us that we have a hopeful future, it doesn't just mean that our hopes are fulfilled in the future, but more importantly, that God's hopes for us are redeemed. Because God's very nature is generous in wisdom, lovingkindness, and forgiveness, one way that we measure the degree to which we've achieved our life purpose is whether what we've accomplished has been conducted with wisdom, lovingkindness, and forgiveness.

What are some of the other qualities that demonstrate that we are aging gracefully? As we mature, we learn to develop an attitude of acceptance. This is not an acceptance of the status quo that oppresses others, and us, from an experience of full humanity regarding the goods of life. For these things, we must keep on fighting. Rather, the attitude of acceptance we reveal is an acceptance of things that we cannot control, as encouraged by the Serenity Prayer, presented here in its full version:

> God grant me the serenity
> to accept the things I cannot change;
> courage to change the things I can;
> and wisdom to know the difference.
> Living one day at a time;
> Enjoying one moment at a time;

Accepting hardships as the pathway to peace;
Taking, as He did, this sinful world
as it is, not as I would have it;
Trusting that He will make all things right
if I surrender to His Will;
That I may be reasonably happy in this life
and supremely happy with Him
Forever in the next.
Amen.

In this fuller version of this prayer, typically attributed to theologian Reinhold Niebuhr, we are to accept the things we cannot change and accept hardships as the pathway to peace. Because of the subtleties of life, there is a thin line between acceptance and change. Some of our greatest life challenges occur as a result of being in struggle. Struggle in and of itself is not problematic; in fact, we have many Biblical examples that demonstrate the importance of struggle (e.g., Moses's struggle with Pharoah for the freedom of the Hebrews; Hannah's resistance against her barren condition; Jacob's wrestling with God). Yet to be effective, we do need to evaluate for what purpose we are struggling. Are we struggling for a divine purpose, or are we struggling to achieve an agenda that is exclusively self-focused? Struggling for the former creates renewal, while struggling for the latter creates bitterness. Have you ever heard an elderly Black woman described as a "mean old woman?" Do you think that she made a conscious decision to establish that reputation? Or might that be the culmination of all of life's hurts and defeats without the sweetness of joy, wisdom, and acceptance? No matter what challenges or traumas we have experienced, we demonstrate that we are aging gracefully when by God's grace we do not allow those experiences to define us.

While aging has a negative connotation in our mainstream, youth-oriented society, we can also view growing older as the unfolding stages of metamorphosis. We elevate from the form of the caterpillar, through the chrysalis, to the emergent butterfly. She flies freely on the winds, transcending the cocoon that once held her captive. Though the lessons of the cocoon were painful, they were necessary for the butterfly to enjoy the liberation to which she has ascended. So, too, are the lessons on our path to freedom. Fly, beautiful, black butterfly!

 Listen to Recording #14, "Black Butterfly"

Epilogue

By now, I pray that you are filled with encouragement and hope about the places in your life where you are already blossoming, and other places where you now have more practical strategies toward blossoming. If you are dealing with a mental disorder, I trust that you will find the courage to pursue support, psychotherapy, and other practices that promote stability and healing. Consistent with the broader message of this book, positive changes work best one step at a time. Regardless of your beginning score on the Blossoming Hope Wellness Inventory, I recommend that you pursue blossoming in one area before moving to the next. Find an accountability partner, perhaps in your small group ministry, book club, or fitness class, who is headed in the same general direction as you are and is prepared for mutual support. Slowly digest the lessons found here, re-reading sections that particularly resonated with you. Listen repeatedly to the recordings for inspiration, instruction, and relaxation. Recognize that it will take both grit and grace to reach your goals. Finally, open your heart to God more fully, and you will receive the guidance, love, and hope that will give way to your fullest blossoming!

References

Ainsworth, M. S. (1967). *Infancy in Uganda: Infant care and the growth of love*. Baltimore: The Johns Hopkins Press.

Akers, D. (1957). You Can't Beat God's Giving. [Vinyl]. Los Angeles, CA: Manna Music.

American Cancer Society (2016). *Cancer facts & figures for African Americans 2016-2018*. Atlanta: American Cancer Society.

American Psychiatric Association (2013). *Diagnostic and statistical manual of mental disorders: DSM-5*. Washington, D.C: American Psychiatric Association.

American Yoga Association (2006). Retrieved from *http://www. americanyogaassociation.org/contents.html*

Armstrong, T. D. (1996). Exploring spirituality: The development of the Armstrong Measure of Spirituality. In R. L. Jones (Ed.), *Handbook of tests and measurements for Black populations* (Vol. 2, 105-115). Hampton, VA: Cobb & Henry Publishers.

Armstrong, T. D. (2016). African American congregational care and counseling: Transcending universal and culturally-specific barriers. *Journal of Pastoral Care & Counseling, 70*(2), 118-122.

Bacharach, B., & Sager, C. B. (1985). That's what friends are for [Recorded by Dionne and Friends]. On *Friends* [Vinyl]. New York: Arista.

Baucom, D. H., & Epstein, N. (1990). *Cognitive-behavioral marital therapy.* New York: Brunner/Mazel, Inc.

Baumrind, D. (1991). The influence of parenting style on adolescent competence and substance use. *Journal of Early Adolescence, 11*(1), 56-95.

Bennett, L., & White, C. (1975). *The shaping of Black America: The struggles and triumphs of African Americans, 1619-1990s.* Chicago: Johnson Publishing Company, Inc.

Biswas, A., Oh, P.I., Faulkner, G. E., Baja, R. R., Silver, M.A., Mitchell, M. S., & Alter, D. A. (2015). Sedentary time and its association with risk for disease incidence, mortality, and hospitalization in adults: A systematic review and meta-analysis. *Annals of Internal Medicine, 162*(2), 123-132.

Black Enterprise (2010). *The Black Enterprise wealth for life principles.* Retrieved from *http://www.blackenterprise.com/money/investing/black-enterprise-wealth-for-life-principles/*

Brantley, J. (2007). *Calming your anxious mind: How mindfulness & compassion can free you from anxiety, fear and panic.* (2nd ed.). Oakland, CA: New Harbinger Publications, Inc.

Boyd-Franklin, N. (2003). *Black families in therapy: Understanding the African American experience* (2nd ed.). New York: The Guilford Press.

Broonzy, B. B. (1951). Black, brown, and white. Retrieved from *http://pancocojams.blogspot.com/2012/06/big-bill-broonzy-black-brown-and-white.html*

Carmona, C., Buunk, B. P., Peiro, J. M., Rodriguez, I., & Bravo, M.J. (2006). Do social comparison and coping styles play a role in the development of burnout? Cross-sectional and longitudinal findings. *Journal of Occupational and Organisational Psychology, 79*, 85-99.

Campbell, J. C. (2002). Health consequences of intimate partner violence. *The Lancet, 359*(9314), 1331-1336.

Center for Behavioral Health Statistics and Quality (2015). *Behavioral health trends in the United States: Results from the 2014 National Survey on Drug Use and Health* (HHS Publication No. SMA 15-4927, NSDUH Series H-50). Retrieved from *http://www.samhsa.gov/data/*

Centers for Disease Control and Prevention (2014). *Death, leading causes of death for 2014.* Retrieved from *https://www.cdc.gov/nchs/fastats/black-health.htm*

Centers for Disease Control and Prevention (2016). *Health, United States, 2015.* Retrieved from *https://minorityhealth.hhs.gov/omh/browse.aspx?lvl=4&lvlid=25*

Chalfant, H. P., Heller, P. L., Roberts, A., Briones, D., Aguirre-Hochbaum, S., & Farr, W. (1990). The clergy as a resource for those encountering psychological distress. *Review of Religious Research, 31,* 305-313.

Chapman, G. D. (2015). *The five love languages: The secret to love that lasts.* Chicago: Northfield Publishing.

Chatters, L. M., Mattis, J. S., Woodward, A. T., Taylor, R. J., Neighbors, H. W., & Grayman, N. A. (2011). Use of ministers for a serious personal problem among African Americans: Findings from the National Survey of American Life (NSAL). *American Journal of Orthopsychiatry, 81*(1), 118-127.

Chryssavgis, J. (2008). *In the heart of the desert: The spirituality of the desert fathers and mothers* (Rev. ed). Bloomington, IN: World Wisdom.

Chua, W. Y. (2001). The pursuit of pallor in Asia. Retrieved from *http://www.frost.com/prod/servlet/market-insight-print.pag?docid=CEHR-4YZUTR*

Clark, R., Anderson, N. B., Clark, V. R., Williams, D. R. (1999). Racism as a stressor for African Americans: A biopsychosocial model. *American Psychologist, 54*(10), 805-816.

Cloud, H., & Townsend, J. (1992). *When to say yes, how to say no to take control of your life.* Grand Rapids, MI: Zondervan.

Collins, P. (2000). *Black feminist thought: Knowledge, consciousness, and the politics of empowerment* (2nd ed). New York: Routledge.

Comer, D. (2012, February 23). Re: Prayer: Yes, no, maybe, and something better [Web log message]. Retrieved from *http://www.hespeaksinthesilence.com/2012/02/yes-no-later-and-something-better/*

Corrigan, P. (2004). How stigma interferes with mental health care. *American Psychologist, 59*(7), 614-625.

Covey, S. R. (1989). *The 7 habits of highly effective people: Powerful lessons in personal change.* New York: Fireside.

Davis, M. Eshelman, E. R., & McKay, M. (2008). *The relaxation and stress reduction workbook* (6th ed.). Oakland, CA: New Harbinger Publications, Inc.

Deal, R. L. (2014). The smart stepfamily: Seven steps to a healthy family (rev. ed.). Bloomington, MN: Bethany House Publishers.

DeGruy, J. (2005). *Post traumatic slave syndrome: America's legacy of enduring injury and healing* (Rev. ed.). Portland, OR: Joy DeGruy Publications, Inc.

Earle, Mary C. (2007). *The desert mothers: Spiritual practices from the women of the wilderness.* New York: Morehouse Publishing, Inc.

Ennis, W., Jr., Ennis, W., III, Durodoye, B. A., Ennis-Cole, D., & Bolden, V. L. (2004). Counseling African American clients: Professional counselors and religious institutions. *Journal of Humanistic Counseling, Education and Development, 43*, 197-210.

Erikson, E. H., & Erikson, J. M. (1998). *The life cycle completed: Extended version*. New York: W.W. Norton.

Evans, R. H. (2012, June 5). Re: Submission in context: Christ and the Greco-Roman household codes [Web log message]. Retrieved from *https://rachelheldevans.com/blog/mutuality-household-codes*

Films Media Group (2006). *When women ruled: Great women leaders in world history* [Motion picture]. US: Worldwide Media.

Flowers, K. C., Levesque, M. J., & Fischer, S. (2012). The relationship between maladaptive eating behaviors and racial identity among African American women in college. *Journal of Black Psychology, 38*(3), 290-312.

Foster, R. J. (1978). *Celebration of discipline: The path to spiritual growth*. San Francisco, CA: HarperSanFrancisco-HarperCollins.

Geronimus, A. T., Hicken, M. T., Pearson, J. A., Seashols, S. J., Brown, K. L., & Cruz, T. D. (2010). Do US Black women experience stress-related accelerate biological aging? A novel theory and first population-based test of Black-White differences in telomere length. *Human Nature, 21*(1), 19-38.

Greenbaum, J., & Crawford-Jakubiak, J. E. (2015). Child sex trafficking and commercial sexual exploitation: Health care needs of victims. *American Academy of Pediatrics, 135*(3), 1-9.

Gottman, J. M. (1989). Marital interaction and satisfaction: A longitudinal view. *Journal of Consulting and Clinical Psychology, 57*(1), 47-52.

Hankerson, S. H., & Weissman, M. M. (2012). Church-based health programs for mental disorders among African Americans: A review. *Psychiatric Services, 63*(3), 243-249.

Hutchins, J., & Smith, L. (1984). Friends [Recorded by Whodini]. On *Escape* [Vinyl]. New York: Jive Records.

Jenkins, M. (2001). There's a bright side somewhere. *African American Heritage Hymnal.* Chicago: GIA Publications, Inc.

Jones, C., & Shorter-Gooden, K. (2003). *Shifting: The double lives of Black women in America.* New York: HarperCollins.

Jones, V. S. V. (1912). The goose that laid the golden eggs (V.S.V. Jones, Trans.). *Aesop's Fables.* London: W. Heinemann.

Kruszelnicki, K. (2001). *News in science: Skin colour 1.* Retrieved from *http://www.abc.net.au/science/articles/2001/03/01/249992. htm?site=science/greatmomentsinscience*

Keating, T. (2009). *Intimacy with God: An introduction to Centering Prayer* (3rd ed.). New York: The Crossroad Publishing Company.

Koch, R.N., & Haugk, K. C. (1992). *Speaking the truth in love: How to be an assertive Christian.* St. Louis, MO: Stephen Ministries.

Lawrence, D. (2011). Spiritual. On *YRM (Your Righteous Mind)* [CD, Vinyl]. Sony Legacy.

Linehan, M. (2015). *DBT skills training manual* (2nd ed.). New York: The Guilford Press.

Martin, W.S. (1904). God Cares. Retrieved from *https://www. blueletterbible.org/hymns/g/God_Will_Take_Care_Of_You.cfm*

Mock, S. E., & Arai, S. M. (2010). Childhood trauma and chronic illness in adulthood: Mental health and socioeconomic status as explanatory factors and buffers. *Frontiers in Psychology, 1*(246), 1-6.

Morse, D. R., Martin, J. S., Furst, M. L., & Dubin, L. L. (1977). A physiological and subjective evaluation of meditation, hypnosis, and relaxation. *Psychosomatic Medicine, 39*(5), 304-374.

Nordqvist, J. (2016). What are the health benefits of tai chi? Retrieved from *http://www.medicalnewstoday.com/articles/265507. php#history_of_tai_chi*

Partnership Against Domestic Violence (2017). Retrieved from *http://padv.org/*

Palermo, E. (2015). *Tai chi*. Retrieved from *https://www.livescience.com/38063-tai-chi.html*

Roberts-Lewis, A. C., & Armstrong, T. D. (2010). Moving the church to social action. *Social Work & Christianity, 37*(2), 115-127.

Rock, C. (Producer), HBO Productions (Producer), and Stinson, J. (Director). (2009). *Good hair* [Motion picture]. US: HBO Films.

Thompson, M. J. (1995). *Soul feast: An invitation to the Christian spiritual life*. Louisville, KY: Westminster John Knox Press.

Thompson, V. L. S., Bazile, A., & Akbar, M. (2004). Americans' perceptions of psychotherapy and psychotherapists. *Professional Psychology: Research and Practice, 35*, 19-26.

Trattner, W. (1970). *Crusade for the children: A history of the National Child Labor Committee and child labor reform in America*. Chicago: Quadrangle Books.

Travis, J. W., & Ryan, R. S. (2004). *Wellness workbook: How to achieve enduring health and vitality* (3rd ed.). Berkeley, CA: Celestial Arts.

Tyler, L., & Tyler, R. (2012). *Still standing: In spite of it all, our marriage still stands* [Motion picture]. US: Tyler New Media.

U.S. Department of Health and Human Services (2008). Retrieved from *http://www.health.gov/paguidelines/*

Van Sertima, I., (Ed.). (1984). *Black women in antiquity*. New Brunswick, NJ: Transaction Publishers.

Walker-Barnes, C. (2014). *Too heavy a yoke: Black women and the burden of strength*. Eugene, OR: Cascade Books.

Wallace, M. (1978). *Black macho and the myth of the superwoman.* New York: The Dial Press.

Wang, P. S., Berglund, P. A., & Kessler, R. C. (2003). Patterns and correlates of contacting clergy for mental disorders in the United States. *Health Services Research, 38*(2), 647-673.

Watson, N.F., Badr, M.S., Belenky, G., Bliwise, D. L., Buxton, O. M., Buysse, D.,…Tasali, E. (2015). Joint consensus statement of the American Academy of Sleep Medicine and Sleep Research Society on the recommended amount of sleep for a healthy adult: Methodology and discussion. *Journal of Clinical Sleep Medicine, 11(8),* 931-952. doi: 10.5664/jcsm.4758

Watson, N. N., Black, A. R., & Hunter, C. D. (2016). African American women's perceptions of Mindfulness Meditation Training and gendered race-related stress. *Mindfulness, 7*(5), 1034-1043.

Welsing, F. C. (1991). *The Isis papers: The keys to the colors.* Chicago: Third World Press.

Weis, R., & Speridakos, E. C. (2011). A meta-analysis of hope enhancement strategies in clinical and community settings. *Psychology of Well-Being: Theory, Research and Practice, 8(5),* 1-16.

West, C. M., & Johnson, K. (2013). *Sexual violence in the lives of African American women: Risk, response, and resilience.* VAWnet: The National Online Resource Center on Violence Against Women.

Wiseman, R. (2007). New Year's Resolution Project. Retrieved from *http://www.richardwiseman.com/quirkology/new/USA/Experiment_resolution.shtml*

Woods-Giscombé, C. L., & Gaylord, S. A. (2014). The cultural relevance of mindfulness meditation as a health intervention for African Americans: Implications for reducing stress-related health disparities. *Journal of Holistic Nursing, 32*(3), 147-160.

Appendix A

Reflection Questions for Vignettes

1. What were the life circumstances that caused challenges for the main character?

2. What were the emotional issues that the main character was dealing with? What were the emotional issues that the main character's family and friends were dealing with?

3. What were the social challenges that the main character encountered?

4. What are some different ways that the main character sought to improve her situation? How well did these strategies seem to work?

5. How did the main character's religious and/or spiritual outlook affect her situation?

6. Are there any ways that you can identify with this main character's struggles?

7. What can you learn from the main character's story?

Appendix B

Additional Mental Illness Vignettes

Panic Disorder

"I feel as if my life is about to fall apart," quivered thirty-one-year-old Erica Rogers over the phone that gloomy afternoon. She shared that she had been on the phone for several hours trying to identify a suitable therapist for her concerns. This proved difficult, as many had full caseloads and/or did not accept her private insurance. She carefully inquired about my level of training, my theoretical orientation(s), my years of clinical experience, and my hours of availability. Once I answered her questions to her satisfaction, she was eager to make an appointment.

Erica had recently moved to the area from a large city where she had practiced for several years as a successful investment banker. She had begun graduate school in order to make a career change, and had found herself encountering some transitions that she had not anticipated. First, the relocation had been much more difficult than she expected because it had greatly affected her social life. Moving from a large to a small city meant sacrificing a number of cultural amenities to which she had grown accustomed. Before moving, she had typically been too busy to take advantage of theater, dance, and symphony concerts. Still, she had managed to take in a couple of ballet performances and an international children's choir concert, and was impressed by the world-class quality of the productions. Since moving to this college town, she had taken a less demanding job to tide her over until she started school. Erica found then that she had lots of time on her hands, but not much to do that interested her.

Not that Erica was alone. She'd been married for seven years to Arnold, a highly celebrated, up-and-coming trial attorney. Arnold had been her high school sweetheart, and Erica had never doubted his love... until now. He worked long hours at the office, and Erica had gotten used to their relatively scarce times together. Arnold stated that he was genuinely sorry that he could not spend more time with her, and promised that things would change significantly after he made partner at the new firm. The way things had progressed since they'd moved there, however, meant Erica wasn't holding her breath. She worried constantly about how Arnold was spending his long hours, and wondered whether he was developing feelings for the attractive business partner who had recruited him. On a regular basis, Erica checked his phone for any suspicious calls or texts. More and more, Erica noticed within herself a growing resentment of Arnold's work, his choice to prioritize work, and his increasing emotional distance from her. She was not alone, but she *was* lonely.

Ironically, one very positive contribution that Arnold had made to Erica's life was in nurturing her faith. Erica's parents had been reared in diametrically opposed faith communities, and they decided before they were married that they would not impose either of their belief systems on their children. Instead, they would allow each of their children to choose her own way. As a result, Erica had encountered very few childhood experiences with organized religion and felt quite confused about issues of faith. In contrast to her own religious confusion, Erica had been struck by the calm assurance of Arnold's abiding faith. He had been raised in a Christian home where his parents took seriously their charge to raise their children in a community of believers. They attended Sunday School, Sunday morning worship, and weekly Wednesday night Bible study. They were proud that Arnold continued his involvement in church activities at the collegiate level, joining a campus group that emphasized outreach as well as fellowship. "Raise a child in the way that he should go, and when he is old, he shall not depart from it" was their mantra.

From the time that they first met, Erica noticed Arnold's dedication to his religious activities, but was even more attracted to his innately spiritual demeanor. She noted that his connection to God transcended his faith claims and religious attendance. Arnold practiced the principles of Christ in his every interaction and decision. His gentleness and serenity were always a great comfort to Erica. Some of Erica's own convictions regarding women's reproductive rights and rights for persons across the sexuality spectrum made her suspicious of organized religion, but through Arnold she was drawn to Christianity and had begun to attend worship with him shortly after they married. She had just joined Arnold's church nine months before they moved. Leaving behind the rhythms of worship at their church, her church family, and the spiritual mentors who had nourished the seeds of her newborn faith was much harder than she had anticipated.

Additionally, Erica's distance from her support system was difficult for her to bear. She had lived in the previous city nearly all of her life, and had accumulated friendships from her church, community, secondary school, and college. She had not always been meticulous about keeping in touch with her friends when they were close by, and found the dynamics of long-distance friendships to be frustrating. Moreover, her friends were less likely to keep in touch with her, as their own lives had gotten busier with greater job and family responsibilities. As she and Arnold did not have children, she felt more intensely the sting of her friends' unintended neglect.

Erica's relationships with her parents were another story. Her parents had divorced during her childhood, following her father Karl's incessant verbal and emotional abuse of her mother. Though Erica remained with her mother Margaret from ages nine to eighteen, she encountered increasing conflicts with her mother as she entered adolescence. She resented her mother for not standing up to her father's abuse, and was frustrated that her mother had not done more with her life. As Erica excelled in her studies during middle and high school, she began to adopt a condescending attitude toward her mother. That Margaret had been diagnosed years earlier with an anxiety disorder only exacerbated Erica's dim view of her mother's capacities. Their conflicts culminated in Erica moving in with her father for two years during adolescence. Her father was extremely critical of Erica, which resulted in a negative relational cycle between them. Karl would insist upon Erica's best performance in everything she did. Following the smallest infraction, Karl would berate and denigrate Erica, no matter who was around. Erica would redouble her efforts to meet her father's exceedingly high expectations, only to disappoint him again and again. Toward the end of her time living with him, Erica had begun to express her anger at her father's impossible standards. As a result, Erica reluctantly spent her senior year of high school living again with her mother.

Since marrying Arnold three years after college, her relationships with her parents had become more civil. She spent less time engaged with them and had fewer issues about which to disagree. However, when Erica would discover that her mother had begun missing work again due to her fear of being in public (i.e., agoraphobia), or when her father would insist that Erica send him a complimentary airline ticket for the holidays, Erica felt transported right back into the tempestuous throes of her adolescence.

Despite having fewer job demands, Erica reported having consistent difficulty with sleep. She was responsible for creating presentations for the small business firm's marketing arm, an area of expertise that she'd developed within investment banking. Even though she probably could have developed these presentations in her sleep, she was ironically deprived of sleep on many occasions while creating them. Erica was often acutely aware of what her various constituencies would think about her presentation: Would it be well received by their clients? Would it seem sophisticated enough for her peers and managers? Would everyone expect more from someone with a track record in investment banking? At first, Erica would awaken around 2 am and worry about many details of the presentation into which she'd already poured hours. After about 90 minutes, she would go back to sleep, only to awaken again around 5 am. After a few months, Erica simply began to get up at the first waking and work on the project at hand. Sometimes, she would go back to bed after two to three hours; sometimes, she would simply stay up, striving to do her best with less than three hours of sleep. On days when she would make presentations to her team, she would experience symptoms of heart palpitations, sweaty palms, shortness of breath, and stomach upset, but these issues usually subsided after her presentation was finished.

Seven months after her move, Erica began graduate school, which further aggravated her anxiety. She was very excited at the opportunity to formally pursue a different career direction in psychiatric epidemiology, yet was immediately beset with other cumbersome concerns: How could she complete the overwhelming volume of assignments? Did she really have the requisite skills to succeed in a doctoral program? Did she have the acumen and the stamina to be competitive with her younger peers? Had she been accepted into the program because of her talents, or because of the program's affirmative action policies? With much trepidation, she launched into her work. From the start, she received positive feedback from her professors, who said that she was exceptionally bright and visibly passionate about her research. She found her professors and mentors reasonably accessible, and met with them frequently to ensure that she understood the objectives and parameters of each assignment. Erica worked assiduously on each assignment, yet began to fall further and further behind as she sought to perfect each task. Plus, she'd begun to have panic attacks. Erica would feel like she was having a heart attack, with tingling sensations in her arms, great difficulty in getting her breath, and feeling as if she were losing her mind. Eventually, Erica became more and more afraid that she would have a panic attack in class and blow her cover with her classmates and professors. Sensing her uneasiness, most professors graciously extended their deadlines, which unexpectedly initiated a negative domino effect throughout the remainder of the semester for Erica. By the time finals were over, Erica was exhausted from the work. Instead of feeling relieved, like most of her peers, Erica was even more anxious about completing work from her previous job that she'd promised to make up at the end of the semester. Thus, despite high marks across all of her classes, Erica was wondering out loud whether she needed to return to school for the following semester.

Erica perceived that her family was not much help in answering this question. Arnold had always been very proud of Erica's accomplishments and supportive of her ambition and career pursuits. Still, he had witnessed Erica navigate what appeared to be sheer torture throughout the semester, and he could scarcely imagine three or four more years of the same. Erica dismissed his concerns, suspecting that Arnold might secretly want to divert any threats to his celebrity status within the family.

Margaret had never understood her daughter's ambitions for attending college, let alone entering the investment world and going to graduate school. She would have preferred that Erica return home to a much richer support system. Erica knew that following her mother's wishes would give Margaret much greater peace of mind; however, Erica was also deeply suspicious of the extent to which she would become entangled in enabling her mother's avoidance of more and more social situations. Karl, on the other hand, was still grappling to understand why Erica had left such a lucrative career in investment banking in the first place. Although his financial support of Erica's college costs had varied unpredictably, Karl always specified that the funds he did provide were given to maximize her earning potential, not to promote a personally satisfying career. The last thing Erica wanted to hear from him was "I told you so."

Therefore, Erica came to a pivotal decision. She was fairly certain that pursuing this degree was the only way that she could fully engage her vocational aspirations. Moreover, she did not want to face humiliation by explaining to her friends and family that she had decided to discontinue her program, a decision that would seem incomprehensible in light of her stellar grades. Nevertheless, Erica knew that she could not continue to function as a victim of her anxiety for the remainder of her program. Erica knew that God was with her, but felt too tentative in her fairly new faith commitment to understand *how* God would make it all work together for good. She was convinced that working around the clock in relentless pursuit of perfection in her work would destroy her marriage with Arnold (especially given her perspective that she was the glue holding it together, anyway) and would consume her physically, emotionally, and spiritually. Something had to give... Erica picked up the phone and reached out for professional help.

Major Symptoms of Panic Disorder

- Repeated panic attacks (featuring heart palpitations, sweating, shortness of breath, chest pain, nausea, dizziness, fear of losing control, and so forth)
- Worry about having more panic attacks
- Changes in behavior to avoid having panic attacks

How Psychotherapy Helped Erica

Early on in her therapeutic work, Erica was diagnosed with Panic Disorder, which helped her therapist identify the most appropriate treatment interventions for her. Erica learned how to practice deep breathing, progressive muscle relaxation, and other stress management strategies to decrease her levels of anxiety. She discovered a way to monitor and to change her self-defeating thoughts so that she could maximize her success in her grad school program. Erica also benefitted from an increased understanding of the relational dynamics between her and each of her parents, and learned how to better navigate her relationships with them through a combination of compassion and assertiveness skills. Therapy gave Erica the clarity she needed to identify and move forward with her own priorities, not just those articulated by her parents. She and her therapist explored the ways that her faith provided a foundation for her every endeavor, a healthy structure for living her life in a godly fashion, and concrete guidance for handling her challenges as she encountered them. It was ultimately her faith, along with her therapist's support, that gave Erica the courage to invite Arnold into marriage therapy to better communicate her concerns and to rely on their mutual faith as an anchor for staying together, not out of duty, but in pursuit of joy.

Borderline Personality Disorder

Keesha, age 27, was raised in a family as the third of four children. Her parents divorced when she was seven, and many changes occurred in her life that year. Her father moved across the country and rarely had any contact with the family. Her mother, unable to support her children on her own, moved back home with her aging parents to a small town that offered no viable job opportunities. Thus, Keesha's mother commuted two hours each day to maintain her job in middle management at a tech company. Keesha started a new school in the middle of the school year and felt that she was never able to make friends with her peers, almost all of whom had lived in that town all their lives and accused Keesha of thinking that she was better than them. Even worse, Keesha's peers began to bully her for her urban accent and her chocolate-toned skin. At home, Keesha rarely saw her mother, and when she did see her, her mother was often tired from the long commute and from striving to meet the incessant deadlines imposed by her boss. Her grandparents, not at all thrilled at the prospect of so many "bad" (read: grieving) kids living under their roof again, were often mean and bitter. When Keesha fell short of completing a chore according to her grandmother's specifications, Keesha would often hear her grandmother mutter under her breath, "Mmm hmm…ya jes lazy, just like yo daddy!" Based on the messages she received from both adults and other kids, Keesha felt that the grief she experienced over so many losses (e.g., her father's presence, her mother's attention, her home and hometown) was not legitimate, and that she needed to "get over it." Additionally, many in her family would denigrate her for her looks, whether it was her skin color, her hair, her body shape, or her facial features:

"It sho is a shame you didn't get your great-grandmother's silky locks. She was half-Indian, you know."

"Chile, when you gone stop growing? You got hips for days!"

"Wear your hat when you go down to the mailbox—you can't afford to get any darker!"

As she matured from adolescence into adulthood, Keesha learned that although she was naturally shy, she could get more of what she wanted in her relationships by making demands, especially if the demands were draped with dramatic flair. Viewed by some as manipulative, Keesha would make statements to her friends that would virtually leave them feeling guilty for needing to end a two-hour-long phone call with her, or for wanting to go home after hanging out with her for most of the day.

Additionally, Keesha often interpreted events in her life in extreme ways. For example, if she were dating someone new, he could be the best thing since sliced bread one day, and the very next day, he might be the devil himself. Most of her boyfriends quickly tired of this intensity in relationships with her. She even had a similar impact on her choir director. Keesha would either be raving about the high caliber of the songs they were learning, or would be murmuring about every single detail that was not in place: having the wrong soloist, or the conductor messing up on the second verse, or the A-V system compromising the quality of their sound.

When she was in a very low mood, Keesha would warn others that she was thinking about harming herself, telling herself that "nobody will miss me when I'm gone." Deep in her heart, Keesha knew that

God loved her, because she'd always heard this message at church. However, in moments of despair, God felt very distant from her. *Yes, God is a loving God,* she thought, *but God doesn't really love me.*

At first, loved ones took her threats of self-harm very seriously. They would stay with her all night to make sure that her knives were out of her reach and that all prescription medication was secured. Once, when Keesha actually did overdose on Tylenol, a friend accompanied her to the hospital and reached out to her loved ones to ensure continual presence of support. However, when Keesha made several more attempts that year, friends and family alike became weary and suspected that they were simply being jerked around. Even though her behavior was eroding her social life and endangering her work, Keesha would tell even her closest friends that the problem was other people, not her. She would point out her virtues of intelligence and qualities of learning new skills. Although she was devastated inside by her loneliness, she would bluntly tell others, "Y'all can love me or leave me!"

Just when she thought that she was done with dating, Keesha met Keith at the hospital where she worked as a clinic receptionist. He worked at the hospital's computer support help desk and would occasionally troubleshoot computer issues in her clinic. They started dating, and although Keith found Keesha quirky at first, he was mesmerized by her beauty and appreciated her fun qualities. After eight months of dating, they became officially engaged. Keith became increasingly confused about Keesha's erratic behavior. She would suddenly become angry with him over seemingly small issues and would impulsively kick him out of her apartment. A day to two later, she would reach out to him, full of apologies and affirmations of how much she loved him. This cycle continued for months. Only after Keith threatened to end their engagement did Keesha agree to see a psychotherapist. After an extended assessment during which I took a careful psychosocial history, examined her family history, and with her permission spoke privately with Keith, Keesha was diagnosed with Borderline Personality Disorder.

Major Symptoms of Borderline Personality Disorder

- Unstable relationships, self-image, and feelings
- Desperate attempts to avoid abandonment
- Alternating between strong feelings of love and hate
- Impulsive, self-damaging behaviors
- Intense feelings of emptiness, anger, sadness, or anxiety
- Paranoid thoughts and feelings under stress

How Psychotherapy Helped Keesha

In Keesha's case, an empirically validated treatment had been formulated for her particular mental illness—Borderline Personality Disorder. Dialectical Behavior Therapy, or DBT (Linehan, 2015), has a series of modules that helped Keesha develop effective skills in four areas: mindfulness, emotion regulation, interpersonal effectiveness, and distress tolerance. While she learned these skills primarily through a DBT group, Keesha was connected with an individual therapist who also had knowledge of DBT skills and who worked collaboratively with her group therapists. Keesha's development of skills in these areas helped her to respond better in situations where she felt invalidated, gave her better control of her emotions, and increased the quality of her relationships, especially her courtship and eventual marriage to Keith.

Conduct Disorder

"We just told Violet on the way here that she was coming to you, and she told us that she's not talking." This was the news I received during my initial appointment with sixteen-year-old Violet Durante and her parents, Edward and Anne. For the last seven years, Ed had been senior pastor of the local community church, and his wife Anne was a schoolteacher and a dedicated leader of the church's women's ministry. Besides Violet, they had two younger children: Fred, a twelve-year-old soccer player and budding trumpeter, and eight-year-old Brittany, a feisty gymnast and self-proclaimed fashionista. I'd invited the entire family to attend the first appointment, but Fred had band practice. After all, the appointment had been scheduled rather abruptly. Violet's teacher had discovered Violet smoking marijuana in the bathroom with two other friends during second period. Violet already had two instances of out-of-school suspensions for fighting at school and skipping class, not to mention a long string of in-school suspensions for tardiness and defiance of teachers. This latest violation, which carried the threat of expulsion, came on the heels of Anne's discovery of Violet's journal, which revealed the lurid details of Violet's sexual promiscuity and "bicurious" adventures in sexual experimentation with males and females in her underground clique. Sadly, Violet had already been expelled from the traditional high school in her community and had been transferred five months earlier to an alternative school. Thus, her parents were deeply troubled by this most recent development, for it signaled the possibility that Violet would potentially be placed in a residential treatment program approximately two hours away.

Ed and Anne were taken completely by surprise with the emergence of Violet's misbehavior over the last four years. As a child, Violet was sometimes headstrong but always attentive to the needs of others. She was an extremely helpful big sister and an eager participant in all of the children's programs of their church at that time, where Ed had been the assistant pastor of missions and evangelism. She was especially kind toward young children and animals, and spent many hours volunteering at the local animal shelter. She'd always told her family that she wanted to become a veterinarian and start a program matching children in poverty with abandoned animals. As an academically gifted student, her pursuit of these ambitious goals seemed reasonable, even natural.

There seemed to be some shift in Violet's attitude when the Durantes moved from Orangeville to another state so that Ed could accept the pastorate at a medium-sized church, but the family attributed Violet's behavioral changes to the hassles of relocation and to the addition of baby sister Brittany to the family. As a sixth grader, Violet was more reticent about making friends at her new school and in their neighborhood. She once expressed her irritation to her mother that other kids didn't want to play with her because they didn't want her snitching on them. The primary mission of Ed's church was reconciliation, and as a result, the church engaged an ethnically and socio-economically diverse congregation, a bold move in that historically segregated city. It was likely that the community's adults possessed distrust of, even opposition to, this "social experiment," an attitude not lost on their children.

Less than a year after the Durante family moved away from Orangeville, they received word that Ed's mother had fallen gravely ill. She was diagnosed with end-stage ovarian cancer and was given two weeks to live. Ed returned home immediately, but the rest of the family was not able to return before Grandma Lynn died, just five days after her grim prognosis. As the oldest grandchild, Violet had been intensely doted on by Grandma Lynn, and immediately felt the impact of this profound loss.

Although everyone in the family attended the funeral, Violet felt invisible at the service. Ed insisted on preaching his mother's eulogy, and after the flurry of casseroles, flowers, and sympathy cards that were shared during the week leading up to the funeral, it seemed that life abruptly went back to "business as usual," at least for everyone other than Violet. Ed was especially busy in the weeks and months following his mother's death, and she found her own mother to be frequently preoccupied with pursuing state certification and competency in a new area of teaching. Violet noticed that Fred and Brittany didn't seem to "get" that Grandma Lynn was gone forever, so she thought that her lingering feelings of sadness, disappointment, and resentment meant that there was something wrong with her.

During Violet's sixth grade year, Ed and Anne noticed that her grades began to drop. Even though Violet's new school was more academically rigorous than her previous school, they were confident of Violet's aptitude and felt that she was becoming lazy. Teachers occasionally reported that Violet was not fully attentive in class; furthermore, she frequently failed to turn in her homework. Considering the adjustments Violet had to make to middle school, Ed and Anne reasoned that Violet would stabilize during the second grading period. Instead, they began to receive reports that Violet was talking excessively in class and being disrespectful and noncompliant with teachers.

Before they knew it, Violet had become sullen and withdrawn at home. She spent much of her time at home in her room, and even though she was not allowed to close her door, she figured out how to rig a secluded "cave" within her "pigsty," as her mother often called it. Both Ed and Anne grew up in an era when their parents firmly believed in the doctrine of "spare the rod and spoil the child." They differed with this child-rearing philosophy on several grounds, namely because they wanted Violet to internalize the right motivation for behaving well. With each month of growing desperation, however, they both found themselves questioning this decision. They once found one of Violet's "friends" sneaking into her room in the wee hours of the morning. Even after removing all of Violet's many privileges for a month, her bold, entrenched defiance seemed indifferent to these negative consequences and to the embarrassment inflicted on her family. During one truant episode, Violet was discovered shoplifting condoms at the neighborhood convenience store. The store pressed charges, and even Ed's powerful position in the community did not prevent a conviction. Fortunately, Violet was sentenced to 200 hours of community service, which she was able to fulfill at an animal shelter.

Violet seemed to be reformed in the weeks following her conviction; however, her parents painfully discovered that her exploits slowly but surely returned. By this point, Ed had become convinced and increasingly vocal that Violet was bound and determined to "chase sin." Growing up as the son of a pastor, he recalled the pressures of being a preacher's kid, or "PK," as his peers nicknamed him. To relieve these pressures, he had often stepped into the role of the class clown, a role not often appreciated by his teachers. Ed was often sent to detention, but his parents saw to it that he would never misbehave to the extent of being suspended. Even after he graduated from high school as a mediocre student, he was able to matriculate at a reasonably respected college. Looking back, he reckoned that he'd had his share of "devilment," but was able to get through college without any significant challenges. Besides, he'd begun to clean up his act during his junior year after he met Anne. He could always hear his father's words echoing in his ear: "Ed, he who finds a good wife finds a good thing and obtains favor from the Lord."

Anne was a beautiful, smart, and talented young woman whose reputation preceded her. She was an early childhood education major who came from a long line of teachers. Her family members, of modest means, were hailed as hardworking, salt-of-the-earth paragons in their working-class community. Anne learned the values of faith, determination, and sacrifice from her paternal and maternal forebears, and was raised in a community where she assumed that everyone embraced the same values. Cow tipping was the worst offense anyone ever heard of in her community, carried out by only the most hardened of rascals. Among her small high school class of sixty students, everyone graduated according to schedule, and only a handful of students sidestepped societal expectations to continue their training or education through college, trade school, the military, or by assuming the responsibilities of a family business.

Unlike several of her counterparts, Anne did not attend the state college with the chief intent of obtaining her "MRS" degree. Just as she ambitiously pursued her bachelor's degree, she brought a high level of seriousness to every task and expected others to do the same. Ed perceived her organized focus immediately during the English course they shared and viewed her high expectations as positive during their courtship. After college graduation, Anne's philosophy

of life continued to motivate her to do what she was "supposed to do."
She married Ed (both because she loved him, and because she didn't
want to "burn with lust for him"); took a job as an English teacher;
eventually had three children; served as the "go-to" person in her
family; and served her church faithfully as Sunday School teacher,
facilitator of countless outreach projects, and ultimately, First Lady.
She found herself increasingly exhausted by wearing so many hats,
but firmly believed in and anticipated her heavenly reward.

Thus, Ed and Anne's own experiences, even those in ministry, had
not adequately prepared them for Violet's extreme misbehavior.
Violet's baptism at age fourteen was their only consolation during
an otherwise hopeless period. Both parents experienced seemingly
endless embarrassment over Violet's wrongdoing. They desired to
protect her physiologically from the consequences of substance
use and premature sexual activity. They hoped that her flirtations
with crime were over and would not lead to a permanent criminal
record or incarceration. They worried constantly about how her current choices were constraining her future educational and vocational
options. They wondered whether she could rebound morally from the
long-term consequences of acting out. Furthermore, they often faced
the very pragmatic concerns of how to identify educational alternatives for her; how to secure the house to prevent future "break-ins"
and escapes; how to allow Violet continued opportunities for positive socialization without further exposure to the deviant behavior
of the underground clique; how to prevent Violet's behavior from
negatively influencing her younger siblings, the youngest of whom
had already begun to adopt some of Violet's "attitude" in interacting
with her parents.

Ed soon realized the extent of his prior blindness to parents in similar
circumstances in the church. He'd often preached about the wages
of sin as death and had implored young people to obey their parents.
Ed had even counseled many families about "taking their burdens to
Jesus" and had held fervent family prayers for the repentance of way-
ward teens. He'd never stopped to consider that youth misbehavior

was more complex than choosing obedience over disobedience and confessing one's sins.

For her part, Anne had not recognized the extent to which her own misbehaving students in the past were not always simply the products of an uncaring, disorganized home. Although their personality styles had always differed, Anne loved Violet deeply and appreciated the young woman she was becoming, at least before all of the misbehavior. Anne felt that Violet was so very far away, and more than anything, she wanted the real Violet to come home.

Just as she promised, Violet was silent during today's initial session—at least verbally—when her parents were present. Her disdain for both her parents and the counseling process was readily apparent from her constant eye-rolling, teeth-sucking, and her choice to sit on the opposite side of the room from everyone else. She glared at her parents, particularly when they made attempts to interpret her behavior. She simply looked off when Brittany described what things were like at home.

When I asked to speak privately with Violet, however, another side of Violet emerged. After a few minutes of breaking the ice, Violet acknowledged that she regretted that she had caused her family so much pain, and acknowledged her own confusion about why she continued to behave against her better judgment. Violet discussed the deep mistrust that she experienced as a result of her mother having read her journal. She expressed anger over her family's relocation several years earlier and a deep sadness over the loss of her grandmother as well as the symptoms of Alzheimer's Disease that her grandfather was now experiencing. Violet perceived that her past misbehaviors had brought on a complete destruction of her parents' trust, which she could comprehend at some level, but felt that her actions had established an irrevocable chasm between them. She felt that she could do no right, and had essentially stopped trying. Violet confided that she had already begun to explore her options for achieving emancipated minor status. She wanted a clean start, one where she could pursue her GED, get a full-time job at the pet shop, and perhaps study animal science at the community college. She and a friend from the alternative school had talked about finding an apartment in the next town over where she wouldn't have to be bothered by her parents or community members from their church. As she shared her life vision, and even after all the Durantes had been through, I was impressed by how desperately Violet wanted to fight for her dreams.

Major Symptoms of Conduct Disorder

- Threatening or starting fights with others
- Physical cruelty to people or animals
- Use of weapons
- Destroying others' property
- Lying
- Stealing
- Staying out past curfew
- Running from home
- Skipping school

How Psychotherapy Helped the Durantes

My work with the Durante family was consistent with research demonstrating that the best form of treatment intervention for youth with conduct problems is a combination of family therapy and individual therapy. At the family level, helping each member of the family to listen to and express their feelings in a safe, structured place was a key ingredient that laid the groundwork for later problem solving. Given their shared stressors of living in the limelight of ministry and shared experiences of grief, encouraging each member of the family to be transparent in these areas eventually helped to build some mutual compassion. Individually, it was important for Violet to vent about her stressors in a nonjudgmental atmosphere, but also to build practical skills for moving forward into young adulthood. Once she acknowledged the extent of her substance use and abuse and learned that effective and culturally sensitive treatments were available, Violet received and followed through with a referral to an addictions specialist. Also, individual psychotherapy became the space for her to explore her grief, not only for her Grandma Lynn, but also the anticipatory grief that was rising as she witnessed Grandpa Leonard's decline. Finally, providing psychoeducation about Violet's vocational options relieved some of the anxiety commonly felt by late adolescents launching into the world. Violet began to believe again that despite her past negative choices, God still had a hopeful future in store for her.

Grief

From all indications, 41-year-old Aniya Henderson was a model Christian. She was an associate minister at a small church in a rural community that had until recently denied women the opportunity to speak from the pulpit. Thus, she was a "first generational" clergywoman whose comportment was critical. Moving to Smithboro eleven years ago, coming from another small community about 40 miles away, provided yet another reason for having much to prove. Nevertheless, Aniya was up to the challenge. She was an attractive, educated young woman whose seminary education and multiple spiritual gifts finally convinced her pastor that she would be a good fit for his ministerial staff. Aniya was well-spoken, featured excellent administrative skills, and demonstrated a genuine caring, calming spirit toward all.

If anything, Aniya proved to be too helpful to her congregation. She was very active with several ministries and frequently placed the needs of church members ahead of her own. Not only was she involved with the Board of Christian Education, but she also chaired the ministry to aid the sick, and often served as the worship leader. Her pastor often cautioned her to remember that her first ministry was to her family; moreover, her husband Raymond, while extremely understanding, became firmer in his insistence that she protect family time. After all, they had a six-year-old daughter to raise and were expecting another child in a few months. Still, Aniya loved staying busy with the work of the church, and would have been content to maintain her hectic pace were it not for two life-changing events: she miscarried, and six weeks later, her mother died.

About 13 months after the miscarriage, Aniya sought psychotherapy for these losses, particularly after having success in her and Raymond's attempts to conceive again. Understandably, Aniya was anxious about this latest pregnancy, especially during the second trimester, which was when she lost her previous child to a vague medical abnormality. Because of her high visibility in the congregation, she recognized that she would not be entirely successful in avoiding questions about being pregnant. However, each question would raise the pain of the previous loss as well as the possibility of another.

Aniya also struggled to make sense of what she considered a senseless loss, in light of her long-lived faith. She had always strived to live a righteous life; in fact, she had a reputation within her family for being, more favorably, a paragon of virtue; or less favorably, a "Goody Two-Shoes." Although she was the youngest of three children in her family, she functioned as the ever-responsible oldest child. Aniya had become accustomed to her role of bailing her sister out of financial disasters and lecturing her brother following his frequent relapses back into substance abuse.

While she had preached many times on never seeing the righteous forsaken, she had certainly felt forsaken after the miscarriage. It was months after we'd begun our work together that Aniya made a surprising disclosure: she had been raped by a family member at age 17, had conceived a child during this painful episode, and had passively acquiesced with her mother's plan for her to have an abortion. Even after twenty-three years, the shame she felt for this string of events was palpable. Although she understood intellectually that she was not to blame for the rape, she still wondered whether she had contributed to her misfortune in some small way. She felt further traumatized by having lost her virginity so violently, and to someone who was presumably trustworthy.

Then there were her thoughts about the abortion. Both her community church while growing up and her current church were staunchly opposed to abortion. Under the circumstances of her life at that time, Aniya and her mother had both agreed that giving birth to the child would significantly limit what appeared to all to be a bright future for Aniya. How would she explain the pregnancy? How would she avoid bringing further shame to the family if she revealed the perpetrator? How could she bear the constant reminder of her rape in that young child's eyes? Still, Aniya continually felt guilty about the "murder of her child," despite many, many prayers for forgiveness over the years. Some small part of her wondered whether the miscarriage had been a physiological, even a moral, consequence of the abortion she had undergone at age 17. Hadn't she always heard that abortions contributed to fertility challenges later in life? Had God been judging her for what some thought of as murder?

Although Aniya had only revealed her pregnant status weeks earlier to a few church members, news spread quickly, which she perceived as a joyous and excited response to her news. Thus, announcing the news of the miscarriage had been extremely difficult. Aniya felt that there was no adequate or proper forum for discussing miscarriage in the church, or other birth-related issues, for that matter. That reality, combined with her ambivalent feelings and interpretations of the event, resulted in her decision not to make a public announcement. It was not uncommon, then, for Aniya to unexpectedly find herself giving explanations many months following the miscarriage. The pain, not only of the loss, but also of the constant, one-on-one, shocking disclosures, left Aniya feeling that she was often in a hypervigilant mode.

Just as Aniya sensed that the pain of the miscarriage was beginning to subside, her mother Sandra died very abruptly of a heart attack. Aniya had always been very close to her mother, even though their relationship was sometimes strained by what Aniya perceived as her mother's poor choices in relationships. While Aniya's grandmother and mother had raised her in the church, Aniya had always been dismayed by Sandra's cavalier attitude toward attending church and actively practicing her faith. This attitude was particularly apparent to Aniya in Sandra's dating relationships. Since divorcing Aniya's father when Aniya was three years old, Sandra had paraded a string of boy-friends through their lives, many of whom moved into the home for months at a time. Even from Aniya's young eyes, it was obvious that many of these temporary dwellers were little more than convenient companions. Nevertheless, Sandra was the only consistent caregiver in Aniya's life, and they were closely attached. In recent years, Sandra had grown increasingly financially dependent on Aniya, yet showed a desire to build an authentic relationship with Christ. In fact, Sandra had just begun attending Aniya's church on a regular basis.

In helping Aniya to understand the depth of her pain, I noted for her that this very sudden loss had not only triggered her memories of her loss of the child, but had also triggered the loss of her very first child through abortion. Aniya felt very much alone in all of these losses. She had only shared news of the abortion with Raymond, and many years later, with me; thus, this early loss and its related issues were invisible to would-be supporters. A few more people, including her co-workers, knew about the miscarriage, but many did not know what to say to Aniya about this loss. They wondered,

"Did she consider the fetus a child?"

"Would everything be all right again if she simply conceived and had another baby?"

"Given Aniya's advanced age, had this baby been planned?"

"If it wasn't planned, was it really a loss?"

While the death of Sandra was Aniya's most "legitimized" grief, many friends and peers from work and church seemed very awkward in expressing their support during Aniya's grief. First, some were confused about whether Aniya was actually experiencing grief. They knew that she must have been sad about losing her mother, but they also rationalized that her identity as a minister of the gospel must keep her focused on the hope of the resurrection, even eager that her mother had joined Jesus in heaven, resulting in a triumphant "Death, where is thy sting?" outlook. Second, onlookers pondered to themselves, "What words of comfort do you provide for a minister who is usually doing the comforting?" People were used to her providing care and comfort for them, not the other way around. In fact, some could acknowledge to themselves that they were none too comfortable with drawing close to the humanness of their clergy. Other clergy in her church and community knew the pain of isolation in the name of faith and had organized to send flowers for the funeral, yet in their busy-ness, only a couple had offered calls, cards, visits, or other forms of tangible or sustained support. In not knowing what to say, they simply said nothing, which only intensified Aniya's experience of grief.

Characteristics of Grief

- A normal response to the loss of someone or something that has touched our hearts
- May be in response to death or to other types of loss
- Painful
- Isolating
- A range of feelings including sadness, anger, disappointment, guilt, and regret
- A process, not an event
- Experienced by all creatures
- May be anticipatory, disenfranchised, or complicated

How Psychotherapy Helped Aniya

Aniya's grief was not a form of psychopathology. Rather, her grief was a normal response to the losses of her first child to abortion, her second child to miscarriage, and her mother to a heart attack. Psychotherapy provided the safe and confidential space for Aniya to share her secretive stories, the details of which she'd never discussed before at any length. Aniya was able to process how she felt about her experiences and to engage in "real talk" about how her feelings may have differed from the theological or familial messages she'd heard all of her life. Additionally, she received emotional support for how she really felt rather than succumbing to pressures to maintain her stoicism. As Aniya became relieved of the burdens of her secrets and the sharpest pains of her loss, she was able to serve God, her family, and her church in a more authentic way.

Posttraumatic Stress Disorder (PTSD) Resulting from Child Sexual Abuse

"Khadijah needs your help." Her aunt sounded desperate, yet resolved, in the voicemail she left for me one dreary February afternoon. After confirming that she was the legal guardian and could thusly consent to treatment, I learned from Lucille Johnson that she had recently been awarded physical custody of her twelve-year-old niece, Khadijah, and Khadijah's older sister, Katrina. While sixteen-year-old Katrina had decided that she did not desire to abide by the rules of her aunt and uncle's household and was pursuing status as an emancipated minor, Khadijah was glad to be away from her home. For one thing, the house was crowded. Her father, Aunt Lucille's brother, was somewhat connected to his children, but not present in the household. Frank had never been married to Khadijah's mother, Toni, although they had three children together. He had a history of substance abuse and incarcerations for felony drug convictions, and now was primarily involved in transitory day labor. Frank showed up in their lives erratically. When he was involved, he was very involved, but as the saying goes, when he was bad, he was horrid. He would provide child support for months at a time, spend time with the children after school, and even moved back into the home a few times when the children were younger. However, his absence far outweighed his sporadic presence. Although he had been incarcerated twice for drug possession and distribution, Frank was more likely to be living on the streets of their urban setting.

One morning on the way to school, Katrina and Khadijah saw, from their school bus window, their father passed out on a street corner. One of the neighborhood kids recognized him immediately and began to taunt the sisters about their "crack daddy." By the time Katrina was eleven, she had written her father off altogether and explicitly encouraged her siblings to do the same.

Prior to moving in with Aunt Lucille, Khadijah, Katrina, and their two younger siblings, Frankie and Zora, had lived in the home with their mother, in addition to her mother's best friend, Diane, and Diane's two children, Josh and Kelsye. The presence of so many persons overwhelmed the two-bedroom apartment, let alone the psyche of each person there. There was rarely enough space, enough food, or enough peace and quiet for Khadijah, who was an introvert who craved solitude.

Toni worked two jobs just to make ends meet. Toni had dropped out of school after becoming pregnant at fifteen years of age. (What few people knew was that Toni had been raped and impregnated by her mother's boyfriend. Only after severe ostracism did Toni report the rape to her mother. Much to Toni's chagrin, her mother replied, "Don't you ever speak a word of this to anyone! As long as Pete is paying the bills, he's staying right here. You, on the other hand, can get the hell outta my house, with your fast self!")

Despite her hard work living on her own as a single mother and working in the fast food industry, Toni had not been able to develop job skills that could command a job paying much more than minimum wage. Thus, Toni was gone from the home during first and second shifts and relied on her friend Diane to provide supervision for their children in her absence.

Unfortunately, Diane had her own distractions and had perpetrated the worst forms of abuse and neglect. Khadijah later reported that Diane would crowd all of the minors into one bedroom and refuse them food and access to the restroom. Diane was physically and emotionally intimidating, so the children were hesitant to reveal to their mother what they endured. Furthermore, the children had good reason to believe that their mother would not believe them because she was aligned with Diane. Khadijah had witnessed, on three different occasions, a sexual relationship between Toni and Diane, even though neither publicly identified as lesbian. Perhaps because of Diane's dominant personality, she gained control of the household fairly quickly and exercised decision-making over much of their lives, even assuming control of Toni's finances. Yes, it seemed that Diane was preoccupied with abusing power in Toni's household.

Unfortunately, physical, emotional, and financial abuse were not the only forms of maltreatment occurring. It was discovered much too late that Khadijah was being sexually abused by Diane's sixteen-year-old son, Josh. The abuse had begun with occasional fondling, but quickly escalated to full-blown intercourse occurring three to four times per week, on average. This pattern repeated for eight months before Khadijah told her mother about the abuse. Toni responded by asking Khadijah what she was doing to invite Josh's unwanted advances and by reminding Khadijah that the family needed Diane's family's share of the rent money to stay afloat. Because of their close relationship, Khadijah ultimately confided in her Aunt Lucille, who immediately involved Child Protective Services (CPS) of the county office of the Department of Social Services (DSS).

Upon investigation, CPS substantiated the abuse and removed Khadijah from the home. Lucille, who was understood by herself as well as other family members to be the most financially and psychologically stable, agreed to accept Khadijah and Katrina into her home. Lucille was quickly villainized by Toni, who suggested that Lucille only volunteered to take in Khadijah to collect a check from foster care. Khadijah and her sibling were then torn between a constant but ultimately neglectful mother who insisted upon their allegiance and a historically resourceful but demonized aunt who dared to speak up.

During my intake session with Khadijah, I observed what appeared to be inappropriate affect. She smiled nervously as her aunt reported on the history of her abuse. Her aunt reiterated her commitment to keeping Khadijah safe while emphasizing that it was not her objective to achieve permanent legal custody of Khadijah, contrary to what Diane and some other family members had suggested. Aunt Lucille noted that since Khadijah had been in her custody, that Khadijah had been performing well at school but had difficulty following instructions at her home. Furthermore, Lucille had an eight-year-old daughter, Grace, with whom Khadijah often argued. Lucille wanted to know what could be done to help Khadijah become more respectful of her and Grace and more compliant with household rules. Moreover, remarked Aunt Lucille, she understood me to be a woman of faith and hoped that I would be respectful, even encouraging, of their Christian faith that she articulated as the source of their stability in the midst of many trying circumstances throughout the family's history. Aunt Lucille was praying that Khadijah would be healed from this traumatic situation.

As we spoke privately, Khadijah revealed significant ambivalence and a great range of emotions. While she was grateful for what she perceived as her Aunt Lucille's "rescue" of her and her sister from the abusive situation (for Khadijah suspected that Katrina, too, had been sexually abused by Josh), she acknowledged a deep sadness in being separated from the rest of her family. Khadijah felt angry that Josh had violated her and angry that her mother put the family's financial needs before her own needs for safety. Further, Khadijah was frustrated that her mother had not been more protective before the fact of the abuse, or more supportive after the fact. Khadijah shared with me her perspective that her mother was putting her relationship with Diane and their financial needs before Khadijah.

Major Symptoms of Posttraumatic Stress Disorder

- Exposure to death, serious injury, or sexual violence through direct experience, witnessing the event, learning that the event happened to a closed loved one, or repeated exposure to negative details of the traumatic event
- Repeated and negative memories of the traumatic event
- Dreams or nightmares related to the traumatic event
- Flashbacks during which it seems that the traumatic event is happening again
- Bodily and emotional reactions to internal or external cues connected to the traumatic event
- Avoidance of thoughts, people, situations, and other reminders of the traumatic event
- Long-lasting negative thoughts, beliefs, and emotions about self and world
- Detachment from others and important activities
- Difficulty experiencing positive emotions
- Hyperarousal as evidenced by angry or self-destructive behaviors, hypervigilance, and sleep challenges

---

How Psychotherapy Helped Khadijah

As we forged a trusting relationship over several sessions, Khadijah and I worked through the avoidance of her mother's home she experienced as a result of flashbacks of sexual assault. Also, we discussed her feelings of detachment from her family and friends and how to overcome her negative view of her world and her future. Later, Khadijah ashamedly admitted that she had begun to enjoy aspects of sex with Josh, and that even now she continued to experience sexual urges that her aunt had referred to as "lust." Moreover, Khadijah felt guilty that she had apparently caused so much difficulty and strain for her immediate and extended families. Khadijah had only begun to attend church since living with Lucille and was confused by how such a good God could allow such a bad thing to happen to her and her family. Khadijah was able to work through her experiences of rape, allowing me to heal her traumas through somatic awareness. Rather than relying only on others' experiences with God, I provided a supportive environment in which Khadijah could safely articulate her questions and doubts about God, listen and watch for God's response in her suffering, and slowly blossom into her own authentic relationship with God.

Appendix C

Mental Health and
Substance Abuse Resources

Please note: This list represents a sample, rather than a comprehensive compilation, of resources across different areas of need. These resources are provided for informational purposes only and do not imply verification or endorsement of these services.

General Mental Health Professional Directories
https://therapists.psychologytoday.com/rms
https://www.betterhelp.com/ (online)
http://finder.psychiatry.org/
http://www.find-a-therapist.com/
https://www.goodtherapy.org/
https://match.talkspace.com/ (online)
https://www.theravive.com/therapedia/

Black Therapists, Counselors, and Psychologists
http://www.Africanamericantherapists.com
http://www.abpsi.org/find-psychologists/
http://www.blackcounselors.com/
http://www.therapyforblackgirls.com/podcast/

Christian Counselors
http://www.aacc.net/resources/find-a-counselor/
https://mycounselor.online/
findchristiancounselor.com

Hotlines and Online Crisis Information

American Psychological Association's Psychology Help Center:
http://www.apa.org/helpcenter/contact.aspx

How to help in an emotional crisis
http://www.apa.org/helpcenter/emotional-crisis.aspx

HopeLine
http://www.hopeline-nc.org/
Call or text 1-877-235-4525

Mental Health America
www.mentalhealthamerica.net
Mentalhelp.net

National Suicide Prevention Hotline: 1-800-273-TALK (8255)
Online chat available at *http://chat.suicidepreventionlifeline.org/*
GetHelp/LifelineChat.aspx

National Alliance on Mental Illness
https://www.nami.org/

HealthyPlace.com
https://www.healthyplace.com/other-info/resources/
mental-health-hotline-numbers-and-referral-resources/

Further Information on Specific Mental Disorders

Anxiety Disorders (including Panic, Agoraphobia, and Specific Phobias)

https://www.mentalhelp.net/articles/
specific-phobias-and-social-anxiety-disorder-social-phobia/

https://www.theravive.com/therapedia/
specific-phobia-dsm--5-300.29-(icd--10--cm-multiple-codes)

http://www.mentalhealthamerica.net/conditions/phobias

https://www.adaa.org/sites/default/files/panic-brochure.pdf

https://www.adaa.org/sites/default/files/July%2015%2020Phobias_ adaa.pdf

https://www.adaa.org/sites/default/files/SocialAnxietyDisorder-brochure.pdf

https://www.adaa.org/sites/default/files/Treating%20Anxiety%20 Disorders.pdf

https://www.psychiatry.org/patients-families/anxiety-disorders/ what-are-anxiety-disorders

Autism Spectrum Disorders

https://www.nimh.nih.gov/health/topics/autism-spectrum-disorders-asd/index.shtml

https://www.autismspeaks.org/what-autism

http://www.asha.org/Practice-Portal/Clinical-Topics/Autism/

https://www.cdc.gov/ncbddd/autism/facts.html

https://www.psychiatry.org/patients-families/autism/ what-is-autism-spectrum-disorder

http://www.thearc.org/learn-about/autism

Dementia/Alzheimer's Disorder

http://www.alz.org/alzheimers_disease_what_is_alzheimers.asp

https://www.alzheimers.org.uk/info/20007/types_of_dementia

https://www.nia.nih.gov/alzheimers/publication/
alzheimers-disease-fact-sheet

https://www.alzheimers.org.uk/info/20007/types_of_dementia/2/
alzheimers_disease

http://www.brightfocus.org/alzheimers/article/
alzheimers-disease-facts-figures

https://alzheimerscareresourcecenter.com/alzheimers-care-crisis-line/

Disruptive Behavior Disorders
(including Attention-Deficit/Hyperactivity Disorder [ADHD],
Oppositional Defiant Disorder [ODD], and Conduct Disorder)

http://www.chadd.org/Understanding-ADHD/About-ADHD/
Coexisting-Conditions/Disruptive-Behavior-Disorders.aspx

https://www.healthychildren.org/English/health-issues/conditions/
emotional-problems/Pages/Disruptive-Behavior-Disorders.aspx

https://www.understood.org/en/learning-atten-
tion-issues/getting-started/what-you-need-to-know/
the-difference-between-disruptive-behavior-disorders-and-adhd

https://www.samhsa.gov/treatment/mental-disorders/
disruptive-behavior-disorders

http://www.psychguides.com/guides/
behavioral-disorder-symptoms-causes-and-effects/

Learning Disorders

https://ldaamerica.org/types-of-learning-disabilities/

http://www.ldonline.org/ldbasics/whatisld

https://www.psychiatry.org/patients-families/
specific-learning-disorder/what-is-specific-learning-disorder

http://www.mentalhealthamerica.net/conditions/
learning-disabilities

https://www.theravive.com/therapedia/
specific-learning-disorder-dsm--5-315-(icd--10--cm-multiple-codes)

https://psychcentral.com/disorders/specific-learning-disorder/

Major Depression and Other Depressive Disorders
(including Dysthymia and Bipolar Disorders)

https://www.ncbi.nlm.nih.gov/books/NBK64063/

https://www.nimh.nih.gov/health/topics/depression/index.shtml?utm_source=BrainLine.orgutm_medium=Twitter

https://www.psychologytoday.com/conditions/depressive-disorders

https://psychcentral.com/disorders/dysthymic-disorder-symptoms/

https://psychcentral.com/disorders/bipolar/

http://www.psnpaloalto.com/wp/wp-content/uploads/2010/12/
Depression-Diagnostic-Criteria-and-Severity-Rating.pdf

Personality Disorders

http://www.mentalhealthamerica.net/conditions/personality-disorder

http://emedicine.medscape.com/article/1519417-overview

https://www.nimh.nih.gov/health/topics/borderline-personality-disorder/index.shtml

https://www.healthyplace.com/personality-dis-orders/personality-disorders-information/ what-is-a-personality-disorder-definition-causes-effects/

https://www.psychologytoday.com/blog/hide-and-seek/201205/ the-10-personality-disorders

Posttraumatic Stress Disorder (PTSD)

https://psychcentral.com/disorders/ptsd/

https://www.ptsd.va.gov/public/ptsd-overview/basics/what-is-ptsd. asp

http://www.mentalhealthamerica.net/conditions/ post-traumatic-stress-disorder

http://www.psychguides.com/guides/ post-traumatic-stress-disorder-symptoms-causes-and-effects/

Schizophrenia

http://www.mentalhealthamerica.net/conditions/schizophrenia

https://www.nimh.nih.gov/health/topics/schizophrenia/index.shtml

https://www.nami.org/Learn-More/Mental-Health-Conditions/ Schizophrenia

https://www.psychologytoday.com/conditions/schizophrenia

http://www.healthline.com/health/ understanding-schizophrenia#Overview1

https://www.theravive.com/therapedia/ schizophrenia-disorder-dsm--5-295.90-(f20.9)

Substance Use Disorders

https://www.samhsa.gov/disorders/substance-use

*https://www.promises.com/resources/addiction-articles/
substance-use-disorder-defined/*

http://www.buppractice.com/node/12351

*https://www.mentalhelp.net/articles/
the-diagnostic-criteria-for-substance-use-disorders-addiction/*

*https://www.drugabuse.gov/publications/media-guide/
science-drug-abuse-addiction-basics*

https://www.ncbi.nlm.nih.gov/pmc/articles/PMC3767415/

Books on Black Women, Mental Health, and Wellness

Brown, D. R., & Keith, V. M. (Eds.). (2003). *In and out of our right minds: The mental health of African American women.* New York: Columbia University Press.

Brown, L. M. (2011). *Strong on the outside, dying on the inside: A Black woman's guide to finding freedom from depression.* Maitland, FL: Xulon Press.

Coleman, M. A. (2016). *Bipolar faith: A Black woman's journey with depression and faith.* Minneapolis, MN: Fortress Press.

Danquah, M. N. (1998). *Willow weep for me: A Black woman's journey through depression.* New York: W. W. Norton & Company.

Evans, S. Y., Bell, K., & Burton, N. K. (Eds.). (2017). *Black women's mental health: Balancing strength and vulnerability.* Albany: State University of New York Press.

Gourdine, M. A. (2011). *Reclaiming our health: A guide to African American wellness.* New Haven, CT: Yale University Press.

Hoyt, E. H., & Beard, H. (2012). *Health First! The Black Women's Wellness Guide.* New York: Smiley Books.

Martin, M. (2002). *Saving our last nerve: The African American woman's path to mental health.* Roscoe, IL: Hilton Publishing Company.

McCloud, M. T., & Ebron, A. (2003). *Blessed health: The African American woman's guide to physical and spiritual well-being.* New York: Fireside.

Neal-Barnett, A. (2003). *Soothe your nerves: The Black woman's guide to understanding and overcoming, anxiety, panic, and fear.* New York: Simon & Schuster.

Swiner, C. N. (2014). *How to avoid the Superwoman Complex: 12 ways to balance mind, body, and spirit.* Durham, NC: Swiner Publishing Co.

Williams, T. M. (2008). *Black pain: It just looks like we're not hurting.* New York: Scribner.

Appendix D

Template for To-Do List

Goals for the Week of:	Deadline	In progress	Complete	Follow-up needed?
Home & Family				
Me				
Work				
Others				
Church				
Hobbies				

Appendix E

Devotional Resources

Books

Banks, M. (2003). *Women of color devotional Bible.* Iowa Falls, IA: World Bible Publishing.

Cook, S. D. J (2003). *Sister to sister: Devotions for and from African American women.* Valley Forge, PA: Judson Press.

Copage, E. (2005). *Black pearls: Daily meditations, affirmations, and inspirations for African Americans.* New York: William Morrow and Company, Inc.

Hammond, M. M. (2011). *Right attitudes for right living: 31 days to making better choices.* Eugene, OR: Harvest House Publishers.

Jenkins, M.C. (2013). *She speaks: Wisdom from the women of the Bible to the modern black woman.* Nashville, TN: Thomas Nelson.

Jenkins, M. C., Moore, S. P., & Countryman, H. (Eds.). (2013). *God's wisdom for sisters in faith.* Nashville, TN: Thomas Nelson.

McDonald, T. A., Allen, B. J., Cousin, M. J. (Eds.). (2003). *How we got over: Testimonies of faith, hope, and courage.* Chicago: Reyomi Publishing Company.

Shirer, P. (2017). *Discerning the voice of God: How to recognize when God speaks* (Rev. ed.). Nashville, TN: LifeWay Press.

Various/Full Cast (2008). *Inspired by the Bible experience: The complete Bible* [Audiobook]. Grand Rapids: MI: Zondervan.

Young, S. (2004). *Jesus calling: Enjoying peace in his presence.* Nashville, TN: Thomas Nelson, Inc.

Blogs

http://www.crosswalk.com/devotionals/girlfriends/

http://www.devotionaldiva.com/faith/top-ten-devotional-books/

http://www.christenacleveland.com/blogarchive/2013/08/people-of-color-blog-too

https://drtonyaarmstrong.com/

Appendix F

Spiritual Gifts Inventories

Spiritual Gifts Test (*http://spiritualgiftstest.com/ spiritual-gifts-test-adult-version/*)

Giftstest in partnership with Beliefnet (*http://giftstest.com*)

United Methodist Church Spiritual Gifts Assessment (*http:// www.umc.org/what-we-believe/spiritual-gifts-online-assessment*)

Team Ministry Spiritual Gifts Analysis (*https://gifts.churchgrowth. org/cgi-cg/gifts.cgi?intro=1*)

Appendix G

Domestic Violence Resources

Childhelp USA/National Child Abuse Hotline
1-800-422-4453
www.childhelpusa.org

National Center on Domestic Violence, Trauma & Mental Health
1-312-726-7020 ext. 2011
www.nationalcenterdvtraumamh.org

National Dating Abuse Helpline
1-866-331-9474
www.loveisrespect.org

The National Domestic Violence Hotline
1-800-799-7233 (SAFE)
www.ndvh.org

National Resource Center on Domestic Violence
1-800-537-2238
www.nrcdv.org and *www.vawnet.org*

National Sexual Assault Hotline
1-800-656-4673 (HOPE)
www.rainn.org

Women of Color Network
1-800-537-2238
www.wocninc.org

Appendix H
Sample Sleep Log

Date	Time to Bed	Time to Sleep	Times(s) Awake	Activity While Awake	Time Out of Bed	Times of Naps	Mood When Getting Up

Appendix I
Food Diary

MEAL	Food & Beverage (description & serving size)	Calories	Fat	Carbs	Protein	Mood before eating
TODAY'S DATE:						
B'fast						
Snack						
Lunch						
Snack						
Dinner						
Snack						

Appendix J

Grief Resources

Association of Death Education and Counseling
*http://www.adec.org/adec/Main/Help_for_the_Grieving/Coping_
With_Loss/ADEC_Main/Find-Help/CopingWithLossNew/
Coping_With_Loss.aspx*

Centering Corporation
https://centering.org/

**The Dougy Center: The National Center for Grieving Children
and Families**
https://www.dougy.org/

Griefshare.org (international grief recovery support groups)

National Organization for People of Color Against Suicide
http://nopcas.org/

Opentohope.com *(online community featuring stories of loss, hope,
and recovery)*

Unspokengrief.com (miscarriage, stillbirth, or neonatal death)

Appendix K

Monthly Budget

INCOME	Amount		
Primary wages/salary			
Secondary wages/salary			
Child support			
Alimony			
Dividends			
Interest			
Investments			
Reimbursements			
Other income			
TOTAL INCOME			
EXPENSES	Due Date	Projected Amount	Actual Amount
Tithes and offerings			
Mortgage/rent			
Car note			
Car insurance			
Transportation costs (e.g., fuel, passes)			
House insurance			
Life insurance			
Other insurance			
Childcare			
Healthcare (e.g., medical, dental)			
Prescriptions			
Charity			
Gas/electricity			
Phone expenses			
Cable			
Internet			

EXPENSES (cont'd)	Due Date	Projected Amount	Actual Amount
Groceries			
Eating out			
Wardrobe & accessories			
Maintenance/repairs			
Pet supplies			
Debt payments			
Self-care			
Entertainment			
Gifts			
Emergency savings			
Retirement savings			
Other savings			
Other			
Total expenses			
Total income -			
Total expenses =			
Difference			

Appendix L

Recording List

About the Author

Tonya D. Armstrong, Ph.D., M.T.S., is a licensed psychologist and founder of The Armstrong Center for Hope, an interdisciplinary group practice in Durham, N.C., providing psychological and spiritual wellness for all ages (*www.armstrongcfh.com*). Additionally, Dr. Armstrong is the Minister of Congregational Care and Counseling at Union Baptist Church and the Dean of the Counseling Studies Department at Apex School of Theology. She holds a double-major in psychology and music from Yale University, a Ph.D. in clinical psychology from the University of North Carolina at Chapel Hill, and a Master of Arts in Theological Studies (*magna cum laude*) from Duke University Divinity School. Dr. Armstrong is the President-Elect of the North Carolina Psychological Association. In her leisure time, she enjoys laughing, harmonizing, and traveling with her husband of 25 years and their two children.

INDEX

A

abortion, 138, 192, 250–53

abuse, 52, 58, 60, 114–15, 170, 175, 248, 256–57; sexual, 114, 138, 170, 175, 184

acceptance, 76, 117, 218–19

ACFH (Armstrong Center for Hope), 3

activities, extracurricular, 154, 169

ACTS, 90, 92, 156, 175

Adams, Yolanda, 147

ADHD (Attention-Deficit/Hyperactivity Disorder), 213

Adichie, Chimamanda Ngozi, 111

adoption, informal,148

adoration, 90, 92

adultery, 69, 83, 174, 182–83

affection, physical, 179

African Americans, 19–20, 76–77, 83, 127, 222–26, 229

agency, 49

aging, 216–19

Alzheimer's Disease, 29–31, 34, 247

Angelou, Maya, 1, 213

anger, 32, 76, 132–33, 151, 154, 190, 234, 241, 253; management, 133

anxiety, 7, 60, 62, 76–79, 141, 151, 223, 235, 237, 241, 249

Apostle Paul, 54, 69, 137, 149–50

assertiveness, 98, 155, 237

attachment, 151, 153

Attention-Deficit/Hyperactivity Disorder. *See* ADHD

authority, parental, 160

Made in the USA
Columbia, SC
23 March 2018